THE SMART GUIDE TO

Freshwater Fishing

By Mike Seymour

The Smart Guide To Freshwater Fishing

Published by

Smart Guide Publications, Inc.
2517 Deer Chase Drive
Norman, OK 73071
www.smartguidepublications.com

For information, address: Smart Guide Publications, Inc. 2517 Deer Creek Drive, Norman, OK 73071

SMART GUIDE and Design are registered trademarks licensed to Smart Guide Publications, Inc.

International Standard Book Number: 978-0-9785341-4-1

Library of Congress Catalog Card Number: 2011936629
11 12 13 14 15 10 9 8 7 6 5 4 3 2 1

Printed in the United States of America

Cover design: Lorna Llewellyn
Copy Editor: Ruth Strother
Back cover design: Joel Friedlander, Eric Gelb, Deon Seifert
Back cover copy: Eric Gelb, Deon Seifert
Illustrations: Lorna Llewellyn
Indexer: Cory Emberson
V.P./Business Manager: Cathy Barker

TABLE OF CONTENTS

INTRODUCTION

Henry David Thoreau said, "Many men go fishing all of their lives without knowing that it is not fish they are after." This quote illustrates that there is much more to fishing than catching fish. Indeed, fishing gets us in the great outdoors where we become active participants in nature rather than simple observers. Fishing is a wholesome activity that offers us time for reflection and the opportunity to commune with nature and to enrich relationships with family and friends.

This book, like other fishing books, cannot contain everything about the subject because fishing is a vast and varied field. To illustrate the amount of information available, consider that my book shelves contain six books focused solely on fishing for a single species, the muskellunge, and those books don't tell all there is to know about muskellunge fishing. Still, *The Smart Guide to Freshwater Fishing* is full of practical information that will help the novice get started in the sport and broaden the knowledge base of experienced anglers. My expectation is that after reading this book, you will have more fish at line's end.

A number of years ago, my brother-in-law, Chris, and a friend had planned a week-long fishing trip into the wilderness region of New York's Adirondack Mountains. At the last minute the friend had to bow out of the venture so Chris made the trip alone. When I asked his wife how she felt about the solo undertaking, she replied, "Of course, I'm concerned, but he always comes back a better person than when he left."

Yes, fishing truly enriches a person's life and makes him or her a better person. Who could ask for more?

PART ONE

Freshwater Fishing

CHAPTER 1

First Casts

In This Chapter

➤ How fishing connects us with nature

➤ Why fishing is a sport for you

➤ What benefits fishing offers

In this chapter, you'll learn that nature is an intrinsic part of fishing. You'll also learn that fishing is a sport for you and for everyone else. Thirdly, you'll see some of the major benefits for those who head to the water in pursuit of fish.

Time in Nature

Most North Americans live in urban areas, and as a result the majority of our population has limited contact with the natural world. We wake to the alarm clock, drive to our place of work via busy roads, work at our assigned tasks, return home on even busier roads, and likely watch television during the evening hours. Weekends may find us catching up on chores around the house, attending local athletic contests, socializing with family and friends, grocery shopping, visiting the mall, and more. Certainly, these activities are important, but what part does nature play in our lives other than when we combat it by controlling the temperature in our cars, workplaces, and homes?

My point is that society's routines and expectations have removed us from the natural world, and this is why you and I need fishing in our lives. Spending time in nature reduces stress and improves one's quality of life, and, most importantly, fishing allows us to be active participants in the great outdoors. Fishing is a natural human act that provides opportunities for our senses to come alive, opportunities to view wildlife in its natural habitat, opportunities to be one with the weather, and opportunities to experience an array of positive emotions.

Arousing the Senses

Fishing allows our senses to come alive. Our eyes view the colors and movements of water, the miracle of a sunrise, the brilliance of a sunset, patterns of drifting clouds, distant shorelines, ascending mountain peaks, and more. Our noses gather the scents of fresh air, the earthy shoreline, nearby vegetation, campfires, and fresh fish. Our ears hear the bubbling brook, lapping waves, chirping songbirds, quacking mallards, calling gulls, splashing fish, and swaying treetops. Our body feels the warmth of the sun, the freshness of the wind, the moisture of the rain, and the gentleness of the earth, sand, and water at our feet. Our taste buds enjoy the delightful flavor of lunch, a meal that is always more enjoyable at water's edge. And if things go well, the angler also gets to enjoy a savory meal of fresh fish at day's end.

Viewing Wildlife

Observing wildlife goes hand in hand with fishing. Common sightings of winged creatures who are also fishermen include terns, fish hawks, ospreys, herons, eagles, mergansers, and cormorants. Then there are gulls, geese, mallards, and more. Muskrats, mink, beavers, and otters inhabit fish-holding waters and shorelines. Chipmunks, squirrels, raccoons, foxes, and white-tailed deer make their way to the water's edge, too. And if you are lucky enough to fish in such places as Yellowstone, Quebec, or Alaska, you will encounter creatures like moose, caribou, elk, black bears, brown bears, and wolves.

Real Fishing

Whenever a fishing trip is in the offing, I stay in tune with weather forecasts. For one thing, I want to make sure conditions are safe for being on the water. Also, conditions may affect my strategy for the day as well as my expectations for success. For example, strong winds might dictate that I troll rather than cast, and easterly winds indicate that fish will be less active so I might expect to catch fewer fish than when the wind blows from the southwest. Because of my keen interest in weather, my two sons tease me that the weather channel is my favorite television show.

Watching the Weather, Too

Except for extreme weather conditions such as wind storms and ice storms, we are pretty much weatherproof as a society today. For anglers, however, weather is very important because our sport demands that we be outside in the natural elements, not in a domed stadium. The weather affects such decisions as whether to even venture forth, where to go, and how to dress. Thunderstorms, drizzles, wind direction, wind strength, and temperatures impact our decision making, so the weather channel and other informational sources become an intimate part of our lives. As an angler becomes more immersed in the sport, he or she will learn how weather impacts fish activity and what conditions make for good fishing and what conditions mean the likelihood of a less productive outing.

Feeling the Emotion

Angling, like other sports, elicits emotional experiences. All ventures begin with anticipation and hopefully end with the thrill of the catch. Experiences may range from total relaxation in a lawn chair at a neighborhood park to extreme adventure at a remote Alaska lake. An individual who fishes is a person who is emotionally alive.

People of All Levels Can Participate

The term *fisherman* has a definite male ring, but fishing holds no prejudices. Fishing is open to all people regardless of gender, age, race, physical ability, income level, or skill level. Certainly a term like *angler* suggests more inclusivity, but a fisherman is not a male; a fisherman is anyone who fishes. The key part of *fisherman* is *fisher*, not *man* so world-class fly caster Joan Wulff is an angler, a fisher, a fisherwoman, and a fisherman.

Open to All

Our age, physical ability, income level, and transportation options influence our activity choices, but none of the four should prevent someone from fishing. If a youngster can turn the reel handle while an adult holds the rod, that child can fish. My eighty-five-year-old aunt and uncle continue to fish together as they have throughout their married life. Fishing ramps, access sites, guides, charter boats, electric reels, and more are available for the physically challenged individual. A week-long lake trout trip to Manitoba may cost thousands of dollars, but less than $50 will get an angler started with a rod, reel, terminal tackle, bait, and fishing license. Not all people have the means to travel to distant fishing destinations, but each of us has fish-holding waters nearby.

Fishing Vocab

An angler is a person who fishes. The term originally referred to fishing with a hook rather than a net, spear, etc. *Angler* is derived from the word *anka* in a now-extinct language of India, and *anka* means bend, which refers to the curved fishhook.

Skill Levels

Like other sports, fishing is a skill, but individuals can participate no matter what their skill level may be. A basic level consists of baiting a hook, casting the offering into the water, and setting the rod in a Y-stick. At the other end of the spectrum is fly fishing, which consists of softly casting a dry fly onto the water and then guiding the offering skillfully into a trout-holding lair by mending the line. Despite the stereotype of the lucky fisherman, it is the skilled angler who routinely catches fish, and improving one's angling skills amounts to making a conscious effort in that direction. Josh Hamilton of the Texas Rangers currently hits one hundred-mile-per-hour fastballs out of major league parks, but he likely began his skill development by hitting plastic balls off a tee. If you want to improve your angling skills, the formula is a simple one: go fishing.

Why People Fish

People fish for different reasons. Some may simply want to relax for a few hours at water's edge or bring home some fresh fish for dinner, while others may want to catch a record fish or compete for millions of dollars in prize money on the professional bass circuit. The majority of anglers, though, have desired goals that lie somewhere in between. What are your objectives?

Benefits of Fishing

Spending time in nature and putting fish on the table rank high on the list of the benefits of fishing, but other noteworthy benefits include the fun of fishing, the development of a lifetime activity, exercise, solitude, and camaraderie.

Plain Old Fun

Fishing gives pleasure to those who take part. Anglers draw pleasure from the entire experience, which includes preparing for a trip, getting away from regular routines, spending time outdoors, being with family and friends, and the act of fishing itself. There is fun in anticipating a bite, the actual bite, the playing of the fish, seeing the fish in the water, and watching the fish swim away upon release or eating fresh fish at the dinner table, whatever the choice may be.

Learning, too, is part of the fun of fishing. If you are like me, you enjoy the act of learning, and fishing is an ongoing, never-ending learning process. Anglers spend their fishing lives learning about various fish species, bodies of water, fishing techniques, and equipment. Speaking of gear, checking out or, better yet, acquiring new equipment that we hope will improve our success on the water is also fun. I enjoy browsing through a fishing catalog, stopping at a local bait shop, or wandering up and down the aisles at a large retail outlet. My attraction to fishing products allows me to appreciate my wife's fascination with shoe stores.

Lifetime Activity

Youth activities typically include sports such as soccer, baseball, softball, basketball, football, hockey, and running. Although we can participate in these sports well into adulthood, we usually move away from them once we finish school. Such is not the case with fishing, though, as fishing is a sport that one can enjoy throughout life.

There is a growing movement in physical education classes to offer students lifetime activities rather than traditional sports such as soccer and softball. In reality, fishing would make an excellent course in such programs, and, indeed, fishing is offered at some schools. No matter where life takes an individual, fishing remains a viable activity.

Real Fishing

Eighty-five-year-old Bob Seymour is the ultimate example of someone for whom fishing has been a lifetime sport. Uncle Bob has a St. Lawrence River cottage, where he keeps a 14-foot boat with a 9.9-horsepower motor. His fishing consists of trolling for northern pike in spring, anchoring and using live minnows for smallmouth bass and yellow perch during the summer, and trolling for walleyes in the fall. This past year he won a local walleye derby with a 7-plus-pound fish. Bob's secret to catching fish is his intimate knowledge of the area he fishes.

Exercise

Despite the stereotype of an angler asleep on the riverbank with a hat pulled over his head, fishing is an active sport that offers the benefit of exercise. Okay, a fishing outing is not like running the Boston Marathon, but the outing does allow us to engage in big-muscle activity that might include walking, hiking, carrying gear, casting and retrieving, getting up and down, paddling or rowing, launching a boat, lifting an anchor, and hopefully hoisting big fish for the camera.

Solitude and Camaraderie

Anglers can go it alone or do it with others. Ironically, fishing is unique in that the sport offers opportunities for both solitude and camaraderie, two important needs of the human spirit. A lone angler casting for rainbows on an isolated stretch of stream in autumn, bobber fishing for crappies on a dock at sunrise, or trolling for muskies on a star-filled evening has the occasion to reflect on his or her lot in life and to revel in solitude. Still, fishing is more about camaraderie than solitude. That camaraderie may be an outing with a regular fishing partner, an annual gathering of friends on opening day, or participating in an ice fishing derby with hundreds of other anglers. Fishermen love to be among others who share their passion for the sport.

A special bond forms between individuals who fish together, so fishing makes an excellent family activity. On a fishing trip, a merging and equality of the generations occurs. Children behave more maturely, and adults become more youthful.

CHAPTER 2

Acquiring Know-How

> ## In This Chapter
>
> ➤ Easy ways to learn how to fish
>
> ➤ What you can learn from experts
>
> ➤ What homework assignments can provide information

In this chapter, you'll learn a variety of ways to acquire fishing knowledge. These methods include observation, conversation, actual fishing, learning from experts, and doing a little homework. Since fishing is a lifelong learning process, the suggestions in this chapter are valid for experienced anglers as well as for novices.

Easy Ways to Learn

Throughout your fishing years, you will continue to learn about fishing as you watch other anglers, converse with other anglers, and actually do your own fishing. These three means are also good first steps to learn how to fish.

Observing

Even though angling is a participatory rather than a spectator sport, individuals can learn by watching other anglers. Such opportunities exist at local parks, public docks, boat launches, marinas, local fishing derbies, and regional tournaments. By observing anglers in action, you can see what the quality of the fishing is like in a certain area and what gear and techniques anglers are utilizing. At marinas and derbies, you can see anglers' catches as well as the gear and lures they are using. Fishing etiquette calls for viewers to do so without crowding or being intrusive.

Conversing

Even better information can be learned by asking questions and striking up a conversation with an angler. Despite the stereotype of fishermen not sharing their knowledge, most anglers love to talk about their sport. To find out how conversant an angler is, politely ask a question and then attempt to assess whether the angler wants to talk or be left alone.

You might begin by asking, "What are you fishing for?" If you get a warm response, you might follow up with, "How has the fishing been so far this season?" If it seems appropriate to carry on the conversation, then continue to converse and acquire know-how. If you get a terse response to the original question, you might want to wish the angler luck and leave him or her alone.

Learn by Doing

You can learn a lot just by going fishing, so don't be shy about grabbing your basic gear (rod, reel, hooks, sinkers, bobbers, worms) and heading to a near-home fishing spot. Hands-on experience is a great teacher. If other anglers are there, don't crowd them. Instead ask, "Mind if I set up here?" or "Mind if I set up over there?" Once at the site, you can continue to learn by observing and conversing. "Do you fish any other places?" is a great conversation starter.

Learning from the Experts

Experienced anglers are all around us, and I contend that any experienced angler can teach us something we don't know. Whenever I spend time conversing with or, better yet, fishing with a fellow angler, I learn something that increases my fishing knowledge.

Experts Surround Us

All of us have family, neighbors, friends, and coworkers who are avid anglers, and these folks are your experts. Ask them about favorite species, fishing places, good times to fish, techniques they use, lures, and equipment. Since anglers like to share their passion for the sport, you may even get an invite to join them on a future outing.

The owners and workers at local bait and tackle shops are also experts. Not only are these people fishermen themselves, but they are knowledgeable about the equipment they sell, and they are in daily contact with anglers. This contact means the folks at tackle shops have a good handle on the local fishing scene, and by becoming a purchasing customer at the store, you can have access to their knowledge. Once you have established a relationship at a bait shop, it's appropriate to call for information such as what is happening on Lake Clear, are the crappies biting, what flies are the rainbows hitting, and is the ice safe yet on Big Bay.

Formal Learning

Among the more formal opportunities to learn from experts are fishing seminars and classes. Local media are the best sources for finding when such offerings are available. Fishing stores, sportsmen's clubs, and sportsmen's shows typically offer informative seminars during the year. Expert presenters include local anglers, licensed guides, professional anglers, and company representatives. Although some of the sessions may be specific or advanced, such as surface lures for largemouth bass or trolling for deepwater muskellunges, most seminars include a lot of basic information that is applicable to a variety of fishing situations.

Real Fishing

I recently stopped at Jones Outfitters, a fly-fishing shop in Lake Placid, New York, to pick up a couple of flies and strike indicators. During the short time I was there, the clerk, a knowledgeable fly fisherman, answered four different phone calls, and in each case he courteously provided the caller with information about water levels and other fishing conditions. I was impressed by the clerk's willingness to share valuable information, and this incident illustrates what's in store for anglers who develop a relationship with local shops.

Seminars are more common than fishing classes or courses, but classes are frequently offered by fly-fishing shops and schools or colleges as part of their adult-learning or continuing-education programs. Typical classes include learning to fly-fish, learning to fly cast, and learning to tie flies. Also, there are weekend and week-long fishing schools, where participants spend time both in the classroom and on the water. Muskellunge and fly-fishing schools are particularly popular.

Guides

Hiring a professional guide is an excellent means of acquiring fishing experience as these guides are fully licensed, have significant experience, provide quality gear, and are willing to share their knowledge and expertise. On a guided trip, you will learn where and what time of year to fish for a particular species. You will also learn what gear and techniques to use. The outing should give you the know-how and confidence to be more successful on future fishing trips on that water and other waters, for that matter. Again, don't hesitate to ask your guide questions as he or she is likely very knowledgeable about additional species, waters, and techniques.

Doing Some Homework

Although there may be no substitute for on-the-water learning, you can glean a lot of fishing knowledge by applying those good work habits from your school days. In fact, you are actually doing such homework by reading this book, but plenty of other reading and viewing assignments lie ahead. The reading assignments include newspapers, magazines, books, and tourism brochures; television shows and CDs constitute the viewing component. The Internet offers both reading and viewing assignments.

Bad Cast

When fishing with a guide, remember that he or she is the guide and you are the client. In addition to poor fishing and lousy weather, conditions over which the guide has no control, two things upset guides. One is when the client wants to do things his or her way rather than follow the guide's instructions, and the other is a client who consumes too much alcohol.

Newspapers and Magazines

The outdoors columns in your local and regional newspapers are prime sources for current what, where, when, and how-to fishing information in the area. Magazine possibilities include state, regional, and national publications. Although the state and regional magazines offer the most relevant information regarding places to fish and species to pursue, national magazines have plenty of how-to information. Also, there are species-specific publications, so if you are into a single species such as crappies, then a crappie magazine is the one for you.

Books and Brochures

Just as books provided a wealth of information in your history classes, books also provide a wealth of information on any conceivable topic related to fishing. You will likely be amazed by the range of available titles when you visit the local library, major bookstore, or Internet store. Tourism agencies are an overlooked source of fishing information, and since an agency's job is to promote its area, most agencies have fishing brochures chock full of valuable information.

Television and CDs

For those who prefer to learn from viewing rather than reading, fishing shows and CDs are the way to go. Major outdoors channels offer a variety of fishing shows across North

America, and local cable channels often carry local fishing shows. CDs are frequently species specific, and you can find them at fishing departments or advertised in fishing magazines.

Internet

My generation did its research in the library, but the current generation logs onto the Internet for information, and there are thousands and thousands of websites that provide fishing information. My frustration with these sites is that many of them are more interested in marketing and making money than they are in providing information to anglers. Still, if you are willing to spend some time searching, quality sites are available. For example, state fish and game departments offer visitors excellent information such as regulations, license requirements, available species, best fishing waters, public-access sites, public boat launches, marina locations, and fish stocks.

The Internet's social networking also opens the door to acquiring fishing know-how. For those who are so inclined, socializing via the Internet opens up a world of opportunities to converse with and learn from fellow anglers.

CHAPTER 3

Getting Started

In This Chapter

➤ What choices you should keep in mind when starting out

➤ What the characteristics of various fishing waters are

➤ How to access fishing spots

In this chapter, you'll learn four important choices an angler makes before heading out to fish, and you'll learn about places to fish and how to access those fishing places.

Important Choices

Prior to actually fishing, an angler must decide how he is going to access the water, where he will fish, what species he will target, and what technique he will employ. These choices are interrelated, constantly changing, and ever evolving during an angler's lifetime. If you consider there are four basic ways to access the water, countless places to fish, dozens of species to pursue, and seven or so standard fishing techniques, the options an angler has on a given outing number in the hundreds. And these possibilities are part of the freedom, fun, challenge, and ongoing learning associated with fishing.

How Will I Access the Water?

The simplest way to access the water for fishing is from shore via banks, beaches, docks, or piers. Wading, too, is an easy means of accessing waters. Cartop boats such as canoes, kayaks, belly boats, and aluminum rowboats open up even more places to fish, and a powered vessel, transported on a trailer, gives you access to larger rivers, lakes, and reservoirs. Although I do most of my fishing from 14-foot and 17-foot aluminum boats during the year, I also spend a fair amount of time fishing from shore, wading streams, and paddling a canoe. More details on accessing fishing spots appear later in this chapter.

Where Will I Fish?

Although the grass sometimes appears to be greener on the other side of the fence, the odds are that some decent fishing exists in your own backyard. Fishing your home waters has two advantages: one is the minimal amount of time required to get there, and the other is the minimal cost of getting there. Near-home waters allow an angler to go fishing when he or she has only a few hours available, such as after work. The opportunity to fish on a workday adds fun to your day that would otherwise be lacking.

You should also consider the regional possibilities, places you can drive to within two hours or so from your home, as every region has some first-rate fishing waters. The investment of time and money is more than it would be when fishing at home, but the quality of the experience may outweigh the cost. Regional trips can be done in a day, but camping or getting a motel room allows for more fishing time. By extending your options to new fishing waters, you may discover a particular location, species, or type of fishing you like and want to pursue in the future. Also, any new angling experience will broaden your fishing knowledge and make you a better angler on your home waters.

A fishing vacation may be a financial luxury, but wherever vacations, business travel, or family visits take you, there will be fishing opportunities. Prior to such trips, do some research by visiting the state fish and game website, contacting the local chamber of commerce, or getting information from your local contact, whether it be a family member or host hotel. Once you arrive at the area, consider some on-site scouting by visiting fishing sites, marinas, and bait shops. If you take annual vacations or make annual visits to a particular location, you may want to adopt an away-from-home water. Even if travel doesn't allow you to actually fish, take time to investigate the fishing in the area as that investigation will augment your angling knowledge; there will likely be some things you can transfer to your fishing waters back home.

What Species Will I Pursue?

Your targeted species of fish will be influenced by the waters on which you fish as well as your means of access. For the most part, though, anglers, particularly novices, pursue panfish and smaller game fish because these species offer advantages for the angler. For example, panfish and smaller game fish are found in most waters, populations are usually plentiful, simple gear and techniques are all that is needed, the fish are easy to catch, and there's always the chance of hooking into a larger predator that is in the area feeding on the smaller fish. Pursuing smaller fish is an excellent way to develop basic skills such as casting, detecting bites, playing fish, landing fish, and handling fish. These same skills are used when dealing with larger fish such as Chinook salmon and northern pike.

Two exceptions exist for pursuing species other than panfish and small game fish. If a particular water is known for particular species of quality fish, catfish or walleyes for example, you may want to target that species. Also, if you have your heart set on catching a particular species such as lake trout, muskellunge, or striped bass, then you should do so by heading to a water that holds that species. See chapters 18–23 for detailed information on over fifty common freshwater species.

What Technique Will I Use?

Again, the technique used is tied to your means of access, where you fish, and the species you're after. Both shore and boat anglers have the options of fishing with a bobber, bottom fishing, and casting lures. Boaters also have the options of anchoring, free drifting, controlled drifting, and trolling. At this point, just keep technique in the back of your mind, as chapter 8 goes into detail on these various fishing methods.

Fishing Vocab

Bottom fishing is a basic and common technique that involves using a rig that is used for fishing on the bottom of a lake or river. Such rigs consist of a weight and a baited hook.

Bodies of Water

North American anglers are blessed in that the continent boasts millions and millions of fish-holding waters. Not all waters are created equal from a fishing perspective, however, as waters vary in type and characteristics such as size, available species, fish abundance, access, and more.

Essentially, waters can be divided into two types: still and moving. The still waters consist of lakes, ponds, reservoirs, and pits, and, as the name suggests, these waters are standing rather than flowing. The moving waters consist of streams and rivers, and likewise these waters are flowing with some degree of current. Here's a look at the types of fishing waters and their basic characteristics.

Natural Lakes

Natural lakes abound in North America as evidenced by Minnesota's slogan, Land of 10,000 Lakes. No two lakes are completely identical, though, as variations exist in shape,

Real Fishing

What causes lakes to age? The obvious answer is human influences. Whereas nature may take hundreds of years to age a lake, mankind can create that same aging in just a generation or two.

size, depth, rock formations, fish species, aquatic vegetation, human development, and more. But lakes do share similarities with other lakes of the same age. Let me explain.

Lakes are classified by their age, but the age is not a chronological one. Rather, age is based on water conditions such as fertility, temperature, depth, bottom content, and fish abundance. Lake ages include young (oligotrophic), middle age (mesotrophic), and old age (eutrophic). Since lakes don't suddenly change from young to middle age or from middle age to old age, there are degrees of each age. For example, we could talk about early-stage oligotrophic, middle-stage oligotrophic, late-stage oligotrophic, and so on, but for our purposes, let's look at the characteristics of the three basic lake ages.

Young, oligotrophic, lakes are primarily distributed throughout the eastern two-thirds of Canada and the very northeast corner of the United States. These lakes are characterized by cold water temperatures, infertility, lack of nutrients, significant depth, clear water, rock outcroppings, rock basin, steep drop-offs, minimal weeds, oxygen in deep water, low fish populations, and shorelines of spruce, pine, and white birch. Oligotrophic lakes hold cold-water species such as trout and whitefish.

Middle age, mesotrophic, lakes exist primarily east of the Rockies in Canada and across the northern United States. These lakes are characterized by rock, sand, gravel, shallow weed beds, slow-tapering shoreline, moderate fertility, nutrients, a thermocline, healthy fish populations, and a shoreline consisting of more hardwoods than spruce and pine. Mesotrophic lakes favor cool-water species such as walleye, northern pike, smallmouth bass, yellow perch, and even deep-water trout in their early stage, but these lakes may also be a home to largemouth bass and crappies.

Old age, eutrophic lakes appear throughout the United States east of the Rockies, especially in agricultural areas. These lakes are characterized by shallow depths, mucky bottoms, a dishpan shape, thick weed growth, high fertility, abundant fish populations, and a flat shoreline of hardwoods. Eutrophic lakes hold populations of bass, walleye, crappies, and bluegills in the early stage, but as the lake nears late stage those species give way to bullheads.

Once you learn how to catch fish on a lake of any given age, you should be able to catch fish on unfamiliar lakes of the same age.

Ponds

Millions of ponds exist across North America. Some are natural and others are man-made. Natural ponds are just smaller versions of lakes and can be classified, like lakes, by age. For example, mountain ponds tend to be oligotrophic, so they hold trout populations and lowland ponds tend to be mesotrophic or eutrophic so they typically hold populations of bass and sunfish. Man-made ponds are common on farms, where the ponds serve to enhance productivity by creating a watering hole, facilitating irrigation, or controlling erosion. No matter what the pond's purpose is, these waters are excellent places for young and novice anglers because of accessibility and easy-to-catch species such as largemouth bass, bluegills, bullheads, and catfish.

Reservoirs

Reservoirs, sometimes called impoundments, are actually impounded bodies of water that are created by damming up rivers. A reservoir takes on the personality of the landscape along the river prior to the installation of a dam. For example, a reservoir created in a mountainous region will be long and narrow with steep slopes, and a reservoir created in flatland tends to be extremely wide with gradual slopes.

Reservoirs are much like natural lakes in that reservoirs can be classified by their age or fertility condition. Less fertile impoundments hold trout, and more fertile waters may hold everything from striped bass to bullheads.

But reservoirs differ from lakes in several ways as well. For one, reservoirs often see significant fluctuations in water level as water is either released from or poured into an impoundment, and these fluctuations stifle the weed growth that might otherwise occur in natural lakes. Also, impoundments may have some current flow particularly in their upper reaches. Too, impoundments may have subsurface man-made structures that existed along the river prior to damming and flooding. Such common structures include building foundations, roadbeds, riprap, and stone fences, all of which make excellent fish-holding habitat. Another unique feature of reservoirs is flooded timber, a favorite holding place of both baitfish and game fish such as largemouth bass and black crappies. Finally, all reservoirs contain the old riverbed, and except for very deep reservoirs, this riverbed makes for a natural travel corridor and fish-holding location.

Generally, reservoirs can be looked at in thirds. The upper third contains shallower water, less varied depth, sunken and above-water islands, and the major inlet or headwater. The middle third tends to be the widest portion of the reservoir, and this section typically has the most varied structure and offers the best fishing. The lower third, located just above the dam, has the steepest slopes and the deepest water.

Pits

Anglers don't readily think of pits when looking for fishing places, but abandoned pits once used for the mining of coal or iron ore or once used for digging stone can make for good fishing destinations. Pits require fish stocking initially, and some pits are stocked on a regular basis; others are populated by natural reproduction as well as by stocking. Deep-water pits may hold trout, and the shallower pits commonly contain bass, crappies, and catfish.

Streams and Rivers

Streams and rivers are moving, flowing waters, and from a fish's perspective, current translates to oxygenated water, food passing by, and out-of-the-current holding places. Streams and rivers exist in a variety of sizes and lengths. Like lakes, streams and rivers are characterized from young to old based on their environmental conditions. Young flows are those trout-holding mountain streams characterized by noticeable gradient, a rock streambed, limited nutrients, and low fish populations. Mature or middle-aged rivers contain slower, warmer, less clear, more meandering water that is home to species such as walleye, smallmouth bass, and northern pike. Old rivers are shallow, slow-flowing, warm, expansive waters that support largemouth bass, carp, and catfish.

Fishing Vocab

An eddy is a current that varies from the main current of a river or stream. Water obstructions cause these variants, which appear as whirlpools and make excellent fish-holding areas.

Streams and rivers, like lakes, have degrees of age. For example, we could have young streams in stages varying from infancy to the verge of adulthood, and we could have old rivers varying from just past middle age to very, very old. Also, a single stream or river may have varying ages as it flows from its headwaters to its mouth, where it empties into a larger water body. No matter what a river's age, though, inhabiting fish love to hang out along current edges, eddies, and current breaks. (See chapter 9 for information on locating fish in various waters.)

Pay-to-Fish Places

Unlike University of Auburn football games and Los Angeles Lakers basketball games, there are no admission fees for anglers taking to the water. Still, if your budget allows and you are so inclined, pay-to-fish places do exist. These places come in a variety of forms, but here's a look at the two standard types.

The most common pay-to-fish option consists of heavily stocked ponds, where the angler pays a standard fee for each fish caught or for each pound of fish taken. Anglers must keep every fish caught as there is no catch and release. Common species in pay-to-fish ponds include trout and catfish, and anglers have the option of taking the fish home to clean or having their catch cleaned on-site for a set fee per fish. Some ponds may be restricted to fly-fishing only. Because pay-to-fish places want return customers, these businesses are clean, friendly, and well run.

The advantages of pay-to-fish ponds are:

> ➤ They are good for youngsters and novices as the fish are usually easy to catch.

> ➤ They are a lot more fun than going to the supermarket to buy fish for dinner.

> ➤ The catch is fresh.

> ➤ They offer a chance to enjoy the fishing and catching experience.

The disadvantages of pay-to-fish ponds are:

> ➤ A cost is involved, although it is likely similar to the price of store-bought fish.

> ➤ You might catch the fish too easily.

> ➤ They offer less of a nature experience than fishing on a traditional pond, lake, stream, or river.

Another type of pay-to-fish place is where the pond, lake, section of stream, or section of river is privately owned, and the owner charges an access fee for shore fishing, wading, or launching a boat. Additional services may include a bait shop, fishing guides, lodging, and boat rentals. These waters may have natural fish reproduction, but the waters likely receive regular stockings, too, and a variety of species are commonly available.

In contrast to the pay-to-fish ponds previously mentioned, these businesses do not charge a fee per fish caught or per pound of fish. Instead, they often have stricter rules than those set by the state or province. For example, some waters may be fly-fishing-only or catch-and-release-only waters; others may have minimum lengths that exceed state regulations or maximum creel limits that are lower than state regulations. Owners of private waters want to offer their clients quality fishing, so the owners operate in a way to do just that. Because private waters see less pressure than public waters, anglers may find better fishing there. If your budget allows, there are no apparent disadvantages other than cost when fishing private waters.

Fishing Vocab

Creel limit refers to the number and/or size of fish that an angler may legally take in one day.

North American anglers are blessed in having the option to fish public or private waters. In many countries, public fishing options are extremely limited and only the wealthy can afford the pay-to-fish places.

Accessing Fishing Waters

Anglers have four basic options for accessing fishing waters, and those choices are shore fishing, wading, using a small boat, or using a motorized boat.

Shore Fishing

Possibilities for fishing from shore are numerous, and they include, but are not limited to, community waterfront, public parks, public docks, fishing piers, boat ramps, marinas, campgrounds, bridges, dams, canals, waterfront businesses, break walls, walking paths, and roadside turnoffs. For the most part, there is no charge for accessing the water at public sites, but privately owned locations may or may not charge a fee for fishing from the waterfront.

Many communities and waters have fishing piers specifically designed for the physically challenged. When fisheries' biologists are involved in the planning for such piers, you can bet they are constructed in a location that offers good shore fishing.

Shore fishing is an excellent way to go for novices and youngsters because panfish and small game fish commonly inhabit shoreline areas, and these fish readily strike worm-baited hooks suspended below a bobber or fished on a bottom rig. Also, fishing from shore allows youngsters the opportunity to have some fun exploring the surroundings. Spring is usually the best time for shore fishing because that's when large concentrations of fish invade the shallows and tributaries in search of spawning habitat, warmer water, and food. Shore angling for panfish is particularly popular in springtime.

Shore fishing is not limited to small fish, though. For example, largemouth bass spawn along shorelines, catfish move to the shallows in the evening to feed, northern pike cruise the shorelines in pursuit of prey, walleyes corral schools of baitfish along shorelines in autumn, and various trout and salmon

Fishing Vocab

Commonly called a life jacket or life vest, a PFD is a personal flotation device. PFDs come in a variety of styles and sizes, and it's important to have a properly fitting PFD. Navigational regulations require that boats carry a PFD for each passenger on board, and in some cases youths under a certain age must wear the PFD while the boat is underway. Generally speaking, it's always a good idea to have youngsters wear a PFD when around deep water.

species migrate to tributaries for feeding and spawning purposes. Prime shore-fishing spots are often characterized by such features as a tributary, adjacent deep water, an extending point, or a developing vegetation.

There are some ethics and safety rules of thumb for shore fishing.

> ➤ Always verify that fishing is allowed at the site.

> ➤ Always get permission before fishing on private waterfront.

> ➤ Be courteous to other anglers, and avoid crowding them.

> ➤ Leave the area cleaner than it was when you arrived.

> ➤ Always put safety first.

> ➤ If banks are steep or water is deep, consider wearing a PFD; at the very least, have youngsters wear their life jackets and have a flotation device handy.

> ➤ When fishing near dams, honor the designated stay-back areas.

> ➤ Be wary of slippery, moss-covered rocks.

Wading

For fly fishermen, wading is the standard means of accessing streams, but for some reason, wading is an approach typically overlooked by other anglers. Yet wading is an inexpensive means of expanding your fishing opportunities.

The main limitation to wading is water depth. Current flow, if it is too strong, can also be a deterrent. If the water is shallow enough, though, anglers can wade fish at most of the sites mentioned above for shore fishing. Wading allows an angler more mobility up and down the shoreline than standard shore fishing, and it also allows an angler to get the lure or bait out a greater distance. For example, a wader might be able to reach a weed line or drop-off that is unreachable from shore.

Minimal extra gear is needed for wading. During the summer months, anglers can wade in a pair of sneakers and shorts. Otherwise, hip boots or chest waders are the way to go. Hip boots are good for water depths up to mid-thigh, and chest waders are effective to depths up to mid-chest. Hip boots extend to the top of the thigh, and the boots are held up by straps that are attached to your belt. Chest waders extend to just below the arm pits, and these waders have suspenders to hold them in place. Some chest waders are booted, and others are of the stocking style so the boots must be purchased separately. The general rule for purchasing hip boots or waders is the same as purchasing most gear and that is to buy the best quality your budget can afford. If you're going to wade in waters that are boulder strewn, have a moss-covered bottom, or have significant current flow, it's wise to have studded soles.

Serious waders commonly acquire three additional pieces of gear:

➤ A fishing vest to hold tackle and other items.

➤ A wading staff for checking water depths before moving forward and for support when wading in trickier spots.

➤ A pair of polarized glasses for spotting fish and getting a better view of subsurface features.

The first rule for waders is to take it slow. Carefully check the footing before taking that next step. Do enough wade fishing, however, and you will likely take a spill. In most cases, you can easily upright yourself because of the shallow depths. If the current sweeps you downstream, just go with the flow and keep your feet out in front for protection. Tight-fitting waders or those cinched with a belt prevent waders from filling up with water and make recovering from a spill much easier and safer.

Real Fishing

My younger son and I were recently checking out spots for spring bullhead fishing when we found an overgrown truck path that led to the water at a state park. The spot proved to be a good one, so when we returned the next evening, we brought a garbage bag and cleaned the area of rusty cans, plastics, and other nonbiodegradable items. Anglers, like campers, are advised to adopt the practice of leaving an area cleaner than it was when they arrived.

Small Watercrafts of All Types

For our purposes, small boats are those watercrafts that can be carried on top of a car, in the bed of a pickup truck, or even in the trunk of a car. Common watercrafts include canoes, johnboats, kayaks, belly boats, kick boats, and inflatable rafts. Any one of these watercrafts serves to open up a variety of fishing opportunities for the angler.

Canoes are typically lightweight and easy to transport, and their light weight makes them ideal for fishing trips that require portages. Also, their streamlined shape makes them ideal for travelling in moving waters, especially those that are boulder strewn. Canoes are powered by paddles, but square-backed canoes can handle a small gas-powered or electric motor. Side-mount brackets are also available for electric motors. Canoes do not handle well in strong winds or waves, so these crafts are better suited for small waters rather than larger, open ones. From a safety perspective, anglers are advised to do their fishing from a sitting position as canoes are most stable when there is a low center of gravity.

Johnboats, also spelled jonboats, come in various lengths, but we're talking about the 12-foot ones here. Made of aluminum, johnboats have their origins in the meandering, shoal-laden rivers of the Ozarks, and the flat bottom, width, and shallow draft make these boats ideal for fishing small rivers and other protected waters. Power options for car-top johnboats include oars, electric motors, and small gas-powered outboards.

Kayaks are fast becoming a watercraft choice for anglers. Originally, kayaks were used for travelling along waterways, but because of the demand, manufacturers are making kayaks specifically designed for fishing. These crafts include such features as rod storage, rod holder, tackle storage, net holder, bait well, fish well, and more. Paddles provide power for kayaks, but some of the more advanced models also have the option of leg power via foot pedals.

Belly boats or, float tubes, are essentially inner tubes with a seat and two holes for the legs. These one-person crafts can be powered by oars, but the user usually provides power with a good set of swim fins. Generally used in warm water, belly boats make for an economical and easily transported means of accessing waters.

Kick boats are constructed of a pair of pontoon-style floats with a seat in the middle. These crafts are heavier, more expensive, and more difficult to transport and assemble than belly boats, but kick boats are easier to maneuver, and they provide a higher seat for easier fishing. Kick boats can be powered by oars or by kicking with fins.

Inflatable rafts vary in quality and are subject to punctures, but a raft's light weight makes it ideal for fishing in remote trout ponds, where it might be too much of a chore to carry in heavier watercrafts.

The advantages of small watercrafts are:

➤ Their cost fits most budgets.

➤ They are relatively light and easy to handle.

➤ They open up a variety of waters for an otherwise shore-bound angler.

➤ They are fun to use.

➤ They provide access to places larger boats cannot go.

➤ They are ideal for making float trips down small rivers.

The disadvantages of small watercrafts are:

> ➤ They hold only one or two anglers.

> ➤ They must be used on small or protected waters.

> ➤ They have limited angler maneuverability.

> ➤ They have limited storage for gear.

Motorized Boats

Outboard engines power fishing boats, and most anglers use boats in the 14- to 21-foot range, although Great Lakes' anglers use larger vessels. Fishing boats are constructed of aluminum or fiberglass. Aluminum boats are light, durable, and easy to transport, but they ride rough in whitecap conditions. Fiberglass crafts, on the other hand, are heavier to handle and transport, but they ride better in rough water conditions. Some owners trailer their boats to fishing sites, others dock their boats seasonally, and across much of the continent boats must be stored during the winter months.

A gas-powered boat opens up tremendous fishing options, so owning a boat is in the hearts of most anglers. Exceptions do exist, though. For example, some budgets may not allow for the purchase price, some anglers might be satisfied fishing trout streams, and some living quarters might not allow for boat storage, although in such cases off-site storage is available for a fee.

Bass boats are the most popular style of fishing boat. Designed for speed and fishing comfort, bass boats are powered by motors in the 100- to 250-horsepower range, and they are commonly equipped with electronics, trolling motor, pedestal seats for casting, rod storage, tackle storage, live well, and more. Bass boats typically have console steering and seating for two or maybe three persons, and they are extremely stable in the water.

Deep-V boats have, as their name suggests, a V-shaped design to their hull from front to stern. Such boats are popular among walleye anglers because the boats handle well in large, open waters. Either tiller or console steering is available, and serious walleye anglers usually have a kicker motor for trolling and better boat control. Because deep-V boats sit low in the water, they are not intended for use in shallow water.

Semi-V and modified-V boats are also available. The semi-V has a V-shaped design in the front section so it rides better than a completely flat-bottomed boat. The semi-V adapts well to waters of various sizes. The modified-V is like the deep-V except that the angle is less sharp so the boat functions well in shallower water. Overall, the modified-V is both maneuverable and stable, making it a good choice for anglers.

Fishing Vocab

Some anglers place a kicker motor on their big-engine boats. A kicker is a small outboard motor used primarily for trolling, although it may also be used for boat control when casting or drifting. The kicker allows for slower speed and a quieter approach than the main outboard motor provides.

The flat-bottomed boat, which is really a big johnboat, is ideal for calmer waters. This boat maneuvers easily and offers plenty of fishing room. A drawback of the flat-bottomed boat is that it rides rough in choppy water.

Pontoon boats are growing in popularity as fishing vessels, especially on lakes. The boat's roominess can easily accommodate six or so anglers, and the size lends itself to a socializing style of fishing. Best suited for still fishing or drifting in quiet water conditions, pontoon boats do not handle that well in windy, rough conditions.

No matter what style of motorized boat an angler owns, it must be registered. When operating the boat, it is critical to abide by the weight and person limits as well as the horsepower limits listed on the boat's capacity sticker. Also, all boats should be equipped with required safety gear as mandated by state, provincial, or federal regulations.

CHAPTER 4

Gearing Up

In this chapter, you'll learn about rods, reels, fishing lines, terminal tackle, and accessories. Gaining a familiarity with the available fishing gear is no simple task; in fact, it's an ongoing process for two reasons. First of all, to appreciate the mega-amount of gear available, all you have to do is walk through the aisles of a major fishing retail store or browse through the hundreds of pages of a major fishing catalog. Secondly, new products arrive on the scene every year, so the available gear is an ever-expanding thing. A person would have to fish 365 days a year to become familiar with all of the fishing gear that is out there. Even though there is a tremendous volume of fishing gear on the market, you can catch plenty of fish with a minimal amount of equipment.

Two Standard Fishing Rods

The fishing rod, sometimes called a pole, is the most basic piece of angling equipment. There are two standard rods: spinning and bait-casting. Although you can find specialty rods and spinoffs of the two standard rod types, probably 90 percent of freshwater anglers use spinning and bait-casting rods. Fishing rods serve a number of purposes, including getting the bait or lure to the fish, working the bait or lure to entice a strike, detecting a bite, setting the hook, fighting the fish, landing the fish, and preventing line breakage.

Spinning Rods

The spinning rod is so named because it works in conjunction with a spinning reel. Spinning rods have the reel mounted on the bottom side, and the line guides face down, too. Spinning rods have larger rings in their guides than other rods in order to facilitate casting of the line while it comes off the reel in loops. Anglers typically hold a spinning rod in their dominant hand and handle the reel with their other hand, so right-handed people hold the rod in their right hand and reel with their left hand. Spinning rods are generally one-piece or two-piece, although multipiece rods are available for travelling anglers.

Bait-Casting Rods

As you would expect, a bait-casting rod is matched with a bait-casting reel. Bait-casting rods have the reel mounted on the top side, and the line guides also face up. Because bait-casting rods don't have to handle the loops or coils associated with spinning reels, the guides are smaller and closer to the rod blank. Bait-casting rods have a trigger grip on the underside of the rod to facilitate casting. Anglers commonly cast a bait-casting rod with their dominant hand and then switch the rod to their weaker hand to allow for handling the reel with the dominant hand. This means right-handed anglers cast with their right hand, put the rod in their left hand, and turn the reel handle with their right hand. More so than spinning rods, bait-casting rods are designed for fighting and controlling fish, particularly the larger species. Bait-casting rods are generally one-piece, but two-pieces rods are available.

All About Rods

Most modern rods are constructed of graphite or a graphite-fiberglass composite. Graphite is light, strong, sensitive, and affordable, ideal qualities in a fishing rod. Length, action, and weight are the basic characteristics in a fishing rod.

The parts of a rod include:

> ➤ The butt: The lower or bottom section of a rod

> ➤ The reel seat: A tightening-down device where reel attaches to rod

> ➤ The grip: The place where the angler holds the rod; it's made of cork or synthetic foam

> ➤ The hook holder: A metal loop above the grip for attaching a hook

> ➤ The blank: The shaft of the rod

> ➤ The guides: The metal ring devices along the rod through which the line passes

> ➤ The ferrule: A male-female connector for joining multi-sectioned rods

> ➤ The tip: The topmost portion of a rod, which plays a role in rod action and sensitivity

> ➤ The tip-top guide: The guide at the end of a rod

Rod Length

Although fishing rods may come in lengths from 4 to 14 feet, the most popular lengths range from 5 to 7 feet. Prior to the use of graphite, long rods lacked adequate stiffness so anglers avoided them. Now the trend is toward longer rods since they cast farther, offer better lure control, and provide the desired stiffness. When used for trolling, longer rods allow for a wider spread of lures. Short rods, on the other hand, are easier to handle. A good middle-of-the-road length for most freshwater fishing situations is 6 feet. As a general rule, higher-quality rods have more guides than lower-quality rods. At the very minimum, expect to have one guide per foot of rod length.

Rod Action

The action of a rod refers to where the rod bends along its length. Basic rod actions include fast, medium or moderate, and slow. A fast-action rod bends mainly near the tip. These rods allow for a quicker and stronger hook-set, and they allow for the detection of subtle bites when jig or bait fishing. Fast-action rods are also good for twitching surface lures. The front half of a medium-action rod bends and offers a good compromise between the advantages of fast-action and slow-action rods. The entire length of a slow-action rod bends, and this characteristic provides a shock-absorber effect when fighting a fish. Because the slow-action rods are quite forgiving, they result in fewer line breaks and allow for the use of lighter lines. Such rods also allow for a softer, gentler casting of live bait.

Fishing Vocab

Jigging refers to a fishing action that moves the lure in an up-and-down fashion. Lures commonly used in jig fishing are the lead-head jig, jigging spoon, and blade bait.

Rod Weight

The weight of a rod refers to its strength or power. Lighter-weight rods are designed for smaller fish and lures whereas the heavier ones are intended for larger species and lures. Although manufacturers may use different terminology, seven common ratings for rod weight or power are ultralight, light, medium light, medium, medium heavy, heavy, and extra heavy. If an angler were limited to a single rod, a medium-weight one could handle most freshwater fishing situations.

Purchasing Rods

When purchasing a rod, look for one that will handle the size of the baits and lures you intend to use and the size of the species you intend to pursue. For starters, an angler can't go wrong with a six-foot, medium-action, medium-weight rod. No matter what, check out how the rod feels in your hand, and go for a quality that fits your budget. Rods need little care except for periodic wiping down and periodic inspection for damage to guides. Damage to rods typically occurs when the rods are laid on the ground instead of leaned against something and when they are being taken in and out of vehicles. Rod cases are good insurance for rods, and rod racks make for safe storage.

Rod Labels

If you look at the shaft just above the reel handle, you will find critical information about the rod. For example, you will see something like this: Model (1221B) MH Rod Medium Action 6.6' ½-1 oz (Lure Weight) 100% Graphite. This information tells you that the rod is a medium-heavy, medium-action, bait-casting rod. Made of graphite, the rod is 6.5 feet long and designed to fish lures weighing from 0.5 to 1.0 ounce.

Bad Cast

When rods are not in use, some anglers place hooks directly in the guides, but this practice can damage the guides so anglers are advised to use the rod's hook holder for securing hooks.

Fishing Reels

Modern fishing reels have come a long way from their earlier counterparts. The three basic types of reels are spinning, bait-casting, and spin-casting, although there are a number of variations of the bait-caster. Among the primary functions of any reel are storing line, casting line, working the lure or bait, retrieving line, and providing a drag system to allow for play between the angler and the fish in order to prevent line break.

Spinning Reels

The spinning reel is arguably the most significant development in the modern fishing era, and these reels are by far the most popular among anglers. Spinning reels mount on the underside of the rod so they feel well balanced in the angler's hand. On most models, the reel handle is interchangeable from side to side so either a right-handed or left-handed person can use the same reel. Many reels also have interchangeable spools so the same reel can be used for fishing with different pound test lines without having to respool.

Fishing Vocab

Drag is an adjustable reel setting that resists the release of line as it is pulled from the reel. Drags can be set at various resistance levels depending on the strength of line being used and the size of the fish being pursued.

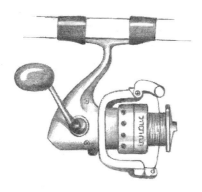

Line is released from and returned to a spinning reel by the use of a metal arm called a bail. To release line, the angler flips the bail over. To retrieve line, the angler turns the reel handle to engage the bail that spins and winds line around a fixed spool, thus the name spinning reel. Also called open-face reels, the drag system consists of a screw-down mechanism on the front or rear of the reel. Most anglers prefer a rear drag. Spinning reels also have an anti-reverse lock that prevents line from going freely off the reel.

The advantages of spinning reels are:

➤ They are easy to use and easy to cast.

➤ There are no backlashes.

➤ They cast lighter lures well.

➤ The same hand can be used for casting and retrieving.

➤ Line tangles are easy to deal with because of the open feature.

➤ They hold a lot of line.

➤ The handle is convertible to right-handed or left-handed retrieving.

The disadvantages of spinning reels are:

➤ Line twist occurs if an angler reels while the drag is going out.

> ➤ Line twist occurs if the angler repeatedly pulls line out without opening the bail.

> ➤ Loops can form on the spool and if not removed, they will cause line tangles on an ensuing cast.

> ➤ Spinning rigs are less effective for strong hook-sets and for horsing fish out of heavy cover.

Bait-Casting Reels

The bait-casting reel was the first modern reel, and current advances in its working mechanisms are contributing to the reel's increasing popularity. The bait-caster, unlike the spinning reel, does have a spool that actually spins to release and retrieve line. Since the weight of the lure pulls on the line to spin the spool, bait-casting reels are better suited for heavier lures than lighter ones.

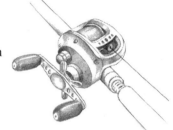

Bait-casting reels can be used for fishing with bait, but the reels are most often used for casting and trolling artificial lures. Sometimes called level-wind reels, bait-casters have an adjustment that allows for increasing or decreasing tension on the spool to match the weight of the fishing lure. Anglers who utilize this function properly are able to eliminate the bane of bait-casting reels, the dreaded backlash.

Fishing Vocab

A backlash is an overrun of the revolving spool on a bait-casting reel. This overrun causes the line to come off the spool in a rolling surge of tangles. Some backlashes are easily untangled; others call for cutting and replacing the line.

Bait-casting reels have a release button, or thumb bar, that the angler pushes in order to cast, and turning the reel handle engages gears that revolve the spool and wind in line. Most bait-casting reels have an adjustable star-drag mechanism located between the handle and the side plate of the reel. Additional features include a line guide that places line evenly across the spool and an anti-reverse mechanism that prevents line from spinning freely off the spool.

When casting bait-casting reels, right-handed people tend to cast with their right hand, switch the rod to their left hand, and then turn the reel handle with their right hand. Basically, a right-handed reel has the handle on the right side of the reel and vice versa for a left-handed reel. In order to avoid having to switch the rod from hand to hand, right-handed people might consider using a left-handed reel. Although this might feel a bit awkward initially, the angler would soon adjust and thus eliminate the need to switch the rod from hand to hand after each cast.

Some bait-casting reels are specially designed for trolling. Such reels don't cast well, but they are larger, heavier, have greater line capacity, and have excellent drag systems. Some models even have a line counter so the angler knows how much line he has out.

The advantages of bait-casting reels are:

➤ Properly adjusted, bait-casting reels are accurate casters.

➤ They allow for thumb control when casting and when applying drag tension.

➤ They allow for the use of heavier lines.

➤ They have quality drag systems.

➤ They are more sensitive to what's happening at line's end.

➤ They allow for more control and power when fighting fish.

➤ Line twist is not an issue.

The disadvantages of bait-casting reels are:

➤ They are harder to learn to use.

➤ Improperly adjusted, they are prone to backlashes.

➤ They are more expensive than other types of reels.

➤ Depending on retrieval hand, the angler may have to put the rod in a different hand after casting.

Spin-Casting Reels

Spin-casting reels are usually a youngster's first reel because they are inexpensive, easy to use, and prespooled with line. These reels are sometimes called closed-face reels because they have a cover over the spool, and they are sometimes called push-button reels because a button is pushed to release and cast the line. Like a bait-casting reel, the spin-caster sits on top of the rod and functions much like a bait-caster in casting approach and use of a star-drag mechanism. Even though spin-casting reels are handled similarly to bait-casting reels, spin-casters are generally lower quality reels, although quality ones are available. Some newer spin-casting reels are seated underneath the rod and have the feel of a spinning outfit. These reels have a trigger release rather than a push-button one.

The advantages of spin-casting reels are:

➤ They are easy to learn to use and cast.

➤ They handle easier than spinning rigs.

➤ They are good for light lines and lures.

➤ They are inexpensive.

The disadvantages of spin-casting reels are:

➤ They don't handle heavy lines.

➤ Drag systems are often of poor quality.

➤ The reel cover has to be removed to deal with line problems.

➤ Line capacity is limited.

Purchasing a Reel

When purchasing a reel, make sure the reel matches the rod. For example, you don't want to put a spinning reel on a bait-casting rod nor do you want to place a large reel on a lightweight rod. Such mistakes are easily avoidable by purchasing a combination rod and reel set where the manufacturer has properly matched the rod and reel. Such sets are typically less expensive than purchasing the rod and reel separately.

Also, check the labeling on the packaging to see that the reel matches your fishing needs. For example, some reels have spools designed for making longer casts or gear ratios designed for faster lure retrieve. Some packaging or labeling on a reel will list the line capacity for various line strengths. When in doubt about a reel purchase, listen to the advice of the experts at the local bait shop or at a major fishing retailer.

Reels demand a moderate amount of care. The best advice is to follow the manufacturer's guidelines, which usually involve periodically applying a supplied lubricant to the moving metal parts as shown in an enclosed diagram. By loosening the drag when the reel is not in use, you can lengthen the life span of a reel's drag system. When reel care or repair is beyond your skill level, take the reel to a local repair shop.

Putting Line on Reels

If line is incorrectly placed on a reel, the line will be full of twists and will perform poorly. When loading line on a spinning reel, place the spool of line on the floor with the label facing up. Thread the line through the guides and make sure the bail is open before attaching the line to the reel spool. For most spinning reels, the spool turns in a clockwise direction. For most spools of line, the line also comes off in a clockwise direction. The proper way to load a spinning reel is to have the line come off the spool in the same direction the reel spool turns. If twists are forming in the line, you need to turn the reel spool over.

When putting line on any reel, place tension on the line by holding it firmly between the thumb and index finger of your off hand as line is reeled onto the spool. Line loosely placed on a reel will perform poorly. General guidelines call for filling the spool to one-eighth inch of its edge.

The spool on a bait-casting reel revolves so line must come off the line spool in a revolving fashion. This is best done by placing a pencil or similar object through the line spool and having another person hold it. The line should come off the top of the line spool and be applied onto the reel spool over the top. The person holding the line spool can apply tension so the line loads tightly.

For spin-casting reels, follow the principles of placing line on a spinning reel. To verify whether the spool is turning clockwise or counterclockwise, though, you will likely have to remove the reel cover.

Fishing Lines

The good news about modern fishing lines is that anglers have plenty of quality products from which to choose. There is no bad news unless it's the pricy cost of some lines, but anglers do face the challenge of making an appropriate selection from the available options. To better understand fishing lines, here's a look at line characteristics and the basic types of lines.

Characteristics of Fishing Lines

Fishing lines are rated by their strength, which is called pound test, and is the number of pounds a line will hold before breaking. In theory, 10 pound test line should handle a 10-pound fish, but most knots weaken a line's strength, and proper drag setting and angler skill are factors, too. For example, a skilled angler can easily land a 20-pound striped bass on 10 pound test line, whereas a less adept fisherman might have a 5-pound smallmouth bass break that same line. The general guideline calls for selecting a pound test to match the rod, reel, and targeted species.

Diameter is another key characteristic, and compared to earlier lines, modern lines are excellent in their low diameter. Anglers prefer low-diameter lines because the lines are less visible to fish, and their thinness means less air resistance when casting and less water resistance when working a bait or lure. When fishing largemouth bass or catfish in brush or other heavy cover, an angler would likely opt for a higher diameter line.

Amount of stretch characterizes lines, too. Nylon monofilament lines may have up to 25 percent stretch, whereas braided lines have minimal if any stretch. Low-stretch lines allow for better sensitivity of lure action and strike detection, and the lines are also good for hook-setting and playing fish. Higher-stretch lines are more forgiving, but lower-stretch is generally a preferred characteristic.

Fishing lines have varying degrees of flexibility. Limp, flexible lines handle well and cast well; stiffer lines cast poorly and create twist problems. Stiff lines tend to have a memory, developing coils that interfere with line performance. This coil effect worsens the longer the line is on the reel. Significant use may reduce the coil effect, but it's best to replace coiling line.

Visibility is another line characteristic, and anglers have an array of choices from low visibility to high visibility. Less visible lines should be the choice in clear waters, and line tints that match water color are always smart choices. I am not one of them, but some anglers like high-visibility lines because the visibility allows for seeing line easily and detecting what's happening at line's end.

Bad Cast

Fishing lines become damaged and worn during regular use. As a result, anglers should routinely examine their lines for nicks and frays. Worn lines rank among the most common causes of losing both lure and fish during the fight. As you might expect, it is usually a favorite lure and a big fish that are lost.

All lines experience wear and tear, so lines merit regular inspection. Wear is very common at line's end because of scraping on rocks or nicks from teeth and hard mouths. Be sure to routinely inspect and retie the last few feet of line. Muskellunge anglers, for example, routinely retie prior to every fishing trip. If line wear shows higher up the line, that wear is likely caused by a faulty guide or worn reel part such as the line guide. In such cases, determine where the problem exists and make the appropriate repair. Sun exposure also weakens lines, so avoid leaving lines so exposed.

Types of Line

Manufacturers are constantly making developments in their fishing lines, and changes occur so frequently the average angler might struggle to make sense of all the available lines. Because of the various hybrid lines out there, categorizing lines by type remains a challenge. Still, here's a look at three main line types: monofilament, braided, and fluorocarbon.

Nylon monofilament line ranks among the most significant advances in modern angling, and three out of every four anglers use this line. Monofilament lines, often called simply mono, are reasonably priced, and unlimited choices are available with variations in characteristics such as pound test, diameter, stretch, flexibility, and visibility. Mono offers the advantages of suppleness, easy handling, and low visibility. The line holds knots well and can be used on all types of reels. Drawbacks of mono might be its stretch, especially when fishing in deep water, its memory, and its weakening when left in direct sunlight for periods of time.

Many lines come under the umbrella of braided, and these are lines manufactured by weaving strands of materials together. Dacron was the original braided line, and Dacron is still in use today, but various materials and space-age fibers are used in today's manufacturing processes. Because of those processes and the materials used, braided lines are more expensive than monofilament. Modern braided lines have earned the description of "super lines" because of their desirable characteristics that include low diameter, low stretch, lack of memory, resistance to sun damage, resistance to abrasion, strength, and excellent sensitivity for feeling lure action and detecting bites. In addition to cost, braided

Fishing Vocab

Backing is any line used to partially fill a reel spool prior to adding the main fishing line. Backing is most commonly used on fly-fishing reels, trolling reels, and spinning or bait-casting reels that have large, deep spools.

line disadvantages might be visibility, tendency of knot-slippage, and strength. Line strength allows for pulling snags free, but some lines are so strong that improper handling may result in broken guides or rods as well as line cuts on hands. Also, braided lines seem better designed for bait-casting than for spinning reels.

Instead of braiding materials in line construction, some manufactures fuse these same materials into a single-strand line rather than the multiple strands of braided line. Because of the simpler manufacturing process, these fused lines are less expensive than their braided counterparts.

Fluorocarbon, the new kid on the line block, is fast growing in popularity because it is the most invisible on the market. In fact, many anglers use fluorocarbon line for making their leaders especially when using braided lines. Actually made of fluorocarbon, the lines are comparatively expensive, but they are excellent for fishing in clear water. Other praiseworthy traits include abrasion resistance, low stretch, and sensitivity to lure action and fish bites. Fluorocarbon's single drawback, other than cost, is its relative stiffness compared to monofilament.

When purchasing line, anglers commonly buy a replacement spool. Such spools hold 100–300 yards of line and are meant to refill a single reel spool, although usually all of the line won't go on the reel. Large spools that hold thousands of yards of line are also available, but megaspools match the needs of professional anglers and guides more so than the needs of weekend anglers. Bait shops and fishing retail stores will install line on a reel, and this service ensures proper installation.

Terminal Tackle

Terminal tackle refers to the items tied on the end of a fishing line, and such basic tackle includes hooks, sinkers, bobbers, snaps, swivels, and leaders. The least expensive of all fishing equipment, terminal tackle is vital to fishing success particularly for anglers using live bait and prepared bait.

Hooks

Hooks come in a wide range of sizes and styles. Hook size is expressed in numbers; a large number represents a small hook and a low number signifies a larger hook. For example, a #16 hook might be used for trout, a #8 for bluegill, and a #2 for smallmouth bass. After size #1, though, the rule changes, and the numbers are followed by a zero, and a larger number indicates a bigger hook so a 4/0 hook is bigger than a 1/0 one. Anglers generally select a hook size to match the size of a fish's mouth and the size of the bait being used. Hooks may be thin wire or heavy wire. Thin-wire hooks allow live bait to move freely and penetrate a fish's mouth more easily, whereas heavy-wire hooks don't bend easily and do a better job of holding large fish once they are hooked.

Hook parts include:

➤ The eye: The loop to which the line is attached. Eyes may be turned up, turned down, or straight; the turned-down eye is the most popular. The shank: Connects the eye to the bend of the hook. Shanks may be long or short. Long shanks bend more easily, but they hold crawlers better and are easier to remove from a fish's mouth.

➤ The bend: The curved part of the hook, which determines the gap (width from point to shank) and throat, or bite (depth from bend to point). A deeper throat means deeper hook penetration, whereas a wider gap allows for the use of bigger bait.

➤ The barb: A reverse point to help keep a fish on the hook. Oversized barbs, though, can make for difficult hook penetration.

➤ The point: Where the hook contacts the fish. A cardinal rule of fishing calls for anglers to maintain sharp hook points.

Numerous hook styles or types are available, and most names aptly characterize the hook. For example, the most widely used hook is the single J-hook, which has a J shape with a single point. A double hook consists of two hooks with a single eye and shank; a treble hook consists of three hooks with a single eye and shank. Double and triple hooks are common on artificial lures but rarely used for fishing with live bait. A snelled hook has a monofilament leader attached, and a weedless hook has a wire arm (weed guard) extending from the eye to the point to keep the hook weed free. A salmon-egg hook has a short shaft and is designed to hold a salmon egg; a bait-holder hook has barbs along the shaft to better hold bait. A circle hook has a circular design and when properly used hooks the fish near the front of the mouth.

The most common hook styles are sproat, O'Shaughnessy, and Aberdeen. The all-purpose sproat hook has a strong parabolic bend, the O'Shaughnessy hook has a strong round bend and offers good holding power, and the Aberdeen hook is a light-wire, round-bend hook that also offers good penetration. Bronze is the standard hook color, but blue, silver, black, and gold are also popular. A growing number of anglers are now using red hooks because this color seems to entice more strikes.

Real Fishing

Barbless hooks have no barbs so the hooks result in less injury to delicate fish that are to be released and make for easier unhooking of fish, too.

Conscientious anglers use only sharp hooks. Dull hooks mean poor penetration and lost fish, so dull hooks need to be sharpened or replaced. Anglers can visually check hook sharpness, but a better method is to slide the point of the hook across your fingernail. A sharp hook grabs a bit and leaves a scratch mark, whereas a dull hook just slides across the fingernail. The general guideline calls for anglers to use the smallest hook possible to do the job. Smaller hooks penetrate better, they are less likely than large hooks to alert fish, and they allow live bait to move more freely.

Unfortunately, fish aren't the only ones to get hooked as anglers sometimes find a hook impaled in themselves or a fishing partner. When this happens, several options exist. If the hook hasn't penetrated past the barb, the hook can be easily removed from the flesh. If the hook has penetrated a sensitive area such as near the eye or if the hook is deeply imbedded or if it's a very large hook, cut it free from the line and seek medical attention.

If the hook has penetrated flesh past the barb, one option is to push the hook through the flesh so that the barb emerges and then use wire cutters to cut the hook below the barb. With no barb, the hook will easily pull free. You should note that this method can be painful, and the wound must be cared for to prevent infection.

A second option for hook penetration past the barb involves five steps. This method works best for small-barbed and thin-wire hooks.

1. Get a 2-foot length of heavy fishing line or cord and tie the two ends together.
2. Loop the line over your wrist and at the other end form a small loop between the thumb and forefinger.
3. Place this small loop over the eye of the hook and bring the loop to the middle of the hook's bend.
4. Press down on the eye of the hook with your other thumb. This step creates an opening and an angle to get the barb clear of the flesh.
5. Give the small loop on the hook's bend a sharp pull directly in line with the hook's shank. The hook should come free with a minimal amount of pain. Again, the wound should be treated to prevent infection.

Weights

Weights, commonly called sinkers, come in a variety of sizes and shapes. Their purpose is to get a bait or lure to a desired depth. Light sinkers may weigh only fractions of an ounce while the heaviest ones used for freshwater fishing may weigh up to half a pound or more. Most weights are made of lead, but environmental concerns have given birth to sinkers made of brass, cadmium, steel, tin, and tungsten. These newer sinkers are generally more costly and less effective than ones made of lead.

Weights may be fixed or free-sliding. Fixed sinkers remain in their attached position; free-sliding, or slip, sinkers ride up and down the line.

The most common fixed sinkers are:

➤ Split shot sinkers: Generally lightweight, split shot sinkers are round with a gap in them that allows for the sinker to be pinched on the line. Split shot are placed on the line ahead of the bait or lure.

➤ Bell sinkers: These bell-shaped sinkers are attached to the end of the line via a metal loop and are generally used for fishing with live bait near the bottom. They hold bottom well and cast well.

➤ Bank sinkers: Although similar in function to bell sinkers, bank sinkers have a molded loop rather than a wire one for line attachment.

➤ Rubbercore sinkers: These sinkers are attached to the line by twisting the ends of the core in opposite directions. These weights are placed ahead of the bait or lure and are easily attached and removed.

> ➤ In-line trolling sinkers: As their name suggests, these sinkers are attached in the line ahead of the lure and are used for trolling. They come in a variety of styles with wire loops at each end that require a connection to the main line and a connection to the length of line that attaches to the lure.

The most common slip sinkers are:

> ➤ Egg, or barrel, sinkers: These weights have a hole through the center and are placed in the line ahead of a swivel or small split shot to keep the weight from sliding down to the hook. They allow a fish to take the bait without feeling the resistance of the sinker.

> ➤ Bullet, or cone, sinkers: These weights also have a hole through the center and are primarily used when fishing with plastic worms for largemouth bass. They are placed directly ahead of the worm; their cone shape helps the rig work in weeds.

> ➤ Walking sinkers: These sinkers function the same way as egg, or barrel, sinkers, but they have a stand-up feature and are designed to move or walk the bait or lure along the bottom.

As with hooks, the best guideline for sinkers is to use the smallest weight that will do the job; excessive weight may result in a fish rejecting the bait or lure.

Floats

Floats, more commonly called bobbers, serve the purpose of suspending a bait or small artificial lure at a desired depth. Floats also allow for drifting bait along the current flow of a stream or across the water with the aid of the wind. In addition to getting an offering where the angler wants it, the movement of a float gives a visual indication of a bite.

Most bobbers are constructed of hallow plastic, balsa wood, Styrofoam, or cork. These light materials are effective for indicating bites but not for casting. For casting efficiency, anglers use light lines, rely on the weight of the bait or lure, add split shot, or use a self-weighted bobber. The basic concept of bobber fishing is quite simple, but the variables of fishing with floats are illustrated in the larger retail stores that will have an entire aisle of float options. Floats are great for kids, and although they are primarily a panfish option, floats are also used for species such as northern pike, walleyes, steelhead, and catfish.

A variety of float styles exist, but the two basic ones are the ball with a round shape and the pencil with a shaftlike shape. Like weights, floats may be attached in a fixed position or allowed to slide up and down the line. Fixed floats work well in shallow water, but slip bobbers must be used for deep-water fishing. Slip bobbers have a bobber stop pinched on the line above the bobber to set the bait at the desired depth. The float slips down the line as the angler winds line onto the reel.

Like selecting hook size and weight size, anglers should opt for the lightest bobber to perform the job. The resistance caused by an oversized bobber commonly results in fish rejecting the bait or artificial lure.

Snaps, Swivels, and Leaders

Snaps, swivels, snap swivels, and leaders have a place in every angler's tackle box. Regarding size, go with the smallest one that will do the job. Common color choices for this terminal tackle include black, silver, and gold. I prefer black.

The most common snap has a loop at one end that attaches to the main line and a safety pin design at the other for attaching to lures. Cross-lock snaps, however, have better holding power than their safety pin cousins. Snaps allow for the easy attachment and change of lures.

A swivel has loops at each end for attaching to the main line and for attaching to a shorter length of line that goes to the lure. Swivels can be used to stop sliding sinkers and to prevent line twist. Barrel swivels work well for sliding sinker rigs, but ball bearing swivels are the way to go to prevent line twist when using spinners and spoons, lures that spin. Three-way swivels have three loops instead of two so they allow for attaching two leaders, one for a weight on the bottom and the other for a lure at a 90-degree angle. Snap swivels, as their name suggests, are a combination of a snap and a swivel. While a snap does not prevent line twist when using spoons and spinners, a quality snap swivel performs that job admirably.

Commercial leaders are generally made of wire, rated by pound test, and come in lengths varying from 6 inches to 3 feet. Common colors are black and silver, and I prefer black. Wire leaders are a mainstay when pursuing toothy fish such as the northern pike, but many anglers make their own leaders using monofilament or fluorocarbon lines. When attached to more visible main lines, these leaders offer low visibility and work well in clear water conditions or for line-shy fish. When using spinners or spoons, a ball bearing leader is the best for prevention of line twist.

Real Fishing

The plastic boxes with adjustable compartments, sometimes called utility boxes, are ideal for storing and transporting terminal tackle. The compartments allow for easy access, and they allow you to neatly arrange all of your terminal tackle by item, size, etc. Some floats, particularly the larger ones, don't fit well in the compartments, though.

Common Fishing

Accessories

The number of available fishing accessories seems to grow every year, but I especially recommend nine.

1. Fishing license
2. Personal flotation device
3. Lake chart to aid in selecting places to fish
4. Clippers for all line cutting, including the trimming of tag ends
5. Set of needle-nose pliers for removing hooks, straightening hooks, pinching down barbs, scrimping shot, tightening loose reel parts, and more
6. Landing net or cradle sized to match the fish you expect to catch
7. Measuring device to verify that a fish meets the minimum legal length if you are keeping your catch for the dinner table
8. Sharp fillet knife for cleaning fish, and for other uses such as cutting a hook free from your clothing
9. Tackle box

The ninth accessory, a tackle box, is used for storing your various fishing items. Tackle boxes come in various sizes, styles, and available storage compartments. The traditional tackle box was metal and then plastic, and consisted of a series of trays where anglers stored all their items. The current trend, though, is toward a soft tackle box or nylon-padded case that holds a number of utility boxes. An angler heading to the water packs the utility boxes suited for the outing. For example, an angler heading out for largemouth bass might take along five separate utility boxes of terminal tackle, plastic worms, jigs and trailers, plugs, and surface lures.

Fishing Vocab

A **plug** is a hard plastic or wooden fishing lure that typically has a minnow shape.

CHAPTER 5

Handling the Rod and Reel

In This Chapter

➤ How to set the drag

➤ How to make basic casts

In this chapter you will learn about the importance of the drag on a reel and how to properly set the drag. You will also learn how to make the overhead, sidearm, cross-body, and underhand casts.

Setting the Drag

The drag is an adjustable mechanism that allows line to come off the spool; a drag can be set at any resistance level to allow the release of line as it is pulled from the reel. Essentially, the drag allows a hooked fish to take line out without the line breaking and without getting any slack in the line. An improperly set drag probably results in more lost fish than any other factor, so checking the drag should be routine on all fishing trips. Properly setting the drag is a fishing fundamental.

Drag Location

A spinning reel may have a front or rear drag. The front drag is a cap, and the rear drag is a knob, and in both cases turning the drag clockwise tightens it or increases the tension, and turning the drag counterclockwise loosens it or decreases the tension. Some anglers prefer the rear drag because it is easier to adjust while fighting a fish; the angler's hand doesn't come in contact with the line as might happen when adjusting a front drag.

Bad Cast

When fighting a fish, some anglers tend to overadjust the drag. If a drag is properly set, it likely needs minimal, if any, adjustment during the fight. By constantly lowering and increasing drag tension during the fight, an angler creates a greater risk of losing the fish.

Bait-casting and spin-casting reels have a star drag situated where the reel handle attaches to the body of the reel. Turning the star drag forward, or clockwise, increases tension while turning the star drag rearward, or counterclockwise, reduces the tension. Bait-casting reels commonly have the smoothest drag systems, so these reels are popular among anglers targeting larger fish such as muskellunge and chinook salmon. Because many spin-casting reels are inexpensive and designed for youths and fishing for panfish, the drag systems are inferior for handling larger fish such as northern pike and striped bass.

Drag Tension

No set rule exists for correct drag tension, but anglers generally like to set the drag somewhere between 50 percent and 75 percent of line strength. If an angler were using 10 pound test line, the drag would be set somewhere in the 5- to 8-pound range. The key is to have the drag set below the breaking point of the line, taking into consideration that your knot has likely lessened that breaking point.

Meticulous individuals might want to attach a scale to line's end to verify the breaking point of the line or to set the drag at a precise poundage, but more realistically anglers put a nonhook item at line's end, step on the item, and then lift the rod to check for a desired drag setting. Most anglers check drag tension by pulling line directly off the reel by hand, but a better method is to pull line with a bend in the rod as that better simulates a fish at line's end.

By letting line slip from the reel when pressure is applied, the drag in conjunction with the rod acts like a shock absorber, so a properly set drag allows an angler to fight and land a fish that exceeds the breaking strength of the line. A drag that is too tight may result in the hook pulling out of a fish's mouth or the line breaking, with the resultant loss of both fish and rigging. If the drag is too loose, poor hook-setting occurs. Some anglers like loose drags because such settings prolong the fight and make the catch seem bigger. A loose drag, however, can result in overplaying the fish, causing it to become too stressed for successful release. Also, when using spinning reels, line twist occurs as line is pulled out during fish runs.

Before storing outfits, it's a good idea to loosen the drag. When not in use over a period of time drags can set up, so they need to be checked and set prior to each outing. Drag systems vary in quality, and generally you get what you pay for. In essence, a good drag allows line to come off the reel smoothly while a poor drag causes line to come off the spool in jerks.

Casting

Casting is the method of throwing a bait or lure where the angler wants it to go. Accuracy and distance are the keys to good casting. Novice anglers tend to put distance ahead of accuracy when casting, but accuracy should be the primary objective. Casting is a skill, and anyone can become a skilled caster. Casting doesn't require great strength, but timing and letting the rod do the work are critical.

There is no right or wrong way to cast. Like the various styles used by a baseball pitcher, casting styles can vary from angler to angler. Also, like a baseball pitcher, it's critical to visualize hitting the target. Here's a look, though, at the general maneuvers employed when casting, and then we'll look at making specific casts including the overhand, sidearm, cross-body, and underhand.

Casting Basics

General casting maneuvers begin with letting the lure extend 6 inches or so from the rod tip and the angler holding the line at the reel. When using a spinning reel, the angler holds the line against the rod with his forefinger. For bait-casting reels, the angler pushes the release button and places his thumb on the spool. For spin-casting reels, the angler controls the line by holding his thumb on the release button.

Bad Cast

Avoid the mistake of focusing on distance rather than accuracy when casting. In nine out of ten fishing situations, accuracy is more important than distance. As a fishing guide, I see too many anglers casting for distance, an occurrence that usually results in poor bait or lure placement as well as a poor feel for what is happening at line's end.

The next steps involve picking out a target and swinging the rod away from the target to let the weight of the lure bend the rod. This bending is called flexing or loading. Then the angler swings the rod in the direction of the target making sure to release the line at the correct point to hit the target. As the lure approaches the target, the angler can control distance by feathering the line and pinching it against the rod for spinning reels or by putting thumb pressure on the spool for bait-casting reels. A spin-caster has to use his or her off hand to feather the line or pinch it against the rod. Once the lure hits the water or sinks to the desired depth, the angler engages the reel by turning the reel handle.

Overhand Cast

The most basic cast is the overhand, which begins with extending the lure 6 inches or so from the rod tip and facing the target. After pointing the rod tip at the target, the angler bends his elbow to raise the rod tip to a position near ten or eleven o'clock at which point the rod tip flexes a bit. Then the angler sharply brings the rod back to the one o'clock or so position. At the end of this backstroke, the rod loads and the angler begins the forward stroke propelling the rod tip toward the target. About midway through the forward stroke, just before the two o'clock position, the angler releases the line and follows through so the rod tip points at the target. If the line is released too soon, the lure will fly high in the air, and if the line is released too late, the lure will slap the water and fall short of the target.

Fishing Vocab

In casting, the rod is pictured as the dial of a clock, and twelve o'clock refers to the point directly overhead of the angler. From there, one o'clock, two o'clock, etc. refer to points in a clockwise direction while eleven o'clock, ten o'clock, etc., refer to points in a counterclockwise direction.

Fishing Vocab

The back cast is that part of the cast when the fishing rod is moved from a position in front of the angler to a position behind the angler. When casting, fishermen must always be aware of their back cast because the back cast results in more partners getting hooks imbedded in their bodies than does any other fishing action.

Sidearm Cast

The sidearm cast is similar to the overhand cast except that the sidearm cast is performed in motions parallel to the water rather than perpendicular to it; it's horizontal in motion rather than vertical. Again let out 6 inches or so of line. If you are right-handed, put your left foot slightly ahead of the right and face the target. Point the rod tip at the target, swing the rod parallel to the water and away from the target to just beyond 90 degrees, feel the rod tip load, and begin the forward stroke. Prior to the rod tip pointing at the target again, at around 45 degrees, release the line. Again, follow through and stop the rod when the tip points at the target.

Cross-Body Cast

The cross-body cast is a mirror image of the sidearm cast. Visualize someone throwing a Frisbee, and you have the basic motions of the cross-body cast. This cast may lack the power of its twin, but when other anglers or objects prevent use of the sidearm cast, the cross-body cast is the way to go.

Fishing Vocab

Loading occurs when a rod takes on the weight of the bait or lure during the back cast. This loading or flexing of the rod gives the rod the potential energy to propel the bait or lure forward.

Underhand Cast

Like the cross-body cast, the underhand cast may lack power, but it's an effective technique when other anglers or overhanging trees prevent use of other casts. Begin by pointing the rod tip at the target and then lift the rod to shoulder height or so to allow the rod tip to slightly load. Perform a downward stroke to a position slightly below the waist so the rod tips loads a bit. Then begin a second upward flex releasing the line as rod tip nears the starting point, at about a 90-degree angle to the water. The underhand cast utilizes a lot of wrist action and minimal arm movement.

Accuracy and Distance

A number of factors affect casting accuracy and distance. Even though these variables are common sense, they merit mentioning anyway. One factor is the wind, and anglers can combat strong winds by using heavier lures or by casting crosswind or downwind rather than directly into the wind, an act that almost guarantees backlashes when using a bait-casting reel. Longer rods cast farther than shorter ones, and lighter lines cast more efficiently than heavier, stiffer ones. Also, a reel spool filled to near capacity will outperform a partially filled spool. Slow-action rods handle light lures better than fast-action rods, lightweight rods are effective for casting lighter lures, and heavy rods are good casters of heavier lures. A rod with quality and properly spaced line guides enhances both distance and accuracy.

Casting Practice

Since casting is a skill rather than an inherited trait, backyard practice sessions serve to make anglers better casters. Always practice in an open area and avoid hard surfaces, which can cause line damage. In addition, use a hookless object such as a rubber casting plug at line's end. Focus more on accuracy than distance, and try mastering a variety of casts. Also, work at making soft casts as they are easier on live bait and less likely to alarm fish. Don't expect perfection in casting because even professional anglers slip up occasionally due to equipment malfunction or angler inattention.

Finally, think safety first when casting. Hooks and lead weights can cause bodily harm, so always be aware of your back cast and use a technique where the forward and backward strokes are at an angle away from other people. Also, pay attention to the casting practices of fellow anglers, and don't hesitate to remind them to watch their back casts.

CHAPTER 6

Fish Senses and Natural Baits

In This Chapter

➤ What senses fish use for survival

➤ What natural baits catch fish

➤ How to acquire and use natural baits

Understanding a fish's senses and using natural baits that appeal to those senses increase an angler's odds for successful catches. Fish primarily use their senses to find available food and to elude predators. Since natural baits appeal to a fish's feeding senses, baits such as worms, minnows, crayfish, insects, etc. are effective fish catchers. Also, knowing what alerts a fish's senses to danger allows an angler to avoid those things.

Fish Senses

Vision and lateral line are the primary tools fish use for finding prey and eluding predation. Hearing, smell, taste, and feel play a part in a fish's survival, but a lesser part.

Vision

Because their eyes are positioned on the sides of their head, fish can pretty much see in all directions except for minor blind spots directly behind, in front, and below. Vision plays a more significant role in clear water than in murky water. In very clear water, fish can see over 100 feet while in very murky water, fish may see only a matter of inches. On the average, fish probably rely on their vision out to the 20-foot or so range.

The size of a fish's eyes also affects the importance of sight. For example, catfish and bullheads have very small eyes and are basically nearsighted, so they rely on other senses for survival. Species like northern pike and brown trout have good long-range vision that helps them when they swim out from hiding places to attack their prey. Large eyes translate to effective feeding in low light conditions, so large-eyed walleyes and muskellunge can see in the dark, conditions under which their prey does not see well.

Fish see colors, too, and colors play a more significant role in shallow water than in deep water, where colors are filtered out. In clear water, prey emit their natural colors, but fish see only a silhouette, rather than natural colors, in murky water.

Lateral Line

The lateral line is a sensory structure consisting of a longitudinal line running the length of a fish's body. The lateral line consists of sensors that enable the fish to detect vibrations from anything moving in the water. Because fish are such vibration-sensitive creatures, the ability of the lateral line to detect vibration plays a key role both in finding prey and avoiding predators. Experts believe the lateral line also plays a role in detecting pressure changes, temperature changes, sound, and current flow.

While the lateral line does play a role in clear water, that role becomes even more important in dark water conditions where fish have to rely less on vision and more on sensing vibrations for survival. No matter what water conditions an angler fishes, he or she is advised to create as little vibration as possible when wading, controlling a boat, or doing anything else because such vibrations will likely put fish in a defensive rather than a feeding mode.

Hearing, Smell, Taste, and Feel

To a lesser degree than vision and lateral line, fish also rely on hearing, smell, taste, and feel for survival. Fish have an inner ear that allows them to pick up sound travelling through the water. Some people believe that talking will scare fish; that is unlikely, though, because the sounds of normal talking do not travel through the water. For the most part, sound is not a concern when using live baits.

The sense of smell varies in different species, but nostrils on either side of the head allow fish to take in water and identify odors of both prey and predator. For feeding purposes, trout and salmon rely on their sense of smell more than other species do. From an avoidance-of-predator perspective, fish go on alert when baits carry foreign odors from humans, when bears are feeding upstream, when baitfish and other fish become alarmed and emit chemicals, and when a larger predator such as a northern pike fins nearby. For many species, the sense of smell plays a more important role in predator avoidance than in feeding. A highly developed sense of smell is necessary for survival of the species among anadromous fish that live in salt water and must return hundreds or even thousands of miles to their native freshwater stream to spawn.

Taste and feel are of secondary importance in fish survival, but fish are capable of detecting taste and feel by sensors in the mouth. Bottom-feeding species such as carp, bullheads, and catfish rely on these senses more so than other fish. Certainly the use of natural baits has the edge over artificial lures when it comes to taste and feel.

Natural Baits

Natural baits, particularly live ones, offer excellent sensory appeal to fish because these baits are a routine part of a fish's diet. These baits look, smell, feel, and taste natural, and they also emit natural, fish-attracting vibrations. Among the most commonly used natural baits in freshwater angling are worms, baitfish, crayfish, insects, amphibians, leeches, grubs, and salmon eggs.

Fishing Vocab

Anadromous refers to fish that live their adult lives in salt water but return to fresh water to spawn. *Anadromous* also refers to salmon and trout that spend their adult lives in the Great Lakes and then return to tributary streams to spawn.

Worms

Worms are the most widely used bait in North America, and the most common types are the night crawler and the common earthworm, often called a garden worm. Night crawlers average 6 inches in length while garden worms average 4 inches. I'm not certain why worms appeal to fish because I have rarely seen them in streams, rivers, ponds, lakes, and reservoirs, but their slow, undulating movements as well as their smell, texture, and taste can seem enticing to a fish's senses. I do know why worms appeal to anglers, though.

For one thing, worms are readily available for a reasonable price at bait shops, convenience stores, and many other locations. Also, anglers can pick their own night crawlers from a damp lawn or dig their own garden worms from moist, damp soils. Find a neighborhood kid who gathers night crawlers, and you'll have the best prices in town.

Worms are also easy to transport and keep alive; just place them in damp bedding in cool, dark storage. Night crawlers are usually sold in cardboard or Styrofoam containers that hold a dozen or two worms, and they will stay lively for a couple of weeks if stored in a refrigerator. On summer fishing trips, avoid leaving worm containers exposed to the heat of the sun. Instead, place them in the shade, or, better yet, place them in a cooler.

Perhaps the most attractive feature of worms is that they catch a variety of fish, most notably panfish, bullheads, catfish, bass, trout, walleyes, carp, and suckers. A small piece of worm placed on a tiny hook will also catch baitfish that can then be used for larger game fish.

Bad Cast

Worms can spoil quickly in warm temperatures. Spoiling also occurs if worms are kept for too long or if they are kept in inadequate bedding. The best way to ensure worms stay is to keep them cool and to check them regularly during a fishing trip and during storage. Immediately discard any worms that show signs of deterioration.

Worms are generally placed in pieces or whole on a bare hook, although they are also used to tip jigs for a variety of species and on crawler harnesses for walleyes. Anglers place worms on hooks in a variety of ways. The most common way is to hook the worm twice in the head area and leave a portion of the tail section trailing freely off the hook. A night crawler hooked once through the collar appeals to larger fish, but smaller fish in the area will often nibble at the worm leaving only that single piece impaled on the hook. Singly hooked garden worms work well for stream trout. When fishing for catfish or carp, anglers commonly ball up the worm by hooking it several times along the worm's entire length. Tipping jigs for panfish and walleyes involves threading a worm piece on the hook. Crawler harnesses have two or three hooks, and night crawlers are attached by extending the worm its full length and inserting each of the hooks along that length.

When using worms, use the smallest hook possible to do the job and avoid using too much worm for the size of the hook because that can impede good hook-setting. Don't be shy about putting a fresh worm or worm piece on your hook to replace a soggy, used worm. Fresh bait translates to more bites. Finally, try to extend the worm's tail from the hook as that action means more fish at line's end, too.

Real Fishing

I often drift crawler harnesses for walleyes during the summer months. When using crawlers, I take a handful from the container and drop the worms in a pail with an inch or two of water. This action keeps worm bedding from getting all over the boat, and the worms swell up, which gives them greater visual attraction.

Baitfish

Baitfish are often called minnows, and though there are hundreds of species in the minnow family, many baitfish used by anglers are actually members of other fish families. Among the dozens and dozens of most popular baitfish are shiners, chubs, smelts, dace, suckers, sculpins, alewives, shad, fatheads, and small panfish. Baitfish are excellent fish catchers because they make up a major part of a game fish's diet, and baitfish have high sensory appeal from the perspective a fish's vision and ability to sense vibrations.

Baitfish can be more difficult to acquire and keep alive than worms, but minnows are readily available at bait shops. Other options for obtaining baitfish include using a drop net, minnow trap, seine, or hook and line. Because some fish and game departments have regulations regarding bait collection, use, and transportation, you should always check those regulations prior to any collecting. To stay alive, baitfish require fresh oxygenated water and that presents a challenge to users. Livewells, battery-operated aerators, and constant water changing are okay for short-term storage, but longer storage requires a large tank with fresh oxygenated water or a baitfish container actually submerged in a stream or lake. Avoid overcrowding baitfish in a minnow bucket or other storage container to prevent undue stress. When minnows start coming to the surface, it is a sure sign they are stressed and need fresh water.

Bad Cast

Never introduce nonnative minnows or fish to a body of water. Leave such decisions to professional fisheries' biologists. Many native fisheries have been ruined by the introduction of nonnative species by well-intentioned anglers.

Baitfish range in size from 1-inch fatheads to 12-inch or longer suckers, and these minnows catch everything from 5-inch crappies to 5-foot muskellunge. Keys are to match minnow size to the size of the targeted species and hook size to size of the minnow. Anglers employ two basic methods for hooking live baitfish, placing the hook through both lips from the bottom up or placing the hook through the back just below the dorsal fin. Generally, the lip hook is used for moving-water situations, and the dorsal hook for quiet-water conditions, so when fishing in current, when drifting, and when using a slow cast-and-retrieve technique, a lip-hooked minnow is the way to go. Minnows hooked below the dorsal fin are forced sideways in moving water, and this action stresses the minnow and gives it an unnatural appearance as the minnow is presented on its side rather than upright.

When using oversize baitfish for larger species, anglers often use minnow harnesses or quick-strike rigs, which have hooks placed along the bait's length that allow the angler to set the hook sooner than a single hook allows. A quicker hook-setting prevents fish from swallowing large baits and thus allows for more effective catch and release.

When fishing with live minnows, try to make a soft presentation because hard-hitting casts will stress the bait. Minnows can also be damaged in the hooking process, so hook them gently. When tipping jigs with minnows, either live or dead ones will work because the angler imparts motion to the minnow as he or she works the jig. Also, dead baits are effective for slow-moving, bottom-feeding species like catfish.

Crayfish

Crayfish, sometimes called crawfish or crawdads, are popular baits for bass, walleyes, yellow perch, and trout. Most anglers purchase crayfish at bait shops, but they can be collected by looking under rocks in shallow water and along shorelines. Seining in ponds also produces crayfish as does setting a wire-mesh trap baited with a chunk of meat. Crayfish are hardier than minnows, but they still require cool oxygenated water.

Crayfish molt, or shed, their shell, and fish prefer soft-shelled crayfish, although hard-shelled ones will catch fish. Some anglers remove the claws from crayfish so they will not grab onto the line or other object, but such removal is generally not necessary. Hooking a crayfish in the tail from the bottom up allows the critter to move freely and is the traditional hooking method.

Terrestrial Baits

Among the most popular terrestrial baits are grasshoppers and crickets, both of which naturally fall into the water and appeal to panfish, trout, and bass. Most bait shops don't carry these insects, but you can collect them by hand or net. Look for grasshoppers in grassy fields, and look for crickets under rocks and logs in shady areas. The two baits hold up well in a ventilated container, and the accepted hooking method is just behind the head under the collar. Because grasshoppers and crickets are fragile, use a fine-wire hook and cast them softly.

Amphibians

Frogs and salamanders aren't widely used as live bait options even though they appeal to a variety of game fish, particularly bass and pike. Amphibians can be collected both by hand or net. Look for frogs in shallow, weedy waters, for terrestrial salamanders in damp, wooded areas under rotting logs, and for aquatic salamanders under rocks in shallow water. If legal, frogs are easily caught at night with the aid of a flashlight. Hook frogs through the lips from the bottom up or use a frog harness, and if you plan on releasing your catch, attempt to set the hook before the fish swallows the frog. Generally fished on the surface, you can also use weights to fish below the surface. Salamanders, sometimes called water dogs or mud puppies, are also hooked through the lips, but they are typically fished near the bottom.

Leeches

Leeches, also called blood suckers, tend to turn people off, but they turn fish on. Leeches are particularly popular among walleye anglers and are available at bait shops in areas near walleye waters. Leeches naturally inhabit still waters such as lakes and reservoirs, but they work well in rivers, too. Hook leeches through the mouth or sucker from the bottom up, and fish them as you would a worm. Be sure to check them periodically because they have a tendency to ball up on the hook.

Grubs

Grubs, mealworms, and other larval stages of various insects are extremely effective for panfish. Commonly sold in small plastic containers at bait shops, these inexpensive baits hold up for weeks in the refrigerator, and they can be used year round. Grubs can be fished on a small hook singly or in groups of three or so, although anglers more commonly use grubs to tip small jigs and spoons particularly during the ice fishing season.

Salmon Eggs

The salmon egg is an effective natural bait since many trout and salmon feed on each other's eggs or reflexively devour them. Anglers can purchase eggs from bait shops or use eggs from a freshly caught and kept fish. Fresh salmon eggs can be hooked singly or tied up in an egg-colored mesh and then attached to a hook by a loop on the rear of the hook shank. Salmon eggs are a go-to bait for rainbow trout, river-run steelhead, and chinook salmon.

Preserved Baits

Some natural baits are available in preserved form, and the most common are minnows and salmon eggs. Minnows may be preserved by freezing, drying, or placing in a liquid, whereas salmon eggs, singly or in bunches, are preserved in a form that makes them firm for staying on hooks. Some preserved eggs are brightly colored for increased visual appeal, and many preserved baits are scented to appeal to a fish's sense of smell.

CHAPTER 7

Artificial Lures

> **In This Chapter**
>
> ➤ The ten variables in lures
> ➤ The five types of lures
> ➤ The characteristics of each lure type
> ➤ How to fish each type of lure

In this chapter you'll learn about the variables that exist in artificial lures and what those variables mean to fish. Also, you'll learn about the five basic lure types (spinners, plugs, soft plastics, jigs, and spoons) and their intended uses.

Shopping Tips for Artificial Lures

The number of artificial lures currently available to anglers is truly overwhelming. When you consider that a company may produce a single lure in six different sizes and twelve different colors, that one lure alone translates to seventy-two options for an angler. Then consider that one company may produce dozens of different lures and that there are hundreds if not thousands of lure makers across North America. How does an angler deal with all of these options?

The best way to start is by selecting lures that are designed for your targeted species. Catalogs and store aisles commonly organize lures in this manner. Also, select lures for different depths. If you are targeting largemouth bass in a reservoir, you might try three lures: a surface plug for fishing over weed beds and in shallow water, a spinner bait for reaching mid-depths of 5 to 10 feet, and a tube jig so you can fish in deeper water, say 15 to 20 feet. Instead of purchasing dozens of lures, anglers are better off having a few for each species and learning how to fish those lures well.

When purchasing lures, the advice of fishing friends and knowledgeable salespeople can be extremely helpful. Tell them the species you are after and the water conditions you'll be fishing, and ask what works for them. No matter what artificial lure you use, two keys to good catches are to work the lure properly and to have confidence in the lure. Angler confidence in a lure is critical to successful fishing, and catching fish is the easiest way to gain such confidence.

And the easiest way to catch fish is to understand how the ten variables in artificial lures appeal to a fish's senses, and how the five different types of lures are designed to be fished.

The Ten Variables in Artificial Lures

Some people say that manufacturers make lures to catch fishermen, but that is not the case. In reality, lure makers invest a lot of money and time in creating and testing lures so that they catch fish. After all, if a lure catches fish, that lure will definitely catch fishermen, too. While artificial lures may not have the natural appeal of live baits, lure makers go to great lengths to make their products appealing to fish. To better understand how lures actually appeal to fish, here's a look at ten common variables in artificial lures.

Depth, Action, and Speed

Primary factors in lure effectiveness are depth, action, and speed. Depth may be the most important variable because a lure won't catch fish unless it gets to where the fish are. Individual lures are designed to work at particular depths from the surface to the lake bottom. Lures such as surface plugs, shallow-running minnow baits, and deep-diving crankbaits have a built-in depth range depending on line diameter. Lures such as spinners, spoons, jigs, and plastics allow the angler to work them at varying depths to 35 feet and more. Of course, adding weights increases depth possibilities for all lures.

Real Fishing

Novice anglers are better off using lures with built-in action such as spinners and diving plugs. As your skills improve, you can turn to lures such as plastic worms and jigs that require angler-imparted action.

Lure action and speed are somewhat interrelated, and both variables play vital roles in lure effectiveness. A lure with the proper action will entice fish with its visual and vibration appeal, and speed plays a part in good action. For example, a spinner retrieved too slowly will not exude the flash to imitate a baitfish, nor will it emit the vibrations of a properly thumping blade. Likewise, poor action occurs when a minnow imitator is retrieved too rapidly and thus swims sideways resulting in the loss of its natural minnow-imitating swimming action and vibrations.

Lures such as spinners, spoons, and plugs have a built-in action while lures such as jigs require the angler to impart proper action. Plastic baits such as grubs commonly have a built-in twister-tail action, whereas others like plastic worms and tube baits demand angler control to impart good action. In truth, the best anglers use a combination of both a lure's built-in action and angler manipulation for peak lure action.

Most lures function best in a narrow range of designed speeds. By observing how a lure works at dockside or boat side under varying speeds, you can see what speed and what movements impart the best lure action. A general speed-related rule is to employ slower speeds in cold water and clouded water and faster speeds in warm water and clear water. Also, varying lure speed during a retrieve often proves irresistible to fish under any conditions.

Size, Vibration, and Color

Additional lure variables include size, vibration, and color. The size factor is pretty obvious: use small lures for panfish and stream trout, use medium-size lures for bass and walleyes, and use large lures for striped bass and muskellunge. Of course, there are no absolutes in fishing, so a large northern pike might hit a tiny panfish jig. Imitating the size and color of native baitfish also pays off as evidenced by the success of striped bass anglers.

Remember that fish are vibration-sensitive creatures, so lures that emit vibrations often attract fish particularly in stained and darker waters. Spinners and plugs emit vibrations while jigs, spoons, and plastic baits rely more on visual than vibrational attraction.

Anglers probably place too much importance on color, although it is a lure variable that plays a role in attracting a fish's attention. Since water filters out colors as a lure descends in the water column, color is a less important factor in deep-water fishing than when fishing in shallow water. Although there are no hard-and-fast rules in color selection, standard guidelines are to use natural colors in clear water, brighter colors in stained waters, and dark colors at night. Another guideline is to select colors that imitate natural prey in the water system. Some anglers are fond of saying things like "Give me any color in your box as long as it's black."

Flash is an offshoot of color, and plugs, spoons, and spinners with silver or gold coloring do emit a flash. Silver seems to work better in clear water while gold works better in stained water.

Sound, Texture, Scent, and Shape

Additional but less important lure variables are sound, texture, scent, and shape. Two types of lures that emit fish-attracting sounds are surface plugs and vibrating crankbaits. Surface plugs work in all shallow waters, crankbaits with built-in rattles work well in most waters, and vibrating crankbaits produce better catches in stained waters than in clear ones. Most lures are made of metal, wood, or hard plastic, evidence that texture is not a fish attractant. Such is not the case with soft plastics and the ever-growing number of swim baits whose softness presents a natural feel in a fish's mouth. Scented soft plastics can also be a fish attractant. Some companies impregnate plastics with scents, some store their plastics in liquid scents, and others offer spray-on and rub-on scents. Regarding shape, some lures like minnow baits strongly resemble minnows while lures like spinner baits have no resemblance whatsoever to a minnow. Shape is likely a more important factor in clear water than in stained water.

Types of Artificial Lures

The five common types of artificial lures are spinners, plugs, soft plastics, jigs, and spoons, and a number of different styles exist within each category. Let's take a closer look at how to use these various styles and why they catch fish.

Spinners

A spinner consists of a wire shaft with a metal blade that spins around the shaft when the lure is retrieved. As the blade spins, it reflects light and emits vibration, actions that are designed to resemble a baitfish in distress. Since most freshwater species feed on baitfish in distress, spinners are effective fish catchers. Spinners are easy to use because an angler simply has to cast them out and then retrieve them. A more experienced angler will want to include some variations in his retrieve, but a novice can catch plenty of fish by simply casting and reeling.

The standard and most common spinner is the in-line spinner. Such spinners have a built-in weight on the shaft behind the blade and a treble hook at shaft's end. The hook may be bare, but hooks are commonly dressed in hair, feathers, or synthetic material intended to give the spinner a longer appearance and a wiggling, tail-like action. Small in-line spinners are a mainstay on trout streams, and the large tandem (two dressed treble hooks) spinners are a favorite of muskellunge anglers. No matter what size in-line spinner you use, be sure to use a quality swivel. Otherwise, serious line twist will occur.

The spinner bait ranks as the second most popular spinner. Spinner baits have a shape that resembles an open safety pin. The top wire holds one or more blades while the bottom wire has a painted weight, hook, and rubber skirt. Spinner baits rank high on the largemouth bass angler's list of must-have lures, but spinner baits are also popular among pike and muskellunge anglers.

Bad Cast

Most in-line spinners cause line twist if the spinner is attached directly to the line. To prevent line twist, always use a quality swivel when casting or trolling a spinner.

The buzzbait and weight-forward spinner are less popular than their in-line and spinner bait counterparts. The buzzbait has a plastic or metal propeller that rotates at the head of the spinner, and the noise-making propeller moving across the water's surface attempts to imitate a swimming struggling creature. The buzzbait is basically a largemouth bass lure designed for fishing over heavy cover, but buzzbaits also have a place in the tackle boxes of anglers who cast for pike and muskies. The weight-forward spinner resembles the in-line spinner except that the weight is ahead of the spinner and it has a single bare hook on which anglers place bait. Weight-forward spinners are most commonly used by walleye anglers, who place a night crawler on the hook.

Because of the built-in weights, spinners are easy to cast and they can be fished at a variety of depths and speeds. To achieve greater depths, simply allow the spinner to sink prior to engaging the reel. Faster retrieves produce well in clear-water and warm-water conditions; slower retrieves catch fish in stained or cold water. Thin blades spin faster and closer to the shaft than heavier round blades that turn slower and farther from the shaft. Spinner blades come in a variety of painted colors, but silver and gold are the most common. A fast-action rod makes for easier retrieving of large-bladed spinners.

Plugs

Made of wood or plastic, most plugs have a minnow shape and are designed to imitate minnows and small fish. The exceptions are surface plugs, which simulate various creatures swimming on the water's surface. Some plugs are stubby and others are slender but all have multiple sets of treble hooks. Plugs offer a number of positive features. For one, they can be fished from the surface to depths of 20 feet or more. Additional depths can be achieved by adding in-line weights or employing other fishing aids. The size of the lip determines depth for most lures, and packaging usually contains information on depth range.

Anglers use plugs for both casting and trolling. Plugs perform well at various speeds and are available in numerous color patterns. Those colors along with shape and action provide strong visual attraction for fish. Plugs come in different sizes and appeal to game fish from small trout to monster muskellunge. If you find a plug you like, you can get different sizes and use them for several species. The multiple sets of treble hooks provide excellent hook-setting, but they also take more time to remove from a fish's mouth and may cause injury, important considerations when you plan on releasing your catch.

Employing a steady retrieve or constant trolling speed when using plugs will catch plenty of fish, but to improve your catches, use erratic and varied speeds, actions, which better simulate the behaviors of live minnows and small fish.

Plugs can be classed by two categories: surface plugs and diving plugs. As their names suggest, surface plugs work on top of the water while diving plugs work below the surface. Also called top-water lures, surface plugs perform effectively in shallow water, around weeds, at night, and under calm conditions. They are essentially a bass lure, although larger models work for pike and muskellunge. Top-water lures attract fish by creating a disturbance on the water's surface. Diving plugs consist of floating, sinking, and neutrally buoyant models, but all of them dive to designed depths upon retrieve and simulate the swimming action of minnows and small fish.

Surface Plugs

The four types of surface plugs are propbaits; chuggers, or poppers; crawlers; and stickbaits. Propbaits have a metal propeller at the front end or propellers at both ends, so propbaits resemble buzzbaits in that they both create a whirling sound to attract fish, particularly largemouth bass. Chuggers, or poppers, have an indented face and when the lure is jerked, it emits a popping or chugging sound. Anglers use tiny poppers for panfish, medium-size ones for bass, and large chuggers for striped bass. Crawlers, sometimes called gurglers, have a metal faceplate or pair of wings in the front portion of the lure. Crawlers create a plopping sound when retrieved steadily across the surface, and the lures appeal to both largemouth bass and northern pike. Stickbaits are usually long and slender, but they rely on angler control for action because the lures have no lips or other features to create a swimming action. Anglers commonly work stickbaits in a side-to-side action known as walking the dog.

Bad Cast

When fishing surface plugs, anglers often set the hook when they see a fish strike the lure. This is a big no-no and will result in a lot of missed fish. Instead of setting the hook when you see the strike, set the hook only when you feel the weight of the fish at line's end.

Diving Plugs

The common types of diving plugs, sometimes called swimming plugs, are minnow plugs, crankbaits, vibrating crankbaits, and jerkbaits. Minnow plugs have a long body shape and a small lip so that upon retrieve they dive and have a side-to-side wobbling action. Crankbaits are similar to minnow plugs except crankbaits are thicker bodied and have larger lips so they dive to greater depths and emit a tighter side-to-side action. Minnow plugs and crankbaits can be either cast or trolled, and both methods will take a wide variety of game fish species. Vibrating crankbaits, also called lipless crankbaits or rattle baits, do not have lips, but they do have built-in rattling sounds and a tight wiggling action. Lipless crankbaits are sinking lures, so they can be fished at a variety of depths depending on how long an angler lets the lure descend before beginning the retrieve. Rattle baits work well for bass and pike particularly in stained waters. Jerkbaits, also called glidebaits, are large plugs that do not have lips, float at rest, and dive below the surface when given a sturdy jerk. These plugs give the appearance of an injured, struggling fish and are most often used by anglers in pursuit of muskellunge.

Soft Plastics

The plastic worm has been around for well over a hundred years, but the modern fishing world has seen an explosion in the soft plastic arena. Available soft plastics include imitations of worms, grubs, minnows, crayfish, frogs, leeches, salamanders, lizards, mice, eels, salmon eggs, insects, and more. Soft plastics are popular for many reasons, most noteworthy is that they catch all species of fish. Still, most soft plastics are primarily bass lures.

Soft plastics are relatively inexpensive, and they can be fished at a variety of depths with the addition of weights. The natural appearance and movement of soft plastics attract fish, and the texture appeal surpasses that of spinners, plugs, jigs, and spoons. In addition, many soft plastics are impregnated with scent. Soft plastics can be fished in a weedless fashion, so they work well in weedy areas, a favorite haunt of largemouth bass. Soft plastics also allow for soft and subtle presentations, and such presentations are often necessary in clear water or in areas where fish experience angling pressure.

The drawbacks of using soft plastics are fairly limited. For one, most soft plastics are not prerigged with hooks as are the other lure types. Also, soft plastics are designed to be fished slowly so an angler cannot cover water as quickly as with spinners, plugs, and spoons. Even though anglers sometimes insert rattles in soft plastics, the lures don't offer the flash and vibration emitted by other lure types. In essence, using soft plastics effectively is a skill since the angler must impart lure action and develop a feel for bites. Unlike faster-moving lures that fish strike, plastic lures are taken more lightly, so the angler has to develop a feel for fish takes that often feel more like taps or ticks than actual strikes.

Worms, Grubs, Minnows, and Tubes

Four popular styles of soft plastics are the worm, grub, minnow, and tube. Plastic worms vary in length from a few inches to over a foot, but bass anglers favor the 4- to 8-inch lengths. The three basic hooking styles are Texas rigged, Carolina rigged, and wacky rigged. The Texas style is a weedless one with the hook point imbedded in the body at the head of the worm and a bullet weight placed on the line ahead of the hook. The Carolina style has an exposed or imbedded hook point and a barrel sinker 2 or 3 feet up the line above a swivel. The Carolina rig allows for heavier weights, so it is used in deep water and in areas with significant current. The wacky style simply involves inserting a hook through the middle of the worm so the hook point is exposed, and since no weight is added, the wacky style is a shallow-water presentation.

Night Crawler

Grubs, commonly called twister tails, come in a variety of lengths and have a cylindrical body in the front portion and a thin tail in the rear portion. When retrieved, the tail wiggles with a fish-enticing action. Grubs are most commonly fished on jigheads to provide weight for casting and for achieving desired lure depth. Some anglers use grubs as trailers on spinners and spoons. Tiny grubs work well for panfish and trout while 3- to 4-inch grubs take bass and walleyes.

Soft-plastic minnows, better known as swimbaits, are fast growing in popularity. These minnows have a lifelike appearance and are available in a variety of sizes for a variety of species. Most swimbaits have a large single hook protruding out the top of the minnow, although some models allow for the hook to fit in a slot to give the lure a weedless feature. Many models have a weight on the hook shank that is prerigged in the minnow's body, a feature that allows the lure to be fished in deep water. Although not as enticing as the tail action on grubs, swimbaits do have tail action.

Tube baits were originally designed as a bass lure in 3- to 4-inch lengths, but now they come in lengths less than an inch for panfish and in lengths up to 10 inches for muskellunge. These soft plastics consist of a hollow tube into which a specially designed jighead, called a tube jig, is inserted. Tube baits have a tentacle tail, which has some movement but for the most part action must be angler induced. When an angler lets the tube bait fall, it does so with a spiraling action; when an angler twitches the lure, it resembles an injured minnow; and when an angler hops the lure along the bottom, it resembles a feeding minnow. Although the tube bait may not look enticing to anglers, its erratic action makes it a fish-catching lure, one overlooked by many anglers.

Jigs

The jig is a simple lure comprised of a hook with a lead head molded near the hook's eye, and the heads are available in various shapes, sizes, and colors. Jighead shapes include round, oval, cylindrical, cone, and flat-sided, and their sizes range from 1/64 of an ounce to several ounces. Jigs catch all species of fish, with tiny jigs taking panfish and stream trout and medium-size jigs appealing to smallmouth bass, walleyes, lake trout, and striped bass. Using large jigs is a fast-growing strategy among muskellunge anglers.

Fishing with a jig requires angler skill since the jig itself has minimal built-in attraction. Also, detecting bites requires good feel because fish do not strike a jig as they might a spinner or plug. Instead, fish usually inhale the jig, and the angler

Fishing Vocab

An eye buster is a small tool that pokes the paint out of the eye on a jighead. Since jigheads are dipped in paint during the manufacturing process, their eyes are coated in paint, and the paint must be removed before the jig can be attached to the line or snap. Some anglers poke the paint out by pushing a hook through the eye, but this practice should be avoided because it dulls hook points.

will feel only a tick at line's end. Slow reaction by the angler may give the fish enough time to eject the lure without getting hooked. Any angler who develops the skill of jig fishing will catch a lot of fish.

Jigs are extremely versatile lures that cast well and can be fished at a variety of speeds and at a variety of depths in the water column. A fast retrieve works when casting to striped bass feeding on a school of shad, whereas a slow retrieve works for bottom-hugging walleyes feeding on crayfish. Light jigs allow for fishing in shallow water, whereas heavier jigs sink quickly for fishing deep-water species such as lake trout. Because of a jig's fast-sinking characteristic, the lure works well in current.

Real Fishing

If I were limited to a single fishing lure, I would pick the jig because of its versatility and effectiveness.

Some anglers cast jigs and retrieve them in a jerking fashion, but a lift-and-drop technique is the standard retrieve whether casting the jig or fishing it vertically. Experienced anglers will tell you that 90 percent of the hits occur while the lure is falling, as fish have difficulty resisting prey that darts away and then swims downward, an action that imitates a struggling baitfish. Jigs may also be hopped along the bottom to imitate feeding baitfish or crayfish. Anglers should avoid retrieving jigs in a steady fashion since it is the irregular, angler-imparted action that makes the jig such an effective fish-catching lure.

Jigs offer the versatility of either soft or aggressive presentations. Soft, slow presentations work under cold-water conditions and at times when fish are inactive; more aggressive presentations work in warm water and when fish are feeding actively or in schools. Anglers commonly give jigs added fish appeal by tipping them with soft plastics, minnows, leeches, or night crawlers. The standard, lead-head jig may have a bare or dressed hook. Deer hair is a common dressing on jigs so such jigs are often called bucktails. Other hook dressings include rubber skirts, marabou, feathers, and synthetics.

Because of their relatively inexpensive cost, versatility, and fish-catching ability, lead-head jigs should find a place in every angler's tackle box. When questioned about what lure an angler would choose if he or she were limited to a single one, the most common response is the lead-head jig.

Jigging Spoons and Blade Baits

In addition to the lead-head jig are two other jigging lures: the jigging spoon and the blade bait. The jigging spoon is a long, slender lure made of heavy metal. The lure has a single or treble hook at the bottom and a hole or split ring at the top for attachment to the line. Jigging spoons are designed to be fished vertically in a lift-and-drop fashion, and their heavy weight translates to fast sinking. The flash and minnow-like motion of jigging spoons imitates injured baitfish. While these lures are sometimes cast into surface-feeding striped bass, jigging spoons are more commonly used at the 50- to 100-foot depths for lake trout.

Blade baits are made of thin metal with molded lead near the front, and they have the profile of a minnow. Blade baits have one or two treble hooks on the bottom and are attached to the line via a hole or split ring on the top. Even though these lures are shaped like a minnow and emit flash, their main attraction is vibration. Blade baits may be fished in a cast-and-retrieve fashion, but they are primarily designed for a vertical lift-and-drop presentation. Blade baits are most widely used by walleye anglers.

Spoons

The first fishing spoons were supposedly made of actual spoons with a hook attached, and modern spoons resemble those first ones because they, too, are essentially concave pieces of metal with a hook at the rear and a hole or ring at the top for line attachment. Although a few models have shapes other than concave, most spoons are the standard concave, a shape that creates a wobbling action and emits a flash to simulate injured or fleeing prey. Thus, spoons catch all species of fish that feed on baitfish.

Some spoons are polished on both sides while others are polished on the back and colored on the front. Common metallic colors include silver, gold, and copper; the painted possibilities include the entire color spectrum. Some spoons are made of hammered metal, a design that reflects light much like the scaled pattern of actual baitfish, and some spoons have a plated surface, a design that better reflects light than a painted surface. Because of the flash they emit, spoons are more effective in clear water than they are in stained and dark waters.

Unlike spinners that are designed to spin, spoons are designed to wobble or move from side to side. To achieve the desired action and flash, spoons must be worked at the proper speed. Too slow or too fast a presentation will result in poor catches, so always verify at what speed a spoon performs best. Speed may be more critical when using spoons than when using any other type of lure.

Bad Cast

Some anglers leave their lures attached to the line at day's end. A better practice is to remove the lures and store them in your tackle box. Drying lures prior to storage helps prevent mildew and rust.

The two basic types of spoons are casting and trolling. Casting spoons are made of heavy metal, and most models have a treble hook, although some have a single hook. These spoons are easy to cast and easy to use because they may be retrieved in either a steady or erratic manner. Also, they can be fished throughout the water column by letting them sink to the desired depth prior to retrieving. Casting spoons catch a variety of species, and an angler simply has to select a size to match the targeted species. Spoons are especially popular among trout, salmon, and pike anglers. Even though casting spoons are designed for casting, the spoons are also used for trolling, particularly for lake trout and northern pike. Some casting spoons have a weed guard, and this weedless feature allows anglers to use the lure to target largemouth bass and pike holding in weeds.

Trolling spoons, also called flutter spoons, are light and have a thin design so they move in a side-to-side manner. Single hooks are more common than treble ones on trolling spoons, whose light weight requires the use of weights or downriggers to get the lures to desired depths. Trolling spoons are especially popular among big-water anglers working the open water for various trout and salmon species.

CHAPTER 8

Basic Angling Techniques

In this chapter you'll learn about the five basic techniques that anglers use to catch fish: bobber fishing, bottom fishing, casting, drifting, and trolling.

Bobber Fishing

Bobber fishing consists of using a bobber, or float, in order to present bait or lure at a certain depth. In addition, the bobber serves as a visual bite indicator. Bobber fishing is often a youth's introduction to the world of fishing because floats are easy to use in shallow water, and they work well for the various panfish species. Perhaps the most fun aspect of using a bobber, for both kids and adults alike, is the excitement that is felt when the bobber moves, a sure indication of fish activity at line's end.

The bobber setup is quite simple. It consists of a baited hook at the end of the line and a bobber placed a selected distance above the hook so that the bait suspends in the water. Then the angler casts the setup to a desired location and waits for the bobber to dip into the water, a sign that a fish has taken the bait. That's bobber fishing at its simplest, but, of course, things can be a bit more complex than that.

Keys to Bobber Fishing

Three keys to bobber fishing are float selection, depth setting, and reading float movement. When selecting a bobber, be sure to choose one that matches the conditions you are fishing, particularly the size of your quarry. The most common error here is using an oversized float, and when a fish feels the resistance from a bobber that's too large, it typically rejects the bait. On the other hand, if you use an undersized float for the bait, the float rides under the surface and you lose your selected depth setting as well as your visual cue of a bite.

Two factors in depth setting are bottom depth and targeted species. For example, if you were fishing for bullhead in 6 feet of water, you might set your bait just a few inches off the bottom. Targeting yellow perch at that depth might see the bait set at 5 feet below the bobber, whereas a 4-foot setting would be more effective for crappies. When fishing in 12 feet of water with 4 feet of weed growth, a 7-foot setting would work for most species, but since a northern pike's eyes are designed to see prey overhead, you might place the bait at only 4 or 5 feet below the bobber.

Interpreting float movement is easy when the bobber disappears. Some experience is required, however, to interpret more subtle movement. Is the bait moving the float? Is a fish causing the bait to move away? Is the bait caught in the weeds? Is a fish nibbling at or nosing the bait? Has a fish taken and then rejected the bait?

Advantages of Bobber Fishing

Fishing with a float has a number of advantages. For one, both shore and boat anglers can use the bobber technique. Since bites are indicated visually, float fishermen don't have to hold the rod in their hands, whereas other techniques require hand-held rods in order to feel the bite. Where multiple rod use is legal, anglers can set out multiple bobbers, or they can set out one bobber and use a different technique on a hand-held rod. The major advantage of bobber fishing, though, is depth control, which allows for a snag-free presentation at anticipated fish-holding depths.

Types of Bobbers

Although variations exist, the three types of bobbers are round, pencil, and slip. The round float has a ball shape and comes in various sizes for all species. These bobbers are particularly popular when using large minnows for northern pike or setting baits on or near the bottom for catfish. As the name indicates, a pencil bobber has a pencil shape and is used for panfish and other light-hitting species because the style lends itself to casting light baits or lures and to indicating light bites.

Both the round and pencil floats are attached directly to the line, whereas the slip bobber has a hole in the center so it can slide up and down the line. A bobber stop is placed on the line to stop a slip bobber so that the bait is set at the desired depth. A slip bobber is designed for fishing in deep water, and anglers commonly use them when a desired bait setting is deeper than the length of the rod. For example, a slip bobber allows an angler to present a live leech to walleyes holding in 18 feet of water.

Bad Cast

Problems can arise if a fixed bobber is set so that the line length exceeds rod length. For example, if you had a bobber set 8 feet up the line when using a 6-foot rod, you would have difficulty casting your bait or lure and landing your catch. Also, when line length exceeds rod length, anglers have a tendency to overreel, which sometimes results in a broken rod tip.

Bobber Fishing Techniques

Anglers can fish any style of bobber in three different ways: cast and wait, cast and work-back, and cast and drift. Cast and wait involves casting out the rig and waiting for a bite. If the action is fast such as when casting into a school of panfish, you can hold the rod in your hand. When the action is slow or when using multiple rods, you can set the rods in a safe and secure position. Cast and wait is an effective strategy when using big minnows for northern pike or when using baits for bottom-feeding species such as bullheads, catfish, and carp. This strategy may require angler patience, but it's also important to check the bait and reset it periodically. When using big baits and targeting large species, fast-action and heavier-weight rods allow for better hook-setting.

The cast and work-back method is most commonly used for panfish, although it also works for larger fish. This technique involves casting out the bobber and letting the bait or tipped jig set for a minute or so. Then the angler moves the bobber toward him or her several feet. After letting the rig set for another minute, the angler again moves the rig closer and continues the process until the rig must be recast. The cast and work-back technique allows an angler to cover a lot of water. When a fish is taken, you should cast back to the same area particularly when targeting schooling species such as yellow perch, black crappies, bluegills, and other sunfish.

The cast and drift method involves casting out the bobber and letting it drift along with the wind or current. The technique allows fishing in shallow water where the angler's presence might otherwise alert fish. Also, this method allows the angler to cover a stretch of water and to drift bait into a specific fish-holding spot such as an eddy. Cast and drift works on still waters when the wind blows, but the method is better suited for the current flow on streams and rivers, especially when targeting trout and smallmouth bass. As a rig moves downstream, the angler can feed out line to lengthen the drift. Be sure to add enough weight, usually in split-shot form, to keep the bait down and the bobber upright. If several drifts in an area turn up fishless, then move on to a new location. If a drift produces fish, continue working the area until the action stops.

When using bait with the bobber technique, or any other technique for that matter, be sure to put on fresh bait occasionally as nine times out of ten, fresh bait outperforms the old stuff.

Bottom Fishing

Bottom fishing is the technique of fishing with a baited hook near or on the bottom. Anglers typically fish from a fixed position on shore or in an anchored boat, so the technique is also called still fishing. Bottom fishing seems to be a more popular term among saltwater anglers, whereas still fishing is commonly used among freshwater fishers.

When still fishing, anglers use an appropriate weight to get the bait to bottom and to keep the bait in a particular location. Still fishing works better than bobber fishing in deep water conditions and in areas where current is a factor. The basic rig, sometimes called a bottom rig or fish finder rig, consists of a bell or bank sinker on the end of the line and a baited hook 6 to 12 inches above the sinker. Three common ways of attaching the hook to the line are via a three-way swivel, an angler-made loop, or a snelled hook. Where legal, anglers sometimes attach two or more baited hooks to the line. An offshoot rig consists of the baited hook at the end of the line and a slip or sliding sinker placed two or three up the line. This rig works for fishing bait directly on the bottom.

The most commonly used baits when still fishing are minnows, worms, crayfish, leeches, and prepared baits. The most commonly pursued species are those that feed on the bottom such as bullheads, catfish, and carp, and those species that hold near the bottom such as yellow perch, smallmouth bass, walleyes, and lake trout. Be sure to use a hook size to match the size of the bait used and the species targeted. Also, use the lightest sinker possible to get the job done.

Bottom Fishing Techniques

Whether fishing from shore or a boat, the bottom rig can be dropped straight down to bottom or cast and allowed to settle to bottom. The most common practice is to leave the bait in a particular place and wait patiently for a bite while holding the rod or setting it in an upright position. Where legal, multiple rods may be used. This sit-and-wait strategy works best for species like bullhead, catfish, and carp. A second strategy involves casting out the rig and waiting two minutes or so for a bite. If none occurs, then the rig is brought 6 feet or so toward the angler, and the process is repeated until the rig is back at shoreside or boat side and must be cast out again. If there is no action, the angler casts to a different spot. Of course, if a fish is caught, then the angler casts again to the same area.

Bad Cast

When bottom fishing with live bait, avoid using a hook that's too large. An oversize hook can limit bait activity, make fish wary, and result in missed hook-sets.

By casting out the bottom rig and working it methodically back, the angler covers a large area. This technique works well for all conditions and species, but it is particularly effective in clear water and for fish that feed by sight such as yellow perch and smallmouth bass. If no fish are caught in an area or if the action slows, then move on to a new location. Shore anglers may be somewhat limited in mobility, but boat anglers have the luxury of moving from spot to spot where the key to good fishing is anchoring in fishy spots such as weed lines, drop-offs, and points. For more details on finding fishy spots, see chapter 9.

Casting

The act of casting is used in bobber and bottom fishing, but here we're talking about the technique of casting out a lure and retrieving it. Even though the technique is called casting, a better title for the technique might be casting and retrieving. Anyway, other than the cartoon stereotype of an angler sitting asleep on shore or in a boat, casting is many people's idea of fishing.

Casting is an enjoyable way to fish as the casting itself is fun as is the working of the lure. Even more fun, though, is the feel of a fish as it strikes the lure.

On the surface, casting seems to be a fairly simple technique: cast out the lure and reel it in, cast again and reel again, etc. In essence, though, casting is a learned skill particularly in the retrieving part of the presentation. Give two anglers identical fishing outfits with the same lure, and the more skilled angler will outfish the other guy nine times out of ten if not ten times out of ten. Contrary to fishing lore, luck plays only a minor role in fishing.

The Retrieve

While casting out the lure is important, retrieving the lure plays a more critical role because of the wide variety of lures available and their various features. Three of the important lure variables when casting and retrieving are depth, speed, and action. The angler must get the lure to the depths where fish are holding. That is easy to do in shallow water, but deep-water situations call for proper lure selection and proper timing. For example, when casting to bass in 4 feet of water, an angler can cast out a spinner or shallow-running minnow plug and begin the retrieve once it hits the water. Casting a spinner to bass in 15 feet of water requires that an angler allow proper sinking time before beginning the retrieve. Casting a shallow-running minnow plug would prove fruitless to bass holding on the bottom at 15-foot depths, where a diving crankbait, tipped jig, or weighted plastic worm would be a better choice.

Speed is another vital retrieve factor. Most importantly, an angler must use a speed at which the lure performs effectively. Most lures work within a range of speeds. Retrieve too fast and the lure may roll over or swim sideways. Retrieve too slowly and the lure will lack proper action. General guidelines call for slower retrieves in murky water, cold water, and at night; faster retrieves are called for in clear water and in warm water. Since worms move slowly, these plastics are best fished in a slow manner.

Lure action, too, is a critical aspect of the retrieve. Many anglers use a steady retrieve when working spinners, spoons, and plugs. Such lures do catch fish when steadily retrieved, especially in stained waters, low-light conditions, and cool water. Lures like jigs, plastic worms, and stickbaits have minimal built-in action so the angler must impart the action, and an erratic action typically outperforms a steady action with these lures. In fact, an irregular, erratic action is a more effective strategy overall because such action better imitates injured or fleeing creatures and an easy meal.

How do you get varied lure action during the retrieve? The options are many, but here are some worth trying. Use a stop-and-go retrieve by pausing for a few seconds when reeling. Give the lure bursts of speed by turning the reel handle faster for several turns. Sweeping the rod forward or backward also creates erratic action. Likewise, raising or lowering the rod tip alters action as well as depth. Fish love a falling action which you can impart to spoons, spinners, weighted plastics, jigs, and sinking plugs by discontinuing your reeling. Perhaps the most effective method of creating erratic lure action is the jerk-and-reel technique. As the name suggests, you jerk or sweep the rod sideways, drop the rod back toward the lure, and reel in the slack line.

Casting Jigs

Casting and retrieving jigs is called jigging, a technique that requires more skill than working most other lures since jigs have minimal inherent action. Jigging involves casting out the jig, letting it settle toward bottom, and imparting a darting, hopping, or lift-and-drop motion as the jig is retrieved. It's easy for the angler to lose contact with the jig as it falls, and since 90 percent of strikes occur on the fall, an angler can miss a lot of fish if contact with the jig isn't maintained. Such contact is best maintained by dropping the rod tip and reeling in the slack line as the jig falls. A fast-action rod and sensitive line are also helpful in maintaining lure contact.

Casting Live Bait

Although live bait is not commonly used with the cast-and-retrieve technique, it remains an effective action. The typical setup includes a baited hook at line's end with a split shot placed 2 feet or so up the line. A soft cast is required so as not to stress the bait, and the bait is allowed to settle to the desired depth. Then the angler retrieves the bait softly by easing it slowly toward the shore or boat.

Drifting

Drifting is the technique of presenting a lure or bait while the boat moves across the water. Originally the term referred to a boat drifting naturally in the current of a river, but I am using a broader interpretation that includes both free drifting and controlled drifting. Free drifting is when the boat moves naturally across the water with the aid of wind and/or current. Controlled drifting is when the angler also uses manmade aids to move the boat along.

Free Drifting

Free drifting works particularly well on rivers where the current moves the boat downstream at a steady pace or on lakes where a mild wind moves the boat across the surface. Such free drifting allows anglers a nonintruding approach. Realistically though, conditions are often less than ideal as winds are too strong, too light, or from the wrong direction. For example, a combination of wind and current might move a boat too fast for effective presentations, or the wind might come from the opposite direction of the current, resulting in a stationary boat. Also, trying to work a shoreline with an offshore wind blowing makes free drifting a pretty fruitless endeavor.

Bad Cast

Free drifting is an easy way to fish, and anglers often get too lax in letting the boat go wherever the current and wind take it. Free drifting should not be an aimless affair. You want to be drifting in an area that holds fish. What is the point of drifting in no-fish waters? The next chapter discusses fish-holding locations, and those are the areas you should do your free drifting.

Controlled Drifting

When less-than-ideal conditions exist, controlled drifting is the way to go because anglers can control the speed and direction of a drift. The most elementary control tool is a paddle or set of oars. Such drifting is silent, but a paddle offers limited control in stronger winds and currents. Paddling or rowing works best with a partner because effectively handling a paddle and a fishing rod at the same time is a near impossibility. The most popular tool in controlling drifts is the electric motor. Such motors can be bow mounted, stern mounted, or even side mounted, and they have speed and directional controls and may be hand controlled, foot controlled, or setting controlled. The electric motor ranks among the most significant developments in the modern fishing era.

Real Fishing

In my earlier fishing years, paddles served as the means of controlling a drift. My fishing partner, Willie Mac Caull, and I fished from a 14-foot aluminum canoe and a 14-foot aluminum boat with a 10 horsepower motor. Each of us had a paddle in his end of the boat, and that paddle provided our propulsion when drifting along or through an area. We caught a lot of pike and bass in those days, and I believe our quiet approach of soft paddling played a key role in the catches, particularly when we were in shallow-water and quiet-water areas. Paddling also created a team atmosphere because we tried to place each other in positions to make good presentations.

Auxiliary and main outboard motors can also be used in controlled drifting. Generally, the motor is left running and kicked in and out of gear to control drift speed and direction. The drift sock lacks the versatility of paddles, oars, electric motors, and outboard motors, but it works to slow a drift that is moving too fast and to position the boat at a desired angle. Drift socks come in various sizes, and although a single sock is generally used, a pair of drift socks, one off the bow and another off the stern, allows for a sideways drift as well as a slower drift.

The key to successful drift fishing is to put the boat in fish-holding areas. Sometimes free drifting with the wind and/or current puts the boat in such areas, but more often than not, boat control is required to facilitate movement along a shoreline, along a weed line, across a flat, over a shoal, through a deep hole, etc. Proper boat control requires constant attention, and such control is often a guide's primary task during an outing.

Fishing Vocab

A drift sock is a cone-shaped device made of nylon. The sock is attached to the boat via straps, and as water funnels from the drift sock's wide mouth to the small opening at its rear, a boat's drift speed is slowed. Drift socks come in various sizes to match boat size, and drift socks are also used to slow trolling speeds as well as drifting speeds.

While drifting, anglers can use the three previously discussed techniques of bobber fishing, bottom fishing, and casting. Of the three, casting is the most frequently used. Drifting is an active style of fishing, and it allows anglers to cover a lot of water in search of either nonschooling or schooling species. Once fish are found, anglers should continue to redrift the area until the action slows. In the case of schooling species such as yellow perch or walleyes, anglers frequently anchor the boat after they find fish. Drifting allows anglers to fish the shallows with minimal disturbance. When fishing the shallows, it's best to cast out in front or off to the side rather than behind the boat, where the boat's passing has likely alerted fish.

Trolling

The trolling technique involves running lures or baited rigs behind a moving boat. Trolling can be as simple as running a spinner and worm rig for brook trout while paddling a canoe in a mountain pond or as complex as operating a 10-rod setup on a Great Lakes charter boat in pursuit of chinook salmon. Some people consider trolling to be a lazy man's style of fishing, when in fact effective trolling is really a skill.

Benefits of Trolling

Trolling offers a number of benefits. For one, trolling allows anglers to cover a lot of water. Because of the amount of water covered, anglers are likely to locate fish more quickly. When on unfamiliar water, trolling is an excellent way to become familiar with that water in a relatively short period of time. Also, the lure is constantly in the water. Where legal, trolling allows for the use of multiple rod setups and fishing with various lures at various depths.

The most common trolling offerings are spoons, plugs, and bait rigs. Trolling is effective for nearly all sight-feeding species from crappies to muskellunge and is especially popular among anglers pursuing larger species such as striped bass, lake trout, chinook salmon, and muskellunge. When trolling, rods may be set in holders or handheld. The advantage of holding the rod is the angler gets to feel the strike, arguably the most exciting aspect of trolling.

Trolling Variables

Like other fishing techniques, the important variables when trolling lures are depth, speed, and action. Some plugs will easily dive to depths of 20 feet or more while in-line weights, in-line diving devices, and downriggers are used to get floating plugs, spoons, and bait rigs to fish-holding depths. The critical aspect of trolling speed is to go at a rate that allows the lure to perform with the proper action. Although subsurface currents, as well as large waves and strong winds, may alter a lure's performance, the standard method for checking lure speed is to observe the lure's action at boat side.

Just as casting anglers impart varied and erratic lure action to entice strikes, trolling anglers can do the same. Such methods include trolling in zigzag fashion so that the inside lure slows while the outside one speeds, putting the engine in neutral to slow lures and allow them to fall, and giving the engine a slight burst in speed to make the lures move faster and rise a bit toward the surface. When holding the rod, an angler can impart varied lure action by raising the rod high, lowering the rod tip to water level, sweeping the rod forward, dropping the rod backward, and giving the rod several short jerks. An angler who works the rod in such fashion will likely catch more fish than an angler who leaves the rod in a holder.

Using flatlines, downriggers, planer boards, and diving planers are the four primary methods of trolling.

Flatlining

Flatlining is the most common trolling method, and it involves using a line that runs directly from the rod to the lure. When flatlining, anglers can control depth by lure selection, adding in-line weights, letting out or taking in line, holding the rod up, and lowering rod tip to the water. Greater depth can easily be reached by using lighter lines and letting out more line. An angler can impart varied and erratic lure action by utilizing the tactics mentioned above. Fast-action rods and low-stretch lines allow anglers to better see or feel that a lure is working properly by the slight thumping action at rod's end.

Backtrolling is a specialized form of flatlining where the boat is maneuvered transom first. This strategy is used for two reasons. One is to slow the presentation of live bait rigs when pursuing species such as walleyes and lake trout; the other is to gain better control of the boat when going into a strong wind that might otherwise easily turn the bow off course.

Downriggers

Downriggers work well in deep water. A downrigger consists of a large reel spooled with cable and a depth counter, and the cable extends out on a boom. At the end of the cable is a heavy lead weight with a line-release mechanism. When downrigging, the angler lets out a desired length of line behind the boat, attaches the line to the release mechanism, lowers the weight to the desired depth, and sets the rod in a holder. The slow action of downrigging rods allows them to be set in a J shape. That way, when the fish strikes, the rod tip straightens out and offers some hook-setting power. Downriggers come in portable units for small boats and mounted units for bigger boats. Anglers have the option of buying manual or electric downriggers, and speed and temperature gauges are also options.

Planer Boards and Diving Planers

Planer boards are designed to present a wide spread of lures. A planer board runs out to the side of the boat on a length of cord that is attached to a large reel spool on an upright metal pole. Individual fishing lines are then attached to the cord by a release mechanism that slides along the cord to a selected distance from the boat. Anglers commonly fish multiple rods off a planer board so by running such boards off each side of the boat, anglers can cover a wide swath of water with their lure presentations. Planer boards work best at shallow and medium depths. In addition to planer boards, anglers have the option of in-line planers, which are attached to the line of a single rod and then set off the side of the boat at a desired distance.

Diving planers are designed for mid-depth and deep-water trolling. Divers are placed in-line ahead of the lure so that the lure can reach greater depths. To make the landing of fish easier, diving planers are set within a rod length or so ahead of the lure. Some diving planers are nondirectional and dive only straight down, whereas the directional ones not only go down but also to the left or right depending on the setting.

CHAPTER 9

 **Finding the Fish**

In This Chapter

➤ What are a fish's needs

➤ How the seasons affect fish location

➤ What edges and structures attract fish

➤ What tools can help you locate fish

In this chapter, you'll learn about the many factors that come into play regarding fish location. You'll learn about a fish's basic needs and how such knowledge aids in locating fish; seasonal influences on fish location; and edges and structure, arguably the most important keys in finding and catching fish. Also, you'll learn about the various tools anglers use to find fish.

Different species have different habitat preferences, so understanding those preferences aids significantly in locating fish. Chapters 18–2 contain detailed information on specific species, which you'll find helpful in locating your targeted quarry.

A Fish's Basic Needs

Four basic needs that affect fish location are food, safety, proper water temperature, and spawning. The food need is obvious and self-explanatory. Regarding safety, all species during their various growth stages must be wary of predators, the most common of which are larger fish; however, fish of all sizes must find safety from nonwater predators such as eagles, osprey, brown bears, and humans. All species have a comfort zone regarding water temperature, and water that is too warm or too cold can result in fish inactivity. Spawning, an annual occurrence for nearly all freshwater fish, ensures a species' survival, and spawning plays a major role in fish location.

Fishing Vocab

Spawning is the act of producing and fertilizing a mass of fish eggs during the mating process. For some species, the process includes building nests and guarding the eggs and fry.

Food Factor

A common fishing maxim goes like this, "Find the bait, and you'll find the fish." Nowhere is this statement better verified than in the practice of striped bass anglers who watch for baitfish activity on the surface or for a flock of feeding birds. Trout fishermen employ a similar strategy on streams, where the anglers look for active hatches and feeding fish. Locating baitfish below the surface proves more difficult, and though anglers can sometimes actually see baitfish and smaller fish, especially in clear or shallow water, fishermen typically rely on electronic tools to find the baitfish and preying fish. Because baitfish seek safety by hiding from predators, anglers can find fish by focusing on hiding places with plenty of cover such as vegetation, rock piles, downed trees, docks, bridges, and other manmade structures.

Fish Need Cover

Those same covers that provide protection for baitfish also provide cover for larger fish. Anglers could confidently say, "Find the cover, and you'll find the fish." Shade and darkness offer protection as does a fish's natural coloring when it lies on the bottom or holds low in the water column. Thus, anglers should check out shady spots and near-bottom areas in their fish searches. In addition to finding safety in cover, species such as crappies, bluegills, yellow perch, and walleyes find safety in numbers. Catch one of these fish, and you have likely located a number of their kin.

Preferred Water Temperatures

Water temperature can also play a part in locating fish as all species have a comfort zone. While regional variations exist, here is a guide listing the preferred temperature range as well as the ideal temperature for many freshwater fish. Species can survive in temperatures beyond their comfort zone, but such fish are often inactive.

Species	Preferred Temperature Range in Degrees Fahrenheit	Ideal Temperature in Degrees Farhenheit
American Shad	60–75	67
Atlantic Salmon	48–62	60
Black Crappie	65–75	70
Bluegill	70–78	74
Brook Trout	50–65	58
Bullhead	70–80	75
Brown Trout	50–70	61
Carp	75–85	82
Catfish	75–82	78
Chinook Salmon	45–60	55
Coho Salmon	45–60	55
Cutthroat Trout	50–65	55
Grayling	45–60	52
Lake Trout	45–60	55
Largemouth Bass	65–80	70
Muskellunge	60–70	65
Northern Pike	50–70	63
Pickeral	65–80	73
Rainbow Trout	50–70	61
Smallmouth Bass	60–72	68
Steelhead	40–60	51
Striped Bass	65–78	72
Sunfish	55–75	70
Walleye	60–72	68
White Bass	65–75	72
White Crappie	70–75	72
Yellow Perch	60–72	68

Spawning

Spawning has a greater influence on fish location than any other single factor. During the spawn, numbers of fish of the same species migrate to shorelines, shallow water, and tributaries, and since most spawning takes place in spring and fall, those are often the easiest times for locating fish. In addition to the spawning fish, species like rainbow trout and steelhead enter the tributaries to feed on fresh fish eggs.

Successful spawning is a key to healthy fish populations. A good spawn means a strong

Fishing Vocab

A year-class refers to fish of a particular species that were produced during the same spawning season. Whenever there is a good year-class of crappies, walleyes, etc., in a particular water, anglers can expect several years of good fishing once those fish reach maturity.

year-class of fish for that particular species, and a good year-class bodes well for anglers several years down the road. In many areas, fish and game departments close the fishing for a period of time or in a particular area to protect spawning fish. Even if fishing is allowed in spawning areas, anglers might consider self-imposing a limit for panfish and releasing larger game fish.

Seasonal Influences on Fish Location

During the course of a year, factors such as water level, water temperature, food availability, and spawning instinct change significantly, and those changes affect fish location. Here's a look at some seasonal factors to help you find fish throughout the year.

Spring

Spring is the easiest season of the year for locating fish because warming water temperatures draw them to shorelines, shallows, and tributaries for both feeding and spawning purposes. Spring means good concentrations of fish in small areas. Smaller waters and protected bays warm first as do south-facing shorelines. Tributaries, too, offer warmer water temperatures than the main water body, and warm water discharges are fish magnets because baitfish hang out there. On trout ponds and lakes, the upper layer of water warms first so spring is a time to look for trout near the surface.

Fishing Vocab

The thermocline is a layer of water in a thermally stratified lake that separates the warmer upper water from the colder lower water. Some species of trout and salmon hold in the thermocline.

Summer

Summer is a time when fish scatter throughout a water system because of the wide availability of food and cover. As a general rule, summer fish move deeper where they seek cooler water. Finding fish now is a matter of identifying edges and structures at a depth where the temperature matches a fish's comfort zone. When targeting most cool-water and warm-water species, an angler can't go wrong by fishing vegetation, particularly around the outside edges. Although difficult to locate, underwater springs are good summer bets for finding fish. On trout lakes, concentrate your efforts on the thermocline.

Fall

Species such as Atlantic salmon, brook trout, brown trout, and Pacific salmon spawn in the fall, so anglers can easily locate them in spawning tributaries. As long as there is green vegetation, both cool-water and warm-water species will move shallower to feed actively in the area. Once the weeds die, both the baitfish and the game fish move to adjacent deep water. Larger waters hold their temperatures longer so fish-holding locations remain fairly stable. As fall progresses, species such as walleyes gather on prime deepwater structures not far from their spawning sites. In fact, most species are more concentrated in fall than in summer.

Winter

Winter usually means looking for fish in quiet water and deep water, although early winter often finds fish in fall locations while late winter finds the fish in spring locations. Four prime winter locations for fish are deepwater edges and structures, areas of green vegetation, underwater springs, and warm-water discharges.

Edges and Structure

A key to finding fish year-round is to locate their favorite hangouts: edges and structure. Buck Perry, legendary angler and father of structure fishing, used the term *structure* to mean an area of the bottom that is different from the surrounding area, and he maintained that fish hung out and travelled along structures. The concept of structure fishing revolutionized the sport of fishing, particularly for bass anglers, and structure fishing is a mainstay of modern anglers.

Edges

Edges occur where two different features or areas meet in any water body. The most prominent edge is a drop-off. Sometimes called a breakline, a drop-off is a place in a body of water where there is a definite change in depth. Other fish-holding edges include weed lines, break walls, river channels in reservoirs, a change in bottom content such as from muck to sand and gravel, and the seam between flowing and quiet waters.

Fish also position themselves near temperature edges and edges of light. For example, fish will hold at the thermocline in thermally stratified lakes and at tributary mouths where warmer or colder water enters the main water body. Also, fish will hold in the shade of both

Fishing Vocab

An edge is a line of division where two different areas meet. Examples of edges are where weeds meet open water and where moving water meets still water.

natural and manmade features to avoid bright light, and many species move shallow at the edge of light created by sunset and move deeper at the edge of darkness created by sunrise.

Structure

Fish are attracted to both natural and manmade structures. The natural features include weed lines, islands, fallen trees, boulder-strewn areas, points, drop-offs, old river beds in reservoirs, deep holes or pools, and underwater humps (also called bars), reefs, and shoals. Among the manmade structures are bridges, docks, dams, break walls, brush piles (where legal), foundations and other underwater features in reservoirs, navigational aids, dredged boat channels, and boat channels winding through weed beds.

If you can locate edges and structures, you will find fish. Because of the variables, though, not all structures are equal when it comes to holding fish. Consider this example. Let's say you decide to fish an island or mainland point that has weeds. Certainly some fish will be

Fishing Vocab

Structure refers to the configuration of terrain, natural features, and manmade features that attract fish by offering food and cover. Examples of structure include islands, shoals, and bridges.

there. If the same point, however, has several boulder-strewn areas, that point will attract even more fish. If that same point also extends out where the prevailing winds blow, even more fish will be there. Add a drop-off into deep water, and the point appeals to even more species.

Consider a second example consisting of a weedy bay. If the bay has openings in the vegetation, that bay offers additional fish appeal. If a tributary flows into the bay, the area becomes a fish magnet, especially during spring feeding and spawning. Add a defined weed line at the mouth of the bay and a boat channel winding through the bay to open water, and the fish-holding quality of the area gets even better.

Let's consider a final example of an underwater hump, bar, reef, or shoal. A small structure will likely hold fewer fish than a larger structure. An isolated hump will attract fewer fish than a hump in an area where several humps are located. A hump that sits under only 2 feet of water is not as good as a hump that sits under 12 feet of water. A barren hump will not hold as many fish as will a hump with vegetation. And a hump in front of a busy marina is less attractive to fish than a hump located in front of a stretch of undeveloped shoreline.

In essence, the very best fish-holding areas in any water body are those with the larger and more varied structures and edges. Your challenge is to identify those areas on your home waters and then familiarize yourself with their features. Two fishing maxims state, "Ten percent of the water holds ninety percent of the fish" and "Ten percent of the anglers catch ninety percent of the fish." Odds are this ten percent of anglers spends their time fishing edges and structures.

Charts and Electronic Aids

To locate structure, Buck Perry used three methods: consulting available lake and river charts, visually identifying weed lines, drop-offs, points, etc., when water clarity allowed, and trolling metal spoons that dove to various depths. In my earlier years, I used those same methods, and they remain useful tools today. The modern angler, though, has electronic tools for locating fish-holding spots, and in some cases for even finding the fish themselves.

Charts

Charts and maps are must-have tools when fishing home waters as well as unfamiliar ones. Charts aid in navigating safely and finding fish by showing water depths, and they indicate structures such as points, shoals, and islands as well as features such as dams, locks, tributaries, channels, boat launches, and marinas. Actual fishing maps are available for larger waters, and such maps often provide detailed information that would take a lifetime of fishing to learn. You can find charts and fishing maps at local stores, fish and game department websites, and tourism agencies.

Sonar

Sonar technology in the form of sonar units called depth finders or fish locators is the modern angler's primary fish- and structure-finding tool. Depth finders use a transducer that sends sound waves to the bottom. The returning signal appears on a display unit indicating such features as depth, bottom content, weeds, objects, schools of baitfish, and fish. Available models include cathode ray tube (CRT), which makes a paper chart; light-emitting diode (LED), which flashes light on a dial; and liquid crystal display (LCD), which presents a picture on a moving screen. Sonar units are a standard feature on most fishing boats, and LCDs are by far the most popular style. Portable fish locators are also available.

GPS

Global positioning system (GPS) units are fast growing in popularity, especially among anglers on large waters. These units mark locations by sending and receiving signals from orbiting satellites, and then displaying the location on a screen. GPS units aid in safe navigation, and they typically provide information such as trolling speed, direction, and distance traveled. The more expensive models commonly offer more features and higher quality graphics. Although handheld units are available, most users opt for a mounted unit.

Instead of having separate sonar and GPS units, anglers can opt for combination units that contain both GPS and sonar features. Obviously, GPS units can facilitate finding of fish since the units allow anglers to return to spots recorded in their units and to find other fishing spots by using GPS coordinates marked on a fishing map. The previous generation used to mark fishing spots by triangulating three above-water features, a technique that still works today unless you're like me and forget the markings because I failed to record them somewhere.

Temperature Gauges and Underwater Cameras

Two additional fish-finding aids include temperature gauges and underwater cameras. Temperature gauges are especially popular among trout and salmon anglers. Stream anglers check temperatures to see if a stretch of water is conducive to holding trout, whereas boat anglers seek to find the thermocline or other depth that contains water of a temperature preferred by the angler's targeted species.

Underwater cameras or viewing systems are finding a place in more and more boats. The most common unit is battery powered and consists of a camera probe attached to the end of cable that is lowered by hand to the desired depth, and a small monitor for viewing what the camera sees. Underwater cameras are an effective and fun scouting tool, and some anglers spend as much time scouting with the camera as they do actually fishing.

CHAPTER 10

Best Fishing Times

In This Chapter

> ➤ What times of day offer the best fishing

> ➤ How seasonal periods affect fish activity

> ➤ How weather affects fishing

In this chapter, you'll learn about the best fishing times from a daily and a seasonal perspective, and that the sun and the moon also play a part in best fishing times. You'll see how weather impacts fish activity as well.

There's a saying among the fishing fraternity that the best time to go fishing is whenever you can. That philosophy bears an element of truth, but certain times do offer better odds for success than others. The very best odds exist when fish are in a positive mood, and the worst odds exist when fish are in a negative mood. Generally, though, anglers will find fish in a neutral mood. Put bait or a lure in front of an active fish in a positive mood, and you'll most likely get a strike. Put bait or a lure in front of an inactive fish in a negative mood, and you'll likely get no response. Make a good presentation of bait or lure to a fish in a neutral mood, and you'll probably entice a strike. Make a poor presentation to that same fish, and your offering will most likely be snubbed.

Daily Influences on Fish Activity

Fish do not spend the twenty-four hours over the course of a day holding tightly to a confined area nor do they spend that twenty-four-hour period roaming randomly from one section of the lake to another. Instead, they remain in a general area where both safety and food are not far away.

Dawn and Dusk

While in their home areas, fish become active at dawn and dusk, obvious times of change in the degrees of light and dark. At dawn, fish become active as they seek food and then shelter prior to the bright sunlight of midday. Before dusk, fish become active as they do their final feeding before settling in for the night. In muskellunge fishing circles, the hour before dark is often called the magic hour. In essence, low light makes for better fishing, and the hours around dawn and dusk are low-light hours.

Early Morning and Early Evening

Close behind dawn and dusk as prime fishing times are the early morning and early evening hours. The morning hours can be especially productive when water temperatures are warm. While the morning hours see significant activity from nearly all game fish species, that period is prime time for the largest predators in a water system. The best time of day for fishing is during the evening hours when water temperatures are warm. This is when the lakes and rivers seem to come alive with insect hatches, baitfish activity, and feeding fish. On many days where the wind makes for difficult fishing, the evening hours see the wind die down.

Midday

For the most part, the midday hours are considered the poorest fishing period of the day. Exceptions do exist, though, and midday fishing can be good in dark waters where the sunlight increases visibility, in waters with cold temperatures where the sunlight warms the shallows and surface layer, and in spawning areas where fish remain active for longer periods than normal.

Real Fishing

I have long maintained that if an angler changed nothing else in his fishing behaviors except to do his fishing during the evening hours, that angler would double his fish catches.

Night

While many species lie low during the hours of darkness, some species are very active and offer good fishing opportunities. Generally, night fishing is best when water temperatures are warm, although the warming temperatures of late spring and the onset of cooling temperatures in early autumn also lure fish to the shallows where the fish actively feed. Among the species pursued after dark are brown trout in streams, largemouth bass on surface lures, walleyes on shallow structures, bullheads in soft-bottomed areas, catfish in holes, and crappies, white bass, and striped bass around lighted bridges. Night fishing also offers the advantages of escaping the summer heat and avoiding hours that see high recreational traffic.

Seasonal Influences on Fish Activity

Waters experience seasonal variations that impact fish location and activity. Among those seasonal changes are differences in water temperatures, baitfish availability, oxygen levels, abundance of vegetation, and water levels. Here's a brief look at how fish behave seasonally.

Spring

Spring can be the best time of the year for catching many species. Not only does spring kick off another fishing season, but it also sees increased fish activity, and active fish translate to good fishing. Primary causes of fish activity in the spring are warming water temperatures, increased urge for feeding, and the spawn, all three of which bring fish into the shoreline shallows and tributaries. For anglers, this means large numbers of fish in fairly concentrated areas, and fish that are looking for food at a time when the available prey is at its lowest point of the year. Smaller waters offer the advantage of warming first, whereas larger waters offer the advantage of high fish numbers. Trout lakes see fish moving to the warming surface layer as well as to the warming shallows.

Summer

Summer has a dispersal effect rather than a concentrating one on fish. After all, areas with abundant food and suitable water temperatures are commonly available throughout a water system. As a general rule, summer fish move deeper in search of cooler water and low-light conditions. Fish also seek cover for the same reasons. Although scattered, deep, and hiding fish might sound like grim news for the angler, summer offers quality opportunities. Keep in mind that fish activity will be greatest when recreational traffic is at its lightest, so do your fishing in the early morning or in the evening. Also, consider fishing weedy and vegetated areas as they offer both food and cover. Such areas, too, promise the best surface fishing action of the year. Summer is the season for structure fishing, so find the quality structures on your waters and you'll find fish. On thermally stratified lakes, fish will gravitate to the thermocline, and that's where you want to get your lure.

Fall

After the stability of summer water conditions, fall is a time of change. As waters begin to cool in early autumn, many species move shallower to feed, but the colder water temperatures of late fall send fish deep. As vegetation dies, both baitfish and game fish migrate to deeper water, but vegetation that remains green will continue to attract fish. Fall is a time when fish become fairly mobile as they pursue schools of baitfish.

Despite the challenges of changing conditions, the season offers a number of advantages. For one, recreational traffic subsides once school gets underway. For another, fall scenery is unmatched in many parts of North America. Also, fish feed actively before winter, so feeding windows are longer than they are in the summer months. Fall finds fish gathering in schools, so once you locate fish, the action can be some of the fastest of the year. Finally, some tributaries come alive with anadromous species that return to their native streams to spawn as well as other species that follow to feed on the eggs.. In many cases, this means small waters with big fish.

Real Fishing

Many anglers love opening days and the start of another fishing season. I have a different perspective, though. I love "closing days," so fall is my favorite angling season. As autumn winds down I relish those final outings on trout streams and ponds and those last few ventures pursuing walleyes and muskellunge on the St. Lawrence River.

Winter

Winter sees water temperatures cool and food supplies dwindle from summer's abundance. In response, a fish's metabolism slows, and it moves to deeper water where water conditions are stable and where it feeds less actively. Still, there is no reason to put away your fishing gear. Instead, seek quiet water, use a slower presentation, and fish deeper structures. Winter means being more species conscious, and instead of targeting warm-water species, go after cool- and cold-water species such as northern pike, walleyes, yellow perch, and lake trout as they remain fairly active throughout the winter. If you have access to tributaries with steelhead, you have the opportunity to experience some of the most challenging and exciting fishing winter has to offer. If you have access to waters with an ice cover, winter opens up a whole new world of fishing possibilities. See chapter 17 for the scoop on ice fishing.

How Weather Impacts Fishing

A good fisherman is very likely a weather-conscious individual who checks the weather when planning a trip and again just prior to actually heading out on the water. Knowing the weather forecast serves three purposes: verifies that conditions are safe for the outing, helps determine where to fish, and gives an indication of likely fish activity. For example, an expected thunder and lightning storm tells you to stay off the water, a moderate west wind means the east shore of an island should be more productive than the west shore, and a strong cold front indicates that fish will likely be inactive and holding tight to cover or bottom.

Wind

Over the years, fishermen have created short verses that capture the general effects that weather, expressed in terms of wind direction, has on fishing. Here is such a verse: "Wind out of the north, don't leave port/wind out of the east, fish bite the least/wind out of the south, a fish opens its mouth/wind out of the west, fish bite the best." These words don't mean that we should fish only when the wind blows from the west or south, but they do suggest that fish will be less active when winds come from the north and east. On those outings we might lower our expectations, fish slower, fish deeper, fish closer to cover, use smaller baits or lures, and expect softer hits.

Bad Cast

Many anglers head for calm, protected areas when the wind is blowing. In reality, though, fish are more active in areas where the wind is blowing. If you concentrate on fishing wind-blown shorelines and structures, you will likely see your catch rate improve dramatically.

Velocity is another important wind factor. When winds are too strong, they present a safety issue especially on large, open waters and on shallow waters because of wave buildup. A wise angler follows the creed, "When in doubt, don't go out." In addition to the safety issue, strong winds present other difficulties for anglers such as making boat control a real chore when trying to work a structural edge, moving at a comfortable fishing speed, or moving in a desired direction.

Strong winds also raise havoc with casting effectiveness, lure presentation, maintaining a good feel of jigs or plastic worms, assessing bites, and trying to keep offerings near bottom. A complete lack of wind eliminates these negatives, but windless conditions allow fish to easily detect angler intrusions especially in shallow water and in clear water conditions. Two techniques that somewhat combat windy conditions are trolling and anchoring, although big waves can result in inconsistent lure speed and an up-and-down ride. Rough conditions also make it difficult to anchor in a precise spot.

Strong winds do have an upside, though. They blow organisms into the shallows where baitfish follow and where anglers will find active fish at any time of the day. Also, wind action oxygenates shallower lakes, another factor that activates fish. Windy conditions are a time, too, when big fish often roam the shallows.

Overall, light and moderate winds are the most angler friendly as they allow for good boat control and effective bait or lure presentation. Furthermore, breezes create lower light conditions, an occurrence that puts fish in a more positive mood. The term *walleye chop* illustrates this point because walleyes are a light-sensitive species, and when there's a mild chop on the surface, walleye fishing is at its best.

Rain

A common belief exists that rainy weather means good fishing, but that is not always the case. For example, a cold rain in the spring will likely have a negative impact on fish activity, whereas a cold rain in the summer might activate the fish. Likewise, a warm rain in spring will do more to put fish in a positive mood than will a warm rain in summer. In essence, heavy rains make for poor fishing because of discomfort for the angler, a current flow that's too strong in streams and rivers, and discolored, muddied waters caused by runoff. Anglers can expect the fishing to improve, though, as water conditions return to a normal flow and clarity.

On the other hand, a light rain or drizzle typically means excellent fishing. Again, this is a time of low light so fish are generally active. Another excellent time to be on the water is during those prerain hours when a person is apt to say, "It sure feels like rain."

Storms

Maybe it goes without saying, but wind, snow, and thunder storms are good times to stay home. In addition to the safety issue, severe storms put fish in a negative, inactive mood. On a positive note, fishing is typically good in the twenty-four hours prior to a storm's arrival.

Also, minor thunderstorms seem to activate a water's largest predators prior to and after the event. After a significant storm passes, it may take a twenty-four-hour period before most fish return to normal activity levels.

Clouds and Stable Weather

Cloudy, overcast days make for good fishing because of the low-light conditions and the resulting increased fish activity. Low cloud cover creates dawnlike and dusklike conditions all day long. In contrast, bluebird-colored skies and a bright sun make for tough fishing, especially in clear water.

The interplay of various weather factors strongly impacts fish activity levels. Generally though, stable and seasonable weather makes for good fishing, whereas significant weather changes mean poor fishing because fish need time to adapt to those changes.

Sun and Moon

It is generally believed that the position of the sun and the moon in relation to each other and to the earth have an impact on fish activity levels. In fact, a number of tables regularly appear in fishing publications, and the tables predict when fish will be most active and least active for any given day. Many anglers use the tables and swear by their accuracy. Also, fish records indicate that the two or three days on either side of a new or full moon are the best fishing days of the month. Although I believe in the validity of these sun and moon influences, I also believe that local weather conditions are an overriding factor.

CHAPTER 11

Hooking to Unhooking

> ### In This Chapter
>
> ➤ How to detect bites and set the hook
>
> ➤ How to play and land fish
>
> ➤ How to safely unhook fish
>
> ➤ How to release fish

In this chapter you'll learn about the various angling stages from hooking to unhooking a fish, which are detecting a bite, setting the hook, playing the fish, landing the fish, and handling the fish. Also, you'll learn how to successfully release fish. Each of these stages is a skill, and the key to good skill development lies in actually catching and handling fish. Successfully completing each stage from detecting the bite to releasing the fish gives pleasure to the angler, and each stage is a part of the genuine fun of fishing.

Detecting Bites

An angler who develops the skill of staying in touch with the lure or bait at line's end will easily detect bites, whereas an angler who lacks such feel may be oblivious to the more subtle bites and thus will miss out on a lot of fish-catching opportunities. Anglers detect bites in two ways: by sight and by feel.

Sighting Bites

Bites are easy to see. For example, when bobber fishing, a dip means something is there, a submerged bobber means a fish has taken the bait, and a bobber moving to the side means a fish is swimming away with the bait.

When fishing from a dock or boat in clear water, an angler might actually watch a fish take the bait or lure. This method of detecting bites is particularly popular with youngsters.

Lures fished on the surface also give a strong visual evidence of a bite. Other visual clues include seeing the tap-tap-tap movement in the rod tip when a fish takes the bait, and observing the sudden bending of a rod placed in a holder while trolling.

Feeling Bites

Feeling a bite when retrieving or trolling a lure is quite easy because a striking fish usually stops the lure in its path, sending a no-doubt-about-it signal to the angler.

Bites when live bait fishing are less obvious. In some instances the fish may hit the bait hard and thus send an obvious signal to the holder of the rod. Quite often though, the bites are soft ones so that only a tap-tap sensation makes its way up the line to the rod tip. On such occasions having a good feel for what's happening at line's end pays off.

Such a feel is even more critical when fishing with plastic worms or when jigging because slack line occurs in the proper presentation of worms and jigs, and fish usually bite when the worm or jig is falling on that slack line. In such cases, the only bite signal is a tick on the line as the fish inhales the offering. Quality fishing line and a forefinger touching the line are helpful in feeling such ticks. If the subtle tick goes undetected, an angler can still detect the bite by feeling a weight or resistance once the slack line gains tautness.

A skilled angler has developed an ability to stay in touch with what is happening at line's end. He or she has a good feel for detecting bites, and when a bite occurs, the fun part of fishing is just beginning.

Setting the Hook

Because of the variables involved, no single rule exists for when and how to set the hook after detecting a bite. The experts do agree, however, that slack should be taken out of the line and that an angler should feel the weight of the fish prior to setting the hook. They also agree that hook-setting involves using the wrists and arms rather than the entire body and that motions should be quick and firm rather than slow and steady.

Hook-setting Variables

Variables playing a role in hook-setting are rods, hooks, lines, baits, and targeted species. Fast-action rods require less force than slow-action rods. Likewise, fine-wire hooks require less force than heavy-wire ones, low-stretch lines require less force than lines that have a higher degree of stretch, and short lines require less force than long lines. When retrieving or trolling spinners, spoons, or plugs, anglers can set the hook immediately upon feeling the strike.

When using live bait, some judgment is involved to determine when a fish actually has the bait in its mouth. General guidelines call for setting the hook more quickly when using small baits and allowing more time for larger baits, with the caveat that waiting too long may result in a fish swallowing the bait, an unwanted occurrence if an angler intends to release the fish. If you are missing hookups when fishing with live bait, wait a bit longer before setting the hook or try using smaller bait. Also, setting the hook on soft-mouth crappies requires less force than setting the hook on hard-mouth species such as catfish.

Poor Hook-Sets

Poor hook-sets can result from a number of factors, including dull hooks, slack line, slow-action rods, a drag setting that's too loose, angler inattention, angler in a poor position, and rod held too high or too far back prior to setting the hook. Also, a hook-set that's too hard can tear a hole in the fish's mouth, which might result in the fish shaking free of the hook. Setting the hook too hard can also result in line breakage.

Hook-Setting Styles

There are four styles of hook-setting, the most basic of which is simply a sudden lifting of the rod tip overhead. A second style is the drop method in which after detecting a bite, the angler drops the rod toward the fish so it doesn't feel any resistance, reels in the slack, and snaps the rod upward. This technique works well when fishing with a bobber, live bait, jigs, and plastic worms. The sweeping hook-set is effective when retrieving or trolling lures. Here, the angler pulls the rod away from the fish in a sweeping motion parallel to the water. When using top-water lures, the angler uses a downward rather than an overhead hook-setting motion. In this case, the angler points the rod toward the water and sharply pulls the rod away from the fish the moment the fish takes the lure.

Depending upon the amount of force needed for good hook penetration, anglers set the hook with one or both hands. When using a two-hand set, one hand is on the reel and the other is on the fore-grip. When extra force is needed, an angler can stick the rod butt into the stomach or lower chest area while employing the two-hand set. Once the hook is set, avoid the mistake of dropping the rod and giving the fish slack. Instead, keep a tight line as you begin the fun of playing the fish.

Playing the Fish

Detecting the bite and hooking the fish are exciting aspects of fishing as is playing the fish. Some anglers tense up when playing a fish for fear of losing it, but a better approach is to relax and enjoy the experience. Playing a fish should be fun, so take your time. More fish are lost by rushing the process than are by proceeding slowly.

Feeling the Fish

Just as skilled anglers develop a feel for the bait or lure at line's end, so should an angler feel the fish and its movements during the playing process. Try to feel the weight of the fish, the diving, the head shakes, the runs, the changing of directions, the rising to the surface, and the eventual tiring. Feeling the weight of the fish should give you an indication of its size and maybe the species.

When a fish dives or makes a run, bow your rod to the fish and let the drag do its job. When a fish shakes its head, keep the rod tip up and the line taut. When the fish changes direction, quickly maneuver your rod to keep the pressure on, and if a fish swims toward you, pull the rod away from it and reel quickly to eliminate any slack in the line. If a fish rises toward the surface, point your rod down and even stick it in the water if necessary to prevent the fish from jumping.

Some anglers like to see fish jump, and such action is definitely exciting, but it also allows a fish the opportunity to throw the hook and escape. Sometimes angler reaction can't prevent a fish from jumping. In those instances, try to eliminate slack line and exert pressure as quickly as possible.

Getting Control

Skilled anglers allow the flex of the rod and the reel's drag to perform their jobs and tire out the fish. When a decent-size game fish is initially hooked, that fish has some control, but as the fish becomes tired, the angler gets control. As you feel a fish tire, don't muscle it to the shore or boat because too much pressure might pull the hook free. Instead, guide the fish in by pulling upward with the rod, dropping it, and reeling in line without allowing any slack line. Don't overdo the lifting and dropping. A common mistake is to drop the rod too quickly and dramatically so that slack line occurs.

Real Fishing

When I was guiding on the Nushagak River near Dillingham, Alaska, a hooked chinook salmon often made runs during the fight that forced the angler to move from the front of the boat to the rear, from the rear to the front, from the left side to the right, from the right side to the left, and even in a complete circle. We called such activity the Nushagak dance because there was plenty of hooting and hollering, and others in the boat had to move smartly to stay clear of the dancing angler and his rod and line.

Playing smaller fish requires less skill than playing large ones. Still, the acrobatics and fighting ability of 12-inch rainbow trout and smallmouth bass will test any angler's skill. When playing large fish such as striped bass and chinook salmon, an angler has to be ready to react to what the fish does. You may have to stick your rod into the water when a fish dives under the boat, and if the fish goes to the opposite side, you may have to leave your rod in the water as you walk it around to the other side to prevent the line from getting caught in the motor or on the boat bottom.

When playing any fish, a neatly organized boat facilitates your ability to move freely and safely, and moving from one side of the boat to the other and from one end to the other is fairly routine behavior in playing larger fish.

Losing Fish

Most fish lost during the playing process are due to angler error such as poor drag setting or faulty equipment such as frayed lines. In such cases, you have to learn from the experience and avoid those mistakes in the future. Sometimes, however, you can do everything correctly and still lose a fish. Sometimes a hook just comes free, and unfortunately this seems to happen most often when playing a big fish. Such an occurrence can be deflating, but don't get down. Instead, appreciate the experience of playing the fish, and know that there is another fish out there with your name on it.

Landing the Fish

Fish are easily lost during the landing process, a time when both the fish and angler are also subject to injury, but sound landing skills can prevent such losses and injuries. A well-organized boat with landing implements ready for use facilitates landing. As a general rule, anglers should decide whether or not they are going to keep a fish prior to actually landing it. If the fish is to be kept, the goal is to get the fish landed by the most effective means available. If the fish is to be released, the goal is to land the fish in a timely fashion and in a manner that requires minimal handling and does not injure the fish.

Rod Landing

The simplest means of landing small and medium-size fish is using the rod. As the fish approaches the shore or boat, continue that momentum by lifting and swinging the rod in one motion until the fish is in. The method works best when line length is a bit shorter than rod length. If too much line is out, swinging the fish in becomes awkward. For medium-size fish, placing the off hand under the butt of the rod above the reel helps to give good leverage. Rod landing is recommended when keeping the catch. If a fish is to be released, do not let it hit the dock or boat deck during the landing.

Bad Cast

Some anglers like to land fish by grabbing the line and lifting the fish into the boat or onto the dock. I do not recommend this method because it puts significant stress on the line and the knot, and I have witnessed too many fish and lures lost by individuals attempting to land fish by grabbing the line.

Hand Landing

Landing a fish by hand is common practice, especially among bass anglers who insert a thumb into the fish's mouth and grip the lower jaw. This technique of lipping a fish by the lower jaw is safest when using single-hook lures and when landing fish without sharp teeth. When hand landing panfish, trout, and bass, anglers can place their hand under the fish's belly with the fingers on one side and thumb on the other to hold the fish.

For species like walleyes or northern pike, the common hand-landing procedure is to grasp the fish from the top by placing the thumb on one side and fingers on the other side in the area of the gills or slightly behind. When using this method, do not squeeze the gills or put your fingers in the eyes. Simply hold the fish firmly.

Although the technique requires care, large fish such as muskellunge, northern pike, and catfish can be hand landed by getting all four fingers under the gill plate and lifting the fish while providing support with the off hand in the area just ahead of the anal cavity. Just be certain not to damage the gills. No matter what hand-landing technique an angler uses, a wet hand prior to handling any fish that is to be released is essential.

Net Landing

Using a net is the most common fish-landing means. Nets are easy to use and safe for the angler, although nets can cause harm to a fish by removing some of its protective coating. Also, hooks, particularly multiple sets of trebles, can get caught in the netting, and fish become stressed by their thrashing about and by the extra time it takes to remove hooks from tangled netting. A general guideline calls for netting fish head first because that is the direction it will swim. If you net from the rear, the fish will swim away from the net.

One netting technique involves tiring the fish and then easing it into the net by moving the fish with the rod. This works fine for smaller fish. A better technique for larger fish is to lift the fish to the surface and simultaneously scoop it up with the net. Some anglers like to submerge the net in the water and use the rod to guide the fish into the net, but two bad things can happen with this technique. One is the sight of the net may cause the fish to make a sudden burst. The other is that exposed hooks may get caught in the net with the fish on the outside of the net.

Rubber nets resist hook tangles better than mesh nets, but rubber nets are heavy and may be difficult to use with one hand. Instead of submerging any net and trying to get the fish into it, I recommend scooping the fish simultaneously as it is guided toward the net or to the surface. I also recommend tiring a fish instead of hurrying the process and attempting to net the fish when it is still green and full of energy.

Bad Cast

Just as fishing lines fray and weaken with use, so do nets wear out. Be sure to inspect your net regularly, and replace it with a new one if you discover any tears or holes. If there is a hole in the net, you can bet the fish will get its head in the hole, make the hole larger, and maybe even escape.

Cradles, Lip Grips, and Gaffs

Other landing devices include the cradle, lip grip, and gaff. The cradle looks like a stretcher because it consists of netting between two long poles. Cradles are designed for landing large fish such as muskellunge and northern pike. Using a cradle requires two people: one must guide the fish to the surface while the other guides the cradle under the fish. A cradle allows for unhooking and releasing fish without removing them from the water.

A lip grip is a mechanical tool that functions like the hand-landing technique used by bass fishermen, but the device allows for safer handling when treble hooks are an issue and when handling sharp-toothed fish. The gaff is more of a saltwater landing device than a freshwater one, and its use requires care on the part of the angler. Properly used, the gaff lands a fish by hooking it inside the front jawbone from the lower side up.

Unhooking Fish

Like hooking fish, unhooking fish is a skill, too. Handy unhooking tools include needle-nose pliers, line cutters, wire cutters, and mouth spreaders. Unhooking fish is a time of stress for the fish, and it also presents the risk of injury for the angler, so caution is advised.

A firm grip on the fish makes for easier unhooking, although anglers releasing their catch may want to leave the fish in the water. For the most part, single hooks can be removed by hand, especially if they are embedded in the lip area. If the hook is inside the mouth, needle-nose pliers make for easy unhooking. When removing the hook from the mouth of a toothy species such as the northern pike, jaw spreaders and needle-nose pliers are the way to go. If the fish has swallowed a single hook and the fish is to be kept, needle-nose pliers or hook disgorger will remove the hook. If the fish is to be released, experts advise that the line be cut as close to the hook as possible.

Fishing Vocab

A mouth spreader, or jaw spreader, is a handy tool that keeps a fish's mouth open while the angler extracts a deeply set hook. Mouth spreaders are particularly useful for large-mouthed, toothy species such as northern pike and muskellunge.

Removing Treble Hooks

When dealing with a treble hook or multiple sets of treble hooks, avoid the temptation to remove the hooks by hand. Instead, use your needle-nose pliers. When dealing with big lures that have multiple sets of trebles, I use an oversized set of needle-nose pliers to keep my hand further away from the hooks just in case a large fish begins to thrash during the unhooking. Wire cutters are a must-have tool when using large treble hooks if a fish is to be released. Sometimes the safest and quickest way to remove hooks is to simply cut them from the lure. After all, hooks can be easily replaced, but such is not the case for a monster muskellunge.

Sometimes a fish gets hooked in the gills. If the fish is to be kept, such hooking is not a big deal. If the fish is to be released, extreme care must be used so that the gills are not damaged in the unhooking process. I have actually had good luck removing hooks from the gill area by opening the gill plate and using needle-nose pliers to remove the hook by pulling it out through the gill plate and then cutting the line.

Releasing Fish

Catch-and-release fishing is very popular among today's anglers. This practice might be traced back to legendary fly fisherman Lee Wulff, who said, "A good game fish is too valuable to be caught only once." In some waters, catch and release is mandated by regulations, and in other cases, catch and release is required because of closed seasons. For the most part, though, catch and release is a voluntary practice of anglers.

Time Matters

Time and minimizing any handling of the fish is of the essence. A decision to release fish is best made beforehand to allow anglers to take a number of steps to ensure a successful release. The first step calls for a quick hook-set to prevent any swallowing of the bait or lure. When playing the fish, don't prolong the fight since such action may result in a buildup of lactic acid, which reduces the fish's chances of survival. When hand-landing or netting the fish, leave it in the water and unhook it as quickly as possible. If a fish must be handled, wet your hands first, and keep handling to a minimum. If you are going to photograph the fish, a common practice when releasing good fish, have your camera ready to go before removing the fish from the water.

Reviving and Releasing

General release guidelines call for holding the fish upright in the water. Placing one hand under the stomach works for small fish, but larger fish require the support of two hands, one cradling the fish just behind the head and the other supporting the fish near the anal cavity or even holding it just in front of the tail. If there is current or mild wind, face the fish into it. If feasible, avoid releasing fish in heavy current or rough-water conditions.

A fish is ready for release when it can swim away on its own. Key signs that a fish is ready for release are movement of the gill plates and the tail. If a fish needs reviving, support it as mentioned in the previous paragraph, and gently rock it back and forth or even a little from side to side. Be gentle and patient. The forward motion is the important part of the rocking because that pushes water through the gills. Some people make the mistake of overdoing the rocking motion, an action that can actually stress the fish rather than revive it. If a fish rolls on its side when you let it go, the fish needs more revival time.

When releasing fish that don't swim away immediately, I have good luck by opening the gill plates, an action that seems to help fish revive more quickly. When releasing fish that come from deep water, some experts recommend a head-first plunging after reviving the fish rather than letting it swim away on its own.

Watching a big fish swim away after successfully releasing it is very rewarding, and such an event can be fully appreciated only by experiencing it personally. Hopefully, you will have many such experiences.

CHAPTER 12

Fish for the Dinner Table and the Den

In This Chapter

➤ How to select fish to keep and how to keep the catch fresh

➤ How to clean, freeze, and cook fish

➤ How to get good fish photos

➤ What steps to take when getting a fish mounted

By nature, human beings are hunters and food gatherers so there's a sense of accomplishment and fulfillment when catching fish for the dinner table, an act that connects an angler to the natural world and gives him or her a feeling of self-reliance. By nature, human beings are also recorders of special events so it's easy to see why fish photographs and mounts are popular among anglers.

In this chapter you'll learn how to select fish to keep for eating and how to best prepare those fish for the dinner table. You'll learn how to keep the catch fresh, how to clean your fish, how to preserve them for future meals, and how to cook them. In addition, you'll learn how to take quality photographs of your catch and what steps to take if you opt to have your special catch mounted.

Selecting Fish to Keep

Even though catch and release is standard procedure for many anglers, that practice should not deter other anglers from keeping fish to eat. When selecting fish for the dinner table, some basic guidelines come into play.

First of all, the fish must be legal according to the regulations for open season, of legal size length, and within the daily bag limit. Also, anglers should follow all health advisories regarding the eating of fish from waters with such advisories. Anglers should keep only fish that are to be cleaned and eaten with the exception of a trophy fish for mounting. If a legal fish is severely injured or dying, it should find its way to the dinner table.

Selective Taking

When deciding what fish to keep for eating and what fish to release, a growing number of anglers are selectively taking fish. This practice involves keeping small and medium-size fish for the table and releasing large fish. The selective taking of fish makes sense for two reasons. Small and medium-size fish are usually better eating anyway, and large fish that are released have the opportunity to spawn again. While most regulations include minimum-length requirements, anglers who practice taking fish selectively commonly self-impose a maximum-length limit. For example, on occasion I like to keep walleyes for eating, but any fish over 24 inches goes back into the water.

Keeping the Catch Fresh

Fish and fish flesh are quite delicate, so once you have decided to keep your catch, take appropriate measures to keep the fish fresh. The best guarantee of freshness is to keep the fish alive. Most boats today are equipped with aerated livewells, which keep fish alive for the duration of a fishing trip as long as the water is periodically cycled and the fish aren't overcrowded.

Fishing Vocab

A livewell is a watertight compartment on a boat for keeping caught fish alive. Livewells usually have a means of aeration. Baitwells are smaller versions of livewells, and baitwells are intended to keep bait alive.

Fish can also be kept alive on stringers and in wire baskets. Again, the key is not to confine too many fish so that they become stressed. Some anglers like to stringer their fish through the gills, but hooking fish through the lower lip keeps them alive longer.

Cold water is another option for keeping fish alive especially in the cooler months. A 5-gallon bucket or larger container with cold water will hold fish for a couple of hours as long as you limit the number of fish in the container. This method works best for species such as panfish and bullheads.

If fish cannot be kept alive, the next best option is to immediately clean the fish or kill them and cool them down as quickly as possible. A solid knock on top of the head easily takes care of the dispatching, and the most effective cooling method is to get the fish into a cooler with ice. Stream trout anglers commonly cool their catch in a creel containing a bed of moistened vegetation.

Cleaning the Catch

Cleaning fish is a skill, and the best way to learn is firsthand under the direction of an experienced cleaner. Don't expect perfection; your initial efforts will likely be a bit sloppy, and that's okay. Just keep cleaning, and before too long, your skills will improve markedly.

Two fundamentals of cleaning fish are to do so as soon as possible after the catch and to use a sharp knife. Dull knives have no place when cleaning fish. In addition to that sharp knife, other fish-cleaning aids include a sharpening stone, cleaning board or cleaning surface, scaling tool, skinning tool, water for cleaning up, means of carcass disposal, and a container for the cleaned fish. Some marinas, launch sites, and fishing camps have cleaning stations, and they are ideal places for cleaning the day's catch. The same sites sometimes offer fish-cleaning services for a reasonable fee.

Because of the various bone structures and skin makeups of different species, all fish are not cleaned in the same fashion. Three common cleaning methods, though, are scaling and gutting, filleting, and cutting into steaks.

Scaling and Gutting

Scaling and gutting is an easy-to-master cleaning technique, but the method does leave bones in the finished product. Generally, this method is used for panfish and fish that will be baked. You begin by using a knife blade or scaling tool to remove the scales by scraping from the tail to the head of the fish. Next, point the blade toward the head and insert the knife into the anal cavity. Then slit the stomach cavity all the way to the head, but avoid making too deep a cut. After that, remove all the entrails making sure to get the line of dark material under the backbone. The final steps entail slicing off the head and removing the fins.

Some people like to leave the head attached for presentation purposes, but such fish do take up more room in cooking pans. Since trout have such fine scales, they are commonly not removed, and since bullheads and catfish have a tough skin rather than scales, the skin is removed prior to the gutting process.

For bullheads and catfish, simply make a cut through the skin just behind the head and continue the cut down each side of the fish. Then turn the fish over and complete the 360-degree cut by slicing across the belly area. Next, use the point of the knife to split the skin on either side of the dorsal fin. Then use a skinning tool or pliers and remove the skin by pulling it toward the tail. Sometimes the skin comes off in one piece; other times it comes off in two pieces. At this point you have the choice of breaking or cutting off the head and removing the entrails or of filleting the fish. Head removal works better on smaller bullheads and catfish and filleting works better on larger fish.

Filleting

Nearly all species of fish can be filleted although slight variations exist in methods because of different bone structures and fish sizes. Filleted fish offer the advantage of boneless eating.

The basic filleting technique begins with the fish on its side, and the cleaner making a cut halfway through the fish (to the backbone) just behind the head. Then with the blade pointed toward the tail, you slide the knife through the rib cage and along the backbone through the fish's entire length, making sure to stop before getting to the tail. Next, you flip the still-connected slab behind the tail and separate the flesh from the skin by sliding your knife blade between the two. At this point, flip the fish over and repeat the same process on the other side. The final step is to cut out the rib cage from each fillet.

This method works great for species such as bass, bluegills, crappies, yellow perch, and walleyes. Some species like northern pike and salmon, however, have additional bones so some extra cutting is needed. Removing these bones requires a bit of finesse, and having a teacher guide you through the technique is the way to go, although demonstrations are available online. Essentially, you have to guide the knife blade and gently work it along one side of a row of bones and then the other side. Again, a sharp knife allows for proper feel of the bones.

A variation of the basic fillet technique begins with the same cut halfway through a fish just behind the head. Then, instead of cutting through the rib cage, you work the knife along one side of the backbone, cutting to the top of the rib cage. Once you work past the rib cage, push the knife all the way through the flesh and slide the knife along the backbone to the tail as you would when using the standard fillet method. Finish the process by flipping over the still-attached slab and using the knife blade to separate the flesh from the skin. Turn the fish over, and use the same procedure on the other side. This variation of the basic technique works on all species but is used most often for large fish or fish with thick-boned rib cages.

Steaking

Cutting into steaks is another method used for large fish especially when fish are going on the grill. This method begins with the basic cleaning that consists of scaling or skinning, gutting, and removing the head and fins. After determining the desired thickness of the steak, cut through the flesh to the backbone. Then using a thick-bladed knife or cleaver, sever the backbone and complete the cut. Repeat these steps along the length of the fish, realizing that the tail section is better suited for filleting than making steaks.

When cleaning any fish, but particularly larger ones, I advise removing all fatty tissue as well as the lateral line, steps that ensure sweeter-tasting fish. Conclude the cleaning by giving the fish a light rinsing in cold water. Finally, clean up the area, wash the cleaning tools, and properly dispose of the carcass and other fish parts.

Freezing Fish

Because fish are fairly perishable, it's best to cook or store them as soon as possible. If fish are to be eaten within a day or two, they will keep in the refrigerator. Otherwise, freezing is the way to go, and smaller portions are more easily stored than larger ones.

Fast growing in popularity for freezing fish are vacuum sealers. This sealing process keeps fish fresh, and the machines work for other food products as well. A second freezing method involves wrapping the fish using freezer paper, wax paper, or aluminum foil. Less effective at maintaining freshness than vacuum sealing, wrapping will keep fish fresh for a couple of months if sealed tightly, and double-wrapping is recommended. A third freezing method involves placing the fish in a container and covering the fish with water. Commonly used containers include plastic freezer containers, milk cartons, and plastic freezer bags.

No matter which freezing method you use, be sure to label the container with the date so you know what fish should be eaten first. As a general rule, frozen fish hold up well for a couple of months if the packages are well sealed. When freezing fish, I use the plastic freezer bags and cover the fish in water. Fish caught and stored in the fall do maintain their freshness for winter eating.

Cooking Fish

When cooking frozen fish, you should thaw them slowly in the refrigerator. If the fish have been frozen in water, dump off the water periodically and remove any soft ice pieces. Running cold water on a sealed container of frozen fish will speed up the thawing process. Again, remove ice water and ice pieces periodically, and always avoid thawing unprotected fish in water.

General guidelines say to cook fish for a time of ten minutes per inch of thickness. If you overcook fish, the flesh dries and loses its favor. The standard methods for checking doneness are noting when the center turns from a transparency to opaqueness or probing with a fork to see when the flesh flakes apart. Here's a look at eight ways to cook your catch, the most common of which are pan frying, deep frying, baking, broiling, and grilling. Less common methods include making chowder, poaching, and smoking.

Frying

Pan frying and deep-frying fish are simple methods that produce a tasty product. Whole panfish and fillets are good choices for frying. When cooking thicker fillets, I recommend cutting them into smaller pieces rather than frying the entire slab.

Fish coatings add flavor, and coating possibilities include flour, pancake mix, homemade concoctions, and store-bought coatings. Some people like to roll the fish in the coating, but I like to coat the fish by shaking them in a bag containing the coating, a process that is less messy and makes for easy cleanup.

Cooking directions amount to heating the oil to 370°F, putting a coating on the fish, placing the coated pieces into the oil, and removing the fish when it's done. Pan-fried pieces need to be turned over halfway through the cooking process. If you are pan frying a 1-inch piece of fish, you would turn it over after five minutes and cook the other side for five minutes. If you are deep-frying a 1-inch piece, you would remove it after five minutes since the piece is being cooked on the top and bottom sides simultaneously. Disadvantages of frying fish are the cholesterol content and cleanup of the cooking oil.

Real Fishing

Most cookbooks contain a number of fish recipes, and you can't go wrong using them or adapting them to your own liking. I confess, though, that my favorite recipe is a simple one whether I'm cooking fillets of perch, crappie, bullhead, or walleye. I dip the fillets in egg, coat them in pancake mix or a commercial coating, and pan fry them in olive oil.

Baking

Baking is an easy single-dish method of cooking fish. Mild fish work well, and any size fish that fits in the dish will yield a healthful product. Simply preheat the oven to 375–400°F, place butter, cooking oil, marinade, or white wine in the bottom of a covered dish, add the fish, and cook until done allowing ten minutes per inch of thickness. Baked fish allow for seasonings of choice.

Broiling

Broiling is especially popular for cooking steaks and large fillets, but fish of any size lend themselves to broiling as long as you do not overcook them. Broiling amounts to turning the broiler on high, putting oil, marinade, or white wine in the bottom of the pan, basting the fish with the liquid, and cooking until done, using the rule of ten minutes per inch of thickness. Place thicker fillets farther away from the heat source. Like baking, broiling allows for flavoring the fish with seasonings of choice.

Grilling

Grilling is a fun way to cook fish, and the method works well when using steaks and large fillets. The drawback of grilling is that cooked fish tends to fall apart and then fall through the grating. Aluminum foil prevents this, but the foil also limits some of the grilling flavor in the fish. Other options include using a perforated rack on the grating or a special holder with long handles that cooks one side and then is flipped over to cook the other side. The key to successful grilling is keeping the fish moist with repeated basting. When marinating fish for grilling, an hour or so usually suffices. Like baking and broiling, grilling allows for seasonings of choice, although lemon is the most popular.

Making Chowder

Fish chowder is another cooking option, and be sure to use only small pieces of boneless fish. Chowders are either tomato or milk based, and both have potatoes and corn added. Bacon slices, too, are standard in milk chowders.

Poaching

Poaching or boiling works best for mild species and small fish pieces. Fish may be dropped into the boiling water, but using a poacher works better. The poacher is simply a rack with a handle, and the rack can be lowered into and removed from the boiling pan. Poached fish may be served hot or cold with a mild seasoning of choice. My favorite is cold with shrimp cocktail sauce for dipping. Despite earning the name of poor man's shrimp, this dish is rich in taste.

Smoking

Smoking is a lesser-used method of preparing fish but one of the tastiest. While homemade smokers are an option, most people use commercial smokers as well as commercial marinades. For best results, follow the directions that come with the smoker, and you are in for a special treat.

Fish for the Den

Fishermen have always liked to show off their special catches, so keeping such fish for showing and then eating or keeping the fish for a wall mount have been standard procedure. Today's anglers still have those options, but more popular display methods include photographs and replica mounts, choices that bear a conservation-oriented motivation.

Catch-Photograph-Release

CPR (cardio pulmonary resuscitation) is an everyday medical abbreviation, but the same letters also have a place in the fishing world, where CPR stands for catch-photograph-release. CPR allows anglers to show their special catches to others, to have a visual record of the catch, and to enlarge that record for display in the den, office, shop, or elsewhere.

Since a prime objective of CPR is to successfully release the fish, anglers must take steps to avoid stressing the fish by minimizing the time it is actually out of the water. First of all, have the camera handy and get ready to take the picture prior to removing the fish from the water. This may mean placing the fish in a livewell, leaving it in a cradle or net in the water, or actually holding it in the water, although holding a fish in the water involves the risk of it swimming free of your hold. For large fish, cradling results in less stress than netting. Prior to removing the fish from the water, decide on how you want to set up the photo.

Real Fishing

I often find myself on fishing ventures with fellow outdoor writers, and when someone hooks a nice fish, an odd thing happens. Instead of going for the net as most anglers would, these writers go for their cameras because a picture is worth a thousand words.

The best times of the day for getting natural colors in your photos and eliminating shadows are early in the day and again late in the day. If your catch occurs during the midday hours, then use the fill-flash to eliminate shadows. If the catch occurs at night, it's sometimes difficult to frame the picture, but the auto flash takes care of the lighting issue.

Bad Cast

When getting their picture taken, some people hold the fish out in front with arms fully extended. While this does make the fish look bigger, a viewer easily sees that the setup exaggerates the fish's size. For a more realistic photo, hold the fish out in front of your body with arms partially, rather than fully, extended.

If the angler is holding the fish vertically, make sure it's at chest level and not in front of his or her face. When holding a fish horizontally, the angler's fingers should be under the fish's belly rather than on the front side where they detract from the fish's natural features. In all photos, make sure the angler holds the fish squarely to the camera because you want the fish to look good. Unless you are trying to include some scenery in the background, fill the frame with the fish and the holder's face. Here are some more photo-taking tips:

➤ Make certain the background is clean.

➤ Wipe away any blood.

➤ Make sure the fish is clean and wet.

➤ Remove the subject's sunglasses.

➤ Tilt the hat up to eliminate shadow over the holder's eyes.

➤ Position the holder so the sun is on him or her and the fish.

➤ Use the fill-flash if there are shadows.

➤ Shoot from a lower angle than the subject.

➤ Fill the frame with the fish and the subject's face.

➤ Shoot quickly and efficiently because successful release is critical when performing CPR.

Mounting Fish

A fish mount provides a lasting memory and makes for an impressive room decoration. For any angler, the choice to have a fish mounted is a personal one. The most common factor in deciding to mount a catch is size. For example, some anglers set personal goals such as a 20-inch brown trout, a 10-pound largemouth bass, or a 50-inch muskellunge. Some anglers opt for mounting because a fish is the biggest he or she has ever caught of a particular species. Unique catches such as first of a species or a rarity in a particular area, too, are motivation for mounting. Also, anglers commonly mount fish caught on special trips, whether it's a Florida largemouth bass, Labrador Atlantic salmon, Manitoba Northern pike, Alaska rainbow trout, Texas striped bass, Quebec brook trout, Minnesota muskellunge, or Washington chinook salmon.

Taxidermists offer two options: the skin mount or the replica mount. The skin mount requires keeping the fish and the replica mount allows for releasing the catch. When doing a skin mount, the taxidermist removes the skin from the fish and preserves the skin. That skin is placed over a Styrofoam form, and then the taxidermist paints the skin to match the original look of the fish.

Real Fishing

For both types of mounts, the ballpark charge is somewhere in the range of $10 an inch. Depending on the taxidermist's schedule, turnover time runs from several months to a year.

When landing a fish that is to be skin mounted, be careful not to damage the fish, especially any fins or the tail as they are hard to repair. Using a cradle or landing by hand causes less damage than landing with a net. Taking photographs of the fish will help the taxidermist paint the original look. If possible, keep the fish in cold water or dispatch it with a rap to the head. Then wrap it in a wet towel or towels, making sure to protect the fins and tail. Place the wrapped fish in a plastic bag, and then place it in a chest freezer or take it immediately to the taxidermist.

When doing replica mounts, the taxidermist uses photos and measurements from the catch to reproduce a painted fiberglass mount that looks like the actual fish. The replica mount offers a win-win situation because the fish is released and the angler gets the mount.

When landing and handling fish for a replica mount, you want to impart as little stress as possible to allow for successful release of the fish. Replica-mounted fish require a bit of handling because photographs and measurements are necessary for the taxidermist. Realizing that time is of the essence, you should take photographs of the fish, measure its length from tip of the snout to the tail, and measure its girth at the widest part. A soft measure tape works better than a stiff one, especially when measuring girth. If you don't have a measuring tape, use a shoelace or piece of fishing line or rope as a measuring device. Then record the measurements and any other noteworthy characteristics of the fish that might aid the taxidermist.

When selecting a place to display your mount, two rules come into play. First of all, get spousal approval. Secondly, hang the fish where it is out of direct sunlight and away from sources of heat and moisture. Fish mounts require little care except for periodic dusting.

CHAPTER 13

 # Rules, Ethics, Safety, and Health

In This Chapter

➤ How fishing regulations protect the resource

➤ Why licenses are important

➤ What role safety plays in boating regulations

➤ How anglers should treat fellow anglers and the environment

➤ What the cardinal rules of safe angling are

➤ How to prevent and treat nine possible ills

In this chapter you'll learn about fishing regulations and how they protect our resource. You'll learn about different types of licenses and why they are important. There is also information on boating regulations and boating safety. You'll also learn how ethical anglers treat their fellow fishers and the environment. Finally, you'll learn the basic rules for safety as well as how to prevent and treat nine possible ills.

Regulations Protect Fish

The primary purpose of angling rules and regulations is to protect the resource to ensure its viability in the future. For the most part, freshwater fishing regulations are established by the fish and game departments of states and provinces. By law, anglers have the responsibility of knowing what the regulations are for the water they are fishing. Booklets containing fishing regulations are commonly available from fish and game departments by mail or online, and from license-issuing agents at the time of license purchase. Of most interest to anglers are the rules concerning open seasons, daily limits, minimum size limits, and special waters.

Season

Some fish species are open to year-round fishing, whereas others have a specified calendar period when it is legal to fish for them. The primary purpose of a closed season is to protect fish during the spawn, a time when fish are often congregated in shallow water and subject to overharvest. A second reason for a closed season is if fish of a particular species are below a desired level, and fisheries personnel feel that a closed season will help fish numbers rebound. In some cases, catch and release is allowed during closed seasons, but in other cases, an angler may not intentionally target a species during a closed season even if the angler intends to release the catch. Obviously, incidental catches of out-of-season fish do occur, but if an angler is repeatedly catching such fish, he or she should change fishing tactics or, better yet, change fishing location.

Daily Limits

The daily limit, also called the creel limit, is the number of fish of a particular species that an angler may legally keep in a single day. Daily limits vary from species to species and sometimes from water to water.

Species that commonly have daily-limit restrictions are largemouth bass, smallmouth bass, striped bass, northern pike, walleyes, muskellunge, trout, and salmon. Species with no or very liberal daily limits generally include bullhead, yellow perch, black crappies, white perch, bluegills, pumpkinseeds, and rock bass. In some cases, such as with sturgeon, the daily limit may be none.

In addition to daily limits, there may be seasonal limits. For example, a river in Alaska may have a seasonal limit of four chinook salmon. Also, sometimes there are possession limits. This limit usually consists of two or three daily limits and is intended for anglers who go on weekend fishing trips and want to take more than a single day's limit home.

Size Limits

Size-limit regulations tend to be more complicated than the season and daily-limit regulations. The most common size restriction for fish is a minimum-length requirement, which determines what length a fish must measure before it is legal. This protects younger fish that are generally easier to catch and subject to overharvesting. Allowing these fish to reach maturity and have the opportunity to spawn is an investment in future populations.

In cases where fisheries personnel want to allow older fish spawning opportunities, maximum-size limits may be in effect, requiring anglers to release any fish exceeding the legal length. Another size limit is the slot limit, which allows anglers to keep only those fish that measure within a certain range, or require anglers to release all fish measuring within a certain range. Slot limits are usually water-specific management tools. In many cases where a maximum-size rule exists, anglers are entitled to keep a single fish. This one-fish rule allows anglers to keep a trophy fish.

Real Fishing

How do you measure a fish? While the answer may seem obvious, manipulating the fish a bit can alter its measured length. For example, widening the tail shortens a fish's length while slightly pinching the tail makes the fish measure longer. Because this is a gray area, I once asked a veteran environmental conservation officer how to correctly measure fish. He responded, "I don't care how you measure it. If you can show me it's a 12-inch bass or an 18-inch walleye, then it's a legal fish."

Special Regulations

In addition to open seasons, daily limits, and size limits, most areas also have special water regulations. Examples include waters that only allow catch-and-release fishing, fly-fishing, or fishing with artificial lures. Also, some waters have certain sections closed to fishing in order to protect spawning fish. These sanctuaries may be closed seasonally or even year-round. Waters that contain brood stock for fish hatcheries are often closed to fishing. Border waters between states, provinces, and countries often have varying regulations and license requirements, so it behooves an angler to know those regulations before taking to the water.

Licenses

States and provinces require a license to fish in the waters under their jurisdiction. Some people complain about the cost of fishing licenses, but fish and wildlife agencies use the funds from license sales to support fishing-related programs. Youths sixteen and under typically do not need a license, and licenses are not required for other groups of people such as military personnel on leave, senior citizens, and owners of farm ponds. For the most part, though, states require a license of all individuals, even if the cost is a nominal one, because states receive federal funding based on the number of licenses sold. This funding isn't generated from taxes paid by the general public. Rather, the monies are generated from an excise tax on fishing-related equipment, so anglers are the actual funders.

In addition to a standard fishing license, special stamps must be purchased to fish for certain species or to fish certain waters. Common species stamps include trout, salmon, and muskellunge. In some cases, conservation licenses are available. These licenses cost less than a standard one, but they also restrict the holder to lower daily limits.

Fee structures fall under two categories: resident and nonresident. As you would expect, nonresidents pay higher fees. Licenses are available for varying lengths of time, the most common being for one day, three days, thirty days, and one year. Most states and provinces offer the option of purchasing licenses online. Otherwise, you can buy licenses at fish and game offices as well as from license-issuing agents such as bait shops, sporting goods stores, and municipal offices.

Anglers are required to have their license on their person when they are fishing, and some agencies require that the license be displayed. If you lose your license, replacements are usually available for a nominal fee. Also, anglers should note that some border waters have reciprocal agreements where a license from one side is valid on both. In other cases, a separate license is required to fish each side of the water. On a final note, states and provinces commonly offer free fishing days, where no license is required. The intent of such days is to encourage more people to go fishing. Check with your fish and game department to see if there are free fishing days in your area.

Boating Rules

Boating commandments include think safety first, practice common courtesy, and abide by all regulations. Boating regulations may be municipal, state, provincial, or federal, but no matter the source, the rules relate to speed, wake, vessel size and type, motor size, wearing of PFDs, and most importantly the safety equipment required on board. Depending on the size of the vessel, required safety equipment includes but is not limited to PFDs, flotation cushion or ring, anchor, lights, paddles, fire extinguisher, and signaling devices of both a sound and sight nature.

Safe boating may be best learned by growing up with boats and having responsible adults as your teachers. Otherwise, safe boating courses are the way to go. Youths are often required to take a safe boating course prior to navigating without adult supervision. In some instances, a boating safety course or license is also required of adult operators. Local coast guard auxiliaries offer safe boating courses, and if you are unable to find one in your area, an online course is available at www.BoatUS.org.

Ethics and Etiquette

Ethics and etiquette are an important part of fishing. Fishing ethics refer to the unwritten rules of proper angler conduct, and fishing etiquette refers to the socially expected behaviors of anglers. Fishing ethics and etiquette essentially amount to treating other anglers, the environment, and the fish with respect.

Fourteen unwritten rules and socially expected behaviors are:

➤ Know and obey all fishing regulations.

➤ Do unto others as you would have them do unto you.

➤ Avoid crowding other anglers.

➤ Enter private property only when you have permission.

➤ Leave no trash behind.

➤ Even better, leave the area cleaner than you found it.

➤ Fight, unhook, and release fish quickly and gently.

➤ Avoid holding up others at a boat launch; if not ready, move to the side.

➤ Keep only those fish you will clean and eat.

➤ If someone shares a secret fishing hole, don't make it public knowledge.

➤ Don't be a fish hog.

➤ Support a fishing-related conservation cause.

➤ Share your knowledge with other anglers.

➤ Pass on your love of the sport by taking a kid fishing.

Safety

Accidents, injuries, and sickness occur in fishing just as they do in all areas of life, but fishing is generally a safe activity. The three cardinal rules of safe fishing are to use common sense, to think safety first, and to tell someone where you're going, what you expect to do, and when you expect to return. If you are unable to give the information orally to someone, then leave a note. The note might say, "I'm going fishing with Bob over at Big Lake. We're going to launch at the bait shop, and we expect to be home shortly after dark."

Additional safety insurances include having PFDs, knowing how to swim, carrying a personal fishing bag, and dressing properly.

Wearing PFDs is always a good choice, but at the very least have them readily accessible whenever you are on or near deep water. Make certain the PFD fits properly and you know how to put it on.

The benefit of knowing how to swim is self-explanatory. Most communities offer swimming lessons, particularly for youths.

A personal fishing bag might contain items like first aid kit, sunscreen, insect repellent, sunglasses, hat, rain suit, duct tape, and water bottle. Such bags are easily stored on a boat, but when shore fishing or wading, leave your bag in the vehicle.

Dressing properly is more of a comfort than a safety thing. Layered dressing allows for the removal of clothes as the day warms and for the donning of clothes as the day cools.

Health

Among the injuries and illnesses that might occur when involved in outdoor activities are cuts, dehydration, frostbite, hypothermia, insect bites and stings, lightning strikes, motion sickness, poison ivy, and sunburn. Here's a brief look at how to prevent and how to initially self-treat each ill if it does occur. Whenever one of these conditions appears to be of a serious nature, seek professional medical assistance. Cell phones are especially handy in emergency situations.

Cuts

Fishermen commonly receive cuts because of the handling of hooks, lines, knives, and fish with sharp spines and teeth. Using caution offers the best prevention of cuts, but cuts will occur. When they do, the first step is to apply pressure to stop the bleeding. The seriousness of the cut determines how long pressure must be applied. Then clean the area with soap and clean water, apply an antibiotic ointment, and cover with a sterile gauze bandage.

Dehydration

Dehydration occurs when the body loses more fluids than it takes in, and common causes are a lack of fluid intake, exposure to heat, vomiting, and diarrhea. The best prevention and treatment for dehydration is to drink plenty of fluids, and the best fluid to drink is water.

Frostbite

Frostbite occurs when body tissue freezes and is caused by lengthy exposure to cold. Areas most prone to frostbite are the skin on hands, feet, nose, and cheeks. The best frostbite prevention involves keeping such body parts dry and covered. Numbness in an area is a sign of frostbite, and treatment calls for getting to a warm place and rewarming the frostbitten area as quickly as possible. Avoid rubbing the area in any way because such action only causes further damage to the tissue. Warm liquids of a nonalcoholic and decaffeinated nature also help.

Hypothermia

Hypothermia occurs when the body loses heat faster than it can be produced. The culprits of hypothermia are exposures to cold air, water, rain, and wind. Prevention involves dressing in a fashion that keeps you dry and warm. Interestingly enough, hypothermia occurs less often in winter than in other seasons because people typically dress for winter conditions, but people often get caught off guard by unseasonably wet and cold weather during the other seasons. Checking the weather forecast prior to an outing and dressing accordingly is good insurance against hypothermia. Initial signs of hypothermia include shivering, unsteadiness, and lack of fine motor control. If any of these signs occurs, it's important to take action to prevent the hypothermia from worsening. Get the individual out of the wet, cold, or windy conditions, and get him or her dry and warm using whatever means are available.

Insect Bites

Insect bites from mosquitoes and gnats, and stings from bees, wasps, hornets, and yellow jackets are a part of spending time outdoors. Insect bites are best prevented by using repellents, keeping the skin covered, wearing light-colored clothing, and avoiding perfumes. Stings are best prevented by avoiding perfumed products, not wearing bright clothes, and not agitating the bees by swiping at them or by throwing something at the nest or swarm.

If you do encounter a nest or swarm, simply move steadily away. Most bites and stings heal on their own, but remove any stinger as soon as possible. Ice packs and over-the-counter medications such as antihistamines and lotions should relieve any itching or pain. If someone has an allergic reaction cued by extreme swelling or difficulty breathing, seek medical attention immediately.

Lightning

Lightning is a serious threat to anyone in the outdoors during a thunderstorm. The obvious prevention is to get off the water. In reality, you should be checking weather forecasts just prior to an outing, and if a thunderstorm is in the offing, delay the trip until lightning is no longer a threat. If by chance you do get caught in a storm, avoid open spaces, take cover away from areas of highest elevation and areas with the tallest objects, and wait thirty minutes or so after the storm passes before resuming your fishing. If someone does get hit either directly or indirectly, call 911 immediately and begin CPR if the individual is not breathing and has no pulse.

Real Fishing

When thunderstorms are in the forecast, I do two things: I fish close to my launching site, and I head out in the direction from which the storm is coming. By keeping ears and eyes alerted to an approaching storm, I am able to get back to the launch before the storm strikes. My primary guideline for thunderstorms is to get off the water immediately at the first sign of approaching lightning.

Motion Sickness

Motion sickness, also called seasickness, is usually not a concern of freshwater anglers as it is for ocean goers. Still, motion sickness is a possibility on larger waters such as the Great Lakes. Motion sickness tends to occur on rough waters, where an individual's balance-sensing system, comprising the inner ear, vision, and sensory nerves, sends mixed signals to the brain.

The best prevention is to avoid going out in rough seas. Over-the-counter tablets, wrist bands, prescription tablets, or ear patches work for most people in preventing seasickness.

Once motion sickness sets in, an individual experiences nausea and vomiting. The best cure is to stop the motion. Unfortunately, when a group has planned to stay out fishing for the day, the individual suffering from motion sickness is in for some long hours. In some cases, though, things like fresh air, lying down, eating crackers, and sipping a soda can help.

Poison Ivy

Poison ivy, poison oak, and poison sumac contain oils that cause an allergic reaction in some individuals who come in contact with the plants. Common reactions include a skin rash, itchiness, redness of an area, hives-like swelling, and fluid-filled blisters. People can avoid allergic reactions to the plants by learning to identify them and then avoiding any contact with them. Keeping the skin covered also helps to prevent reactions, although individuals can contact the oils from their clothing.

If an allergic reaction does occur, wash the area in cold water immediately. Suggested treatments to relieve itchiness include cold compresses, soaking in cold water, and over-the-counter antihistamines and lotions. Also, avoid scratching the affected area and don't allow clothing to chafe the affected area.

Real Fishing

While casting for muskellunge on a small river one summer, my spinner got caught in a tree branch that I was unable to reach from the water, so I paddled my canoe to shore. To access the trapped spinner, I had to pull myself up a 6-foot vegetated bank. While ascending the bank, a thought passed my mind that there might be poison ivy in the vegetation. Anyway, I saved my $15 muskellunge spinner, but I got a bad case of poison ivy that I gladly would have paid $25 to have cured.

Sunburn

Sunburn may be the most common ill anglers face. Prevention entails covering up the skin, wearing a hat, using sunscreen with a sun protection factor (SPF) of 30 or more, reapplying the sunscreen periodically, using a lip balm with sunscreen, and being extra cautious during the midday hours, when the sun's rays are at their strongest. Sunburn treatments include seeking shade, over-the-counter relief medications, cool-compress applications, aloe lotions, and drinking fluids.

Again, if any of the above ills seems to be of a serious nature or if you are in doubt about the severity of the condition, seek professional medical assistance.

PART TWO

Fly-Fishing and Ice Fishing

CHAPTER 14

Fly-Fishing

In this chapter, you'll learn why fly-fishing is so popular and how to get started in the sport. You'll also learn about rods, reels, lines, and leaders.

Fly-fishing is a unique method of angling. When presenting a lure or bait with a spinning, bait-casting, or spin-casting reel, the weight of the lure or bait pulls the line off the reel and propels the offering to the fish. When fly fishing, the wieght of the line gets the fly to the fish. Because of this unique aspect of fly-fishing, the sport requires totally different rods, reels, lines, leaders, and lures than those that are used for traditional angling.

Real Fishing

For whatever reasons, a stereotype exists that fly-fishing is a sport for sophisticated, designer-clad anglers, and that the fly-fishing equipment is both expensive and difficult to use. In truth, anyone can learn the basics of fly-fishing in just a short period of time, and the equipment, although different from spinning gear, is reasonably priced.

The Allure

Norman Maclean's novel *A River Runs through It* and the subsequent movie version introduced the general public to the allure of fly-fishing. Since that time, the number of fly-fishers across North America has surged tremendously. For the most part, fly-fishing is more about sport than food. Although keeping trout for the dinner table is perfectly acceptable, the majority of fly anglers practice catch and release. Instead of a fish dinner, fly-fishers seek an immersion in the natural world, where they become participants rather than spectators and where they find temporary refuge from the hectic lifestyle of the modern world.

Picture yourself standing knee-deep in a clear flowing stream at sunset with trout dimpling the water's surface as they feed on an early summer hatch. As you prepare to cast your fly, take a minute to drink in the solitude, scenery, and serenity. In essence, the experience of fly-fishing is a reward in itself, and catching fish is a bonus.

Fly-fishing is a solitary, contemplative pursuit, where the angler enters a world bigger than himself, a world of discovery. Fly-fishing is its own Discovery Channel, where an angler is ever learning and ever growing. After reaching one fly-fishing plateau, another plateau looms on the horizon. For example, an angler may begin by simply learning to make the basic cast. Then he or she might advance to more sophisticated casts. Next comes catching fish on dry flies rather than wet flies. Another plateau might be catching fish of a certain size such as a 20-inch rainbow trout or 4-pound largemouth bass. Of course, there is always the plateau of tying your own flies and catching fish on them. Then there is the challenge of catching anadromous species such as steelhead and chinook salmon rather than traditional stream trout. What about the plateau of landing the highly prized Atlantic salmon?

Anyone Can Fly-Fish

Although fly-fishing can be a series of lifelong plateaus and challenges, you can get started in the sport with just a few hours of instruction from someone who fly-fishes. Even better would be spending a couple of outings actually on the water with such a person. If your budget allows, consider taking fly-fishing classes; most fly-fishing shops offer such instruction. Other instructional options include videos, CDs, and books.

In reality, you can make fly-fishing as simple or as complex as you want it to be. For example, you can get started by purchasing a packaged outfit from a reputable manufacturer. Such kits typically include the rod, reel, line, leader, and a couple of flies, and the outfits cost as little as $100. A novice fly-fisher probably can't go wrong with a 6-weight graphite rod, single-action reel, and matching 6-weight and floating fly line. Purchase such an outfit, and you are ready to go fly-fishing. Regarding equipment, keep this maxim in mind: "Successful fly-fishing is 30 percent equipment and 70 percent angler."

To begin fly-fishing, you don't have to visit highly rated trout streams. In fact, starting on a five-star stream would actually be a bad idea because the trout on such streams are highly educated since they see angler presentations day after day. You have to be a good fly fisherman to catch trout on highly pressured waters. Instead, head to the shore of a backyard water, and go for bluegills or pumpkinseeds. Catching such panfish is not only easy and fun, the activity will also develop your fly-fishing skills.

Fly-Fishing Rods

Although once made of bamboo, fiberglass, or boron, most modern fly-fishing rods are made of graphite, a material that is light, strong, flexible, and sensitive.

The rod serves two purposes in fly-fishing. The first is casting a fly, a task the rod accomplishes through its bending or flexing. Rod flex and angler arm motion combine to propel the line, leader, and attached fly to a desired location. The second function of a rod is to set the hook and play the fish.

Like spinning and bait-casting rods, fly rods have eyes along their length, a hook keeper, a cork handle, and a reel seat. Differences in the fly rod include the shape of the inside eyes and the fact that the reel seat is at the very base of the butt end of the rod and below the handle or grip. Most fly rods come in two or three pieces, but rods of four or more sections are available for air travel and backpacking.

Bad Cast

A ferrule is the connection between two parts of a fly rod, and the sections fit together via male and female ends. Sometimes ferrules become stuck. When this happens, anglers tend to grab each section near a guide and twist, but this can result in broken guides. A safer method is to put the rod behind your knees with your arms just outside the knees. Then grip the rod with a hand on each side of the stuck ferrule. When pushing your knees outward against your arms, the two rod parts should come unstuck.

Rod Weights

Fly rods vary in sizes from 1-weight to 15-weight with 4 to 6 being the most common weights. When selecting a rod, you must select one to match the waters you are going to fish and the species you are going to pursue. A 1-weight rod will cast the tiniest of flies and is designed for small fish on small waters, whereas a 15-weight will throw the heaviest of flies and is designed for long casts and large saltwater species. If you are targeting panfish, stream trout, and average-size bass, 4- to 6-weight rods are the way to go. If you are primarily targeting large bass or large trout, you may want to step up to a 7- or 8-weight rod. If pike, muskellunge, and salmon are your primary quarry, then 9-weight is the rod for you.

Here's a closer look at the 4- to 6-weights. A 4-weight rod is considered light and works well for creeks, small streams, and small ponds where the quarry is small trout or panfish. Using 2- to 6-pound tippets and size 10 to 22 flies, this weight easily casts out to 40 feet or so.

Fishing Vocab

Tippet is the terminal and thinnest portion of a fly-fishing leader to which the fly is tied.

A 5-weight rod is considered medium-light and is perhaps the most popular size for trout fishing on medium-size flows. This rod works well with tippets in the 2- to 10- pound test range and for flies varying in size from 8 to 20. The 5-weight rod routinely tosses flies out to 65 feet.

The 6-weight rod is considered to be medium-size and is perhaps the most versatile size as it functions well on medium-size flows, larger rivers, and lakes and can handle trout as well as bass. Using tippets in the 4 to 10 pound range and size 4 to 16 flies, the 6-weight rod casts out to 80 feet or more. Regarding rod size, it's important to note that heavier rods perform better than lightweight ones in windy conditions.

Rod Lengths

The most common lengths in fly rods fall in the 7- to 10-foot range with 8 to 9 feet being the most popular. Long rods allow for easier pickup of line off the water and for longer casting distances, whereas shorter rods sacrifice casting distance, but they make for easier maneuvering in tight quarters such as brushy shorelines. Rod length is a personal preference, although basic recommendations call for 8-feet long for a 4-weight rod, 8 ½-feet long for a 5-weight rod, and 9-feet long for a 6-weight rod. Novice fly-fishers might want to start with an 8-foot rod, though, because that length makes for easy handling.

Rod Action

Rod action refers to how much the rod bends or flexes. A fast-action or tip-flex rod bends near the tip. These rods cast far, but they are unforgiving of poor casting mechanics.

Medium-action or mid-flex rods bend in the upper half. These rods are good for beginners because they are easier to use and somewhat forgiving of casting errors.

Slow-action or full-flex rods bend the length of the rod to the butt. These rods don't cast great distances but are accurate at short distances. Mid-flex and tip-flex rods are more popular than full-flex ones.

Fly-Fishing Reels

Unlike spinning and bait-casting setups, where the reel sits in the middle section of the handle, fly-fishing reels are mounted at the butt end of the rod and below the handle. Right-handed persons hold the rod in the right hand and reel with the left hand, so if you are right-handed, you want a left-handed reel and vice versa.

Fly-fishing reels serve two purposes, and the primary one is to store line. The second purpose is to fight fish through the use of the reel's drag system. Since small fish are usually played by hand, the reel doesn't actually play a role in such cases. The reel does play a role when playing larger fish, though.

Reel Actions

Fly-fishing reels come in three actions, the most popular of which is single action. As the name suggests, these reels turn the spool one revolution with one turn of the handle. Single-action reels have good line capacity.

Again, as the name suggests, multiplying reels turn the spool two or more times per turn of the reel handle. In this respect, multiplying reels are much like spinning and bait-casting reels that have high gear ratios. Multiplying reels work well when retrieving long lengths of line and when fighting larger fish.

Automatic reels, again, as the name suggests, retrieve line by pressing a lever rather than by turning the reel handle. These reels aren't that popular because of their weight and the possibility of mechanical failure, but they work well for retrieving line.

Drag Systems

Fly-fishing reels have either a ratchet-and-pawl drag or a disk drag system. The ratchet-and-pawl drag is the more common of the two, and it works well for panfish and trout. On some reels this drag has a fixed setting; other reels have a dial to increase or decrease the tension on the line. The ratchet-and-pawl drag makes a clicking sound as a fish pulls out line. The disk drag system is recommended for anglers pursuing larger species.

Fishing Vocab

When purchasing a single-action or multiplying reel, look for one that has an exposed spool rim. Such a rim allows an angler to place his or her fingers or palm against the rim to increase tension and support the reel's drag system. This technique is called palming the reel.

No matter which drag system a reel has, it's important that line be pulled smoothly off the spool rather than in jerks.

Other Reel Features

Regarding reel size, common sense says that smaller reels with limited line capacity are fine for small streams and small fish, but larger reels with increased line capacity are the way to go for larger fish. Balance is another consideration. The rod and reel should have balance, which means the pivot point of the outfit should be somewhere along the handle of the rod. When purchasing a reel, consider buying one with interchangeable spools. That way you can use the same reel with different types of line and for different fishing situations.

Fly Lines

Unlike traditional fishing where the weight of the bait or lure facilitates casting by pulling line off the reel, the weight of the line is what casts the fly when fly-fishing. Thus, proper line choice plays a more important role in fly casting than in spin-casting and bait-casting.

The basic principle in selecting fly line is to match the line to the rod. If you are using a 6-weight rod, then you need 6-weight line. In some cases, rods work fine with two line weights, and in such cases, the rod label indicates that.

Fly lines consist of a smooth plastic coating over an inner core of braided Dacron or braided nylon, although in the cases of some deep-sinking lines, the core is made of lead.

Modern fly lines perform very well. Still, you get what you pay for, so go for a quality that your budget can afford. Remember, the line throws the fly where you want it to go, and quality lines allow for easier and more precise casting.

Line Weight

Instead of being rated by strength as traditional fishing lines are, fly lines are classed by weight. Fly-line weights vary from 1 to 15, with 1-weight being the lightest and 15-weight the heaviest.

In selecting a fly line, you must consider the species you will be targeting and the size of the water you will be fishing. As a general rule, lightweight lines will cast small flies designed to catch small panfish and small trout, whereas heavyweight lines are needed to throw the larger flies designed to catch species such as steelhead, pike, stripers, etc.

Select 1- to 3-weight lines if you are casting short distances and targeting panfish and small trout. Such lines, though, are delicate and difficult to cast. A 4-weight line is a good choice for panfish and stream trout, and a 5-weight line works well for trout and small bass. For trout, medium bass, and small pickerel, the 6-weight line is a good option. A 7-weight line will handle flies designed for larger trout, bass, pickerel, average pike, and average stripers. If you are focusing on large freshwater species and tossing bulky flies, then opt for an 8- or 9-weight line. These lines are difficult to cast because of their weight. If a person had to select a single line weight, the 6-weight might be the way to go because it is capable of handling everything from panfish to pike. Still, if you are intent on pursuing bass and pike and not likely to target panfish or stream trout, then a 7-weight line makes sense.

Bad Cast

When stringing up a fly rod, anglers commonly thread a single strand of line through the guides. Quite often, though, the weight of the fly line results in the line falling back through the guides. By doubling the fly line when threading it through the guides, you can eliminate this problem.

Line Shape

Shape or profile is another important feature of fly lines. Although lines come in a number of different shapes, the three main ones are level (L), double taper (DT), and weight forward (WF).

As the name suggests, an L line has the same shape along its entire length. Since these lines are the easiest to manufacture, they are the least expensive, but they are also harder to cast.

The DT line has a taper at each end of the line, and the taper allows for a soft presentation because the line lies easily on the water. This line casts smoothly, and some anglers like the economical feature because when one end of the line shows wear, the line can be reversed on the spool.

The WF line ranks as the most popular due to its inherent design for making easier and longer casts. These lines have 60 feet of thin-diameter, running line, and 30 feet of weighted line in the head. The head is comprised of a front taper, a belly, and a rear taper, and this forward weight carries the running line toward the target.

Fishing Vocab

Taper is the narrowing of a fly line or leader along its length.

Floating or Sinking

Fly lines are either floating or sinking. When fishing dry flies or Bass Poppers, anglers use a floating line. Subsurface flies can also be fished on floating lines, particularly when fishing shallow water or flows with light to moderate current. An angler using a floating line who wants a deeper offering can use weighted flies or add split shot. Because floating line is easy to lift from the water, this line is caster friendly.

As the name suggests, sinking lines sink, so they work well for presenting flies below the surface especially in stronger currents or when flies must get more than a couple of feet down. Sinking lines are either full sinking (FS) or sink tip (F/S).

FS lines sink along their entire length and are designed to get lines down quickly and deep. They work great when trolling flies from a canoe, rowboat, or small boat powered by an electric motor. The disadvantage of these lines is the difficulty in lifting them from the water to begin the next cast.

F/S lines are considered intermediate lines, and they sink slowly. These lines are actually floating lines with a front section that sinks. The sinking portion commonly has a length between 5 and 30 feet. F/S lines are a good compromise because they lift fairly easily out of the water and achieve depth in presenting the fly.

Sinking lines are rated by their sink rate in inches per second, so a 4ips line will sink 4 inches in one second or 1 foot in three seconds.

Length and Color

Fly line comes in lengths from 70 to 90 feet, although 90 feet is the standard length. Prior to putting fly line on their reels, anglers put on 20-pound test Dacron line for backing. The amount of backing may vary from 50 to 200 feet, but 100 feet is the norm. Obviously, minimal backing is required for panfish and stream trout, but plenty of backing is inexpensive insurance for long-run species such as salmon and muskellunge. In addition to allowance for runs made by hooked fish, backing also increases diameter on the reel spool so more line is retrieved for each turn of the reel handle.

Floating lines generally come in bright colors such as yellow, orange, and chartreuse. The bright colors allow for better visibility and angler control. Because these lines can also alert fish, long leaders are the norm. Sinking lines, on the other hand, come in drab colors such as brown, dull green, and gray. Such colors are less likely to alert fish, especially in clear waters and pressured waters. Sink-tip lines often have a bright color in the floating portion and a dark color in the sinking portion.

Line Care

Modern fly lines are well made and will hold up for several seasons with minimal care. First of all, avoid getting any insect repellent or sunscreen on the line. Also, keep the line out of direct sunlight. Finally, clean and dry the line by pulling it through a paper towel as you reel in the line at day's end.

Leaders and Tippets

Leaders are the all-important connector between the fly line and the fly, and they have three parts: the butt, the body, or mid-section, and the tippet. Made of monofilament or fluorocarbon, leaders should be transparent, fairly weightless, and tapered. The tapered feature distinguishes fly-fishing leaders from those used in other types of fishing, and the taper is necessary for the energy of the cast to be carried from the line to the leader and from the leader to the fly.

Knotless or Knotted Leaders

Fly-fishing leaders are either knotless or knotted. Knotless leaders are constructed of a single strand that tapers from the diameter of the fly line to a thin diameter at the fly. After tying on and removing several flies, the tippet loses its original thinness, so you must replace the tippet. By replacing the tippet, an angler might be able to use the same leader throughout the season. Commercially made, knotless leaders are a good choice for beginning fly-fishers.

The taper on knotted leaders is formed by tying together segments of leader material with decreasing diameters. By purchasing several spools of leader material, an angler can make a knotted leader for a fraction of the cost of a knotless one.

The general guideline for knotted leaders calls for 60 percent length in the butt, 20 percent length in the mid-section, and 20 percent length in the tippet. Thus, a 10-foot leader would have a 6-foot butt section and 2-foot sections for the mid-section and tippet. Instead of using a single diameter of leader material for the butt and mid-section of the leader, you can get a better taper by using several segments of decreasing diameters in those sections. For example, a 10-foot leader might have a butt with 30 inches of 25-pound test, 18 inches of 20-pound test, and 18 inches of 15-pound test. The mid-section could have 18 inches of 10-pound test followed by 12 inches of 6-pound test. That leaves a 2-foot tippet.

Tippets

Tippets are measured in sizes from 0X to 8X. The higher numbers reflect a thinner diameter, so the 8X is designed for the tiniest of flies, and the 0X will handle big bass bugs and large streamers. Anglers select a tippet to match the size of the fly being used and the size of the targeted species.

The general guide for selecting tippet size is to divide the size of the fly by four, so you would use a 4X tippet for a #16 fly and a 2X tippet for a #8 fly. Some anglers prefer to use lighter tippets, so these fishers divide the fly size by three to determine tippet size.

Because manufacturers use different materials in making tippets, the strength or pound test for tippets of the same diameter is not always the same. Still, here is a general look at the approximate pound test for various tippet sizes:

> ➤ 0X: 12-pound test
>
> ➤ 1X: 9.5-pound test
>
> ➤ 2X: 8-pound test
>
> ➤ 3X: 6-pound test
>
> ➤ 4X: 5-pound test
>
> ➤ 5X: 4-pound test
>
> ➤ 6X: 2-pound test
>
> ➤ 7X:-1.5 pound test
>
> ➤ 8X:-1 pound test

Bad Cast

Poor knots are a common cause of lost fish. Recommended knots for attaching leader to fly line are the nail knot and surgeon's end loop knot. Recommended knots for attaching tippet to leaders are the blood knot and the surgeon's knot. Recommended knots for attaching flies to tippets are improved clinch knot and the palomar knot.

Leader and Tippet Length

Standard lengths for over-the-counter leaders are 7.5 feet, 9 feet, and 12 feet. Most anglers use the 7.5-foot and 9-foot leaders. Still, some anglers will use leaders of only a few feet while other anglers like 15-foot leaders. General guidelines are to use longer leaders for dry fly-fishing and when fishing in clear water, and use shorter lengths when fishing subsurface flies. The standard tippet length is 18 inches, but longer tippets are used for dry flies and clear water.

CHAPTER 15

Fish-Catching Flies

In This Chapter

➤ Dry flies and wet flies

➤ Nymphs, streamers, bucktails, bass bugs, and terrestrials

➤ Tying flies

In this chapter you'll learn about the different types of flies, the most popular flies of each type, and the allure of tying your own flies. A fly is a lure consisting of various materials tied on a hook and intended to represent something that fish eat.

Flies

The term fly indicates that these lures imitate insects, but that is only part of the picture because flies may also attempt to imitate minnows, crustaceans, worms, leeches, frogs, eggs, and more. Since entomologists have identified some 700,000 species of insect life alone, the possibilities for imitations tied in the form of a fishing fly are nearly limitless.

When selecting flies, though, anglers can make things as simple or as complicated as they wish. For example, you can pick up a couple of traditional patterns and use those flies to catch trout throughout the season. Also, you could ask a local fly shop to recommend a few flies for the water you'll be fishing. At the other end of the spectrum is an angler who becomes something of an amateur entomologist and expert fly tier who spends the off-season creating perfect replicas of nature's insects. Most fly-fishers, though, fall somewhere in between. These anglers rely on several dozen flies, some purchased from a fly shop and some tied by their own hands, to meet their needs throughout the season.

Attractor and Imitator Flies

An attractor fly is one that is not designed to resemble a specific insect or other natural food. Instead, the fly stimulates fish to strike because of shape and size as in the case of the Royal Coachman, swimming motion as in the case of the Mickey Finn streamer, or motion and sound as in the case of a Bass Popper.

An imitator fly is designed to resemble a specific species of insect, minnow, crustacean, terrestrial, etc. that trout and other species eat. An imitator fly represents its natural partner as closely as possible in size, shape, color, and movement.

Surface and Subsurface Flies

As their names suggest, surface flies are intended to be fished on the water's surface and subsurface flies are intended for use below the surface. Dry flies and poppers fall under the category of surface flies, whereas wet flies, nymphs, and streamers are included in the subsurface category. Fishing with dry flies has a special appeal among fly anglers because of the visual thrill of actually seeing the fish take the fly or popper. But since 90 percent of a fish's feeding activity occurs below the surface, anglers have significantly better odds for success by fishing with subsurface offerings.

Fishing Vocab

Floatant is a substance applied to a fly, fly line, or leader to increase buoyancy.

Dry Flies

Dry flies float, and they are intended to simulate insects on the water's surface. Basically, dry flies imitate an adult fly that is rising from the nymph stage to the surface before drying off its wings and flying away, or they represent a spent fly that falls into the water after mating occurs. For the most part, these occurrences are short-lived, but fishing with dry flies is extremely popular among trout fishers, especially when anglers actually see trout feeding on the surface.

Dry flies are tied on light hooks with hackle and water-resistant materials to give them a floating quality. Also, anglers apply a floatant to help the fly's buoyancy, or they make false casts to air-dry the fly. In addition to using light tippets and long leaders, dry fly-fishing calls for anglers to match the hatch.

Fifteen popular dry flies are:

> ➤ Irresistible
> ➤ Brown Bivisible

- ➤ Adams
- ➤ Black Gnat
- ➤ Light Cahill
- ➤ March Brown
- ➤ Quill Gordon
- ➤ Royal Coachman
- ➤ Elk Hair Caddis
- ➤ Blue Wing Olive
- ➤ Blue Dun
- ➤ Gray Wulff
- ➤ Ausable Wulff
- ➤ Pale Evening Dun
- ➤ Dark Cahill

Fishing Vocab

Hackle refers to the feathers from the neck or back of any fowl. These feathers are used to make the collar on flies.

Wet Flies

Wet flies sink and are designed for fishing below the surface. For the most part, wet flies represent waterborne insects swimming to the surface to emerge as adults prior to flying away. These flies have hackle and wings. In addition to imitating insects hatching from the nymph stage and rising to the surface, wet flies may also represent small minnows, egg-laying insects, and drowning or drowned insects. Because wet flies are fished below the surface, anglers typically use heavier tippets and shorter leaders than when fishing dry flies. The standard wet-fly technique is to let the fly drift naturally downstream in the current and then to retrieve it with short pulls on the line with the occasional pause or twitch.

Fifteen popular wet flies are:

- ➤ Black Gnat
- ➤ Gold Ribbed Hare's Ear
- ➤ Royal Coachman
- ➤ Light Cahill
- ➤ Quill Gordon
- ➤ Blue Dun
- ➤ Black Wooly Worm

➤ Dark Cahill

➤ Dark Hendrickson

➤ Hornberg

➤ Professor

➤ Light Hendrickson

➤ Stonefly

➤ Pink Lady

➤ Leadwing Coachman

Nymphs

A nymph is an immature insect in its larval stage, which is between hatching from the egg and shedding its protective coating when it emerges from the water as a winged adult. Nymphs live on stream or lake bottoms. A nymph is also a fly that attempts to imitate an actual nymph in its larval stages. Such flies represent the larval stages of mayflies, caddis flies, stone flies, dragonflies, and damselflies. Some nymph patterns also imitate scuds, which are freshwater shrimp.

Fishing Vocab

Matching the hatch is an expression that refers to the use of artificial flies that closely represent the natural appearance of various insects in various stages of life.

Fishing with nymphs offers a number of advantages to the angler. Nymphs are a major part of a trout's diet and they're in the water year-round. An angler can easily match the hatch by checking the undersides of rocks for actual nymphs easily identified by their scaly, segmented, legged bodies. Best of all, nymphs can be fished anywhere in the water column, although presenting the fly near bottom in a natural drift is the most popular strategy.

Although fishing with nymphs is an extremely effective technique, it has one drawback: detecting bites can be difficult because the strikes are often subtle. Experienced anglers may be able to feel the slight hesitation or tick when a trout hits a nymph, but less-experienced fishers are more likely to miss these takes. Fishing shorter lines is one way to increase the odds of detecting bites. A better method, though, is to attach a strike indicator to your leader.

Fifteen popular nymphs are:

➤ Caddis Nymph

➤ March Brown Nymph

➤ Giant Black Stonefly Nymph

➤ Dark Hendrickson Nymph

➤ Gold Ribbed Hare's Ear Nymph

➤ Montana Nymph

➤ Prince Nymph

➤ Pheasant Tail Nymph

➤ Zug Bug

➤ Green Drake Nymph

➤ Light Cahill Nymph

➤ Bead-Head Hare's Ear Nymph

➤ Isonychia Nymph

➤ Gray Nymph

➤ Midge Nymph

Fishing Vocab

A **strike indicator** is a piece of buoyant material attached to the leader. The strike indicator acts much like a float in that when it hesitates or dips in the current, the angler has a visual clue that a fish has taken the fly below the surface.

Streamers and Bucktails

Streamers and bucktails are flies that imitate baitfish. Streamers have a long, slender profile and are tied on heavy, long-shanked hooks. Both the streamer and the bucktail have thin bodies usually consisting of yarn or tinsel. When the wing is tied with feathers, the fly is called a streamer, and when the wing is made of the hair of a deer tail, the fly is called a bucktail.

Because streamers imitate minnows, the flies function more like lures than the traditional insect-imitating flies. In fact, anglers fish streamers differently than other flies that are often allowed to drift with the natural current. When fishing with streamers, the angler must impart action to simulate the undulating swimming or the injured appearance of a minnow. While some streamers are imitation flies, most streamers are attractor flies whose color, flash, and swimming and darting motions entice fish to strike.

Streamers offer a number of advantages. For one, minnows are a year-round, natural prey of most fish. The general guideline is to work flies erratically in warm water and work them slowly in cold water. Also, streamers are easy for beginners to use because the flies can be retrieved in a variety of ways and don't have to be presented in a natural drift. Another benefit of using streamers is the increased likelihood of catching bigger fish.

Fifteen popular streamers are:

➤ Black Ghost

➤ Gray Ghost

➤ Mickey Finn

➤ Nine-Three

➤ Black Nose Dace

➤ Muddler Minnow

➤ Wooly Bugger (olive, black, or white)

➤ Zonker

➤ Marabou Muddler

➤ Green Ghost

➤ Supervisor

➤ White Marabou Streamer

➤ Olive Matuka

➤ Krystal Bugger

➤ Joe's Smelt

Bass Bugs and Terrestrials

Bass bugs are flies or fly-rod lures intended to imitate frogs, mice, baitfish, and large insects such as dragonflies. Bass bugs are made of buoyant materials like deer hair, cork, balsawood, and hollow plastic. Anglers fish bass bugs on the surface, and their appeal lies in their erratic action, which causes disturbance and commotion. Although called bass bugs, these flies also work for panfish, trout, pickerel, and northern pike. Popular bass bugs include the Dahlberg Diver, Swimming Frog, Mouserat, Bass Popper, and Sneaky Pete.

Terrestrials are flies that imitate life forms whose life cycle occurs on land. While these insects don't live in or on the water, they sometimes fall into the water or get blown, washed, or deposited in the water, where they become prey for fish. Terrestrials commonly imitate grasshoppers, crickets, beetles, inch worms, and ants. These flies work best in the heat of summer, when terrestrial species are most widespread. Because terrestrials are surface flies, anglers fish them as they would dry flies. Popular terrestrial patterns include Dave's Cricket,

Black Fur Ant, Black Beetle, Dave's Hopper, Joe's Hopper, Inchworm, Caterpillar, and Schroeder's Hi-Vis Hopper.

Fly Sizes

Fly sizes are based on the size of the hook on which the fly is tied, so a #12 fly is tied on a #12 hook. Sizes progress in even numbers from #28 to #2 with #28 being the smallest. After #2, fly sizes appear in both odd and even numbers beginning with #1/0 and proceeding to #2/0, #3/0, etc., with a #2/0 being larger than a #1/0 and so on. General guidelines for stream trout call for using #8 to #20 dry flies, wet flies, nymphs, and streamers. For panfish, good bets are #12 to #16 dries, wets, and streamers, and #2 to #8 bass bugs and streamers work well for bass. For northern pike, start out with #2/0 to #1/0 oversize poppers and streamers.

Fly Tying

Since flies are readily available and reasonably priced at fly shops and other stores, one has to wonder why hundreds of thousands of anglers across North America opt to tie their own flies. What attracts anglers to this hobby within a hobby? Plain and simple, tying flies is a fun and relaxing way to spend off-season hours. Also, few things are more rewarding in fly-fishing than catching a fish on a fly that you have tied yourself. Furthermore, tying flies allows an angler the creativity to experiment and design his own flies or make modifications to existing patterns.

Fishing Vocab

Fly tying is the art of imitating insects, minnows, and other natural foods eaten by fish through the skillful application of hair, feathers, fur, tinsel, and other natural and manmade materials to a hook.

Experienced fly tiers can turn out realistic-looking flies even in the smallest sizes, and even though novice fliers lack such skill, beginners can easily produce fish-catching flies. In fact, the basic fly-tying skills can be learned in a short period of time. Such skills are best learned by receiving instruction from a fly-tying friend, a local fly shop, an area fly-fishing club, or a commercial video.

Like fly-fishing itself, you can make fly tying as simple or as complicated as you desire. While items may be purchased individually, starter kits make a lot of sense when you are just beginning. Such kits commonly contain everything you need to start tying flies, and many kits cost less than $100. Contents typically include the vise, various tools, various materials, hooks, and an instructional video. Certainly, you will want to add hooks, tools, and materials to your collection, and many of the materials you can collect yourself while involved in other outdoor pursuits, especially hunting. Since the vice is the most important tool, it makes sense to purchase a quality one that matches your budget. Other basic tools include a bobbin, scissors, hackle pliers, hair stackers, whip-finish tool, tweezers, bodkin or dubbing needle, hair packer, and hackle gauge.

CHAPTER 16

Fly Casting

In This Chapter

➤ Learning to cast

➤ Basic types of casts

➤ Reading the water

In this chapter, you'll learn about the different casting techniques and how to read the water so you know just where the fish are located.

Fly Casting

Fly casting is the most important skill in fly-fishing. Even though fly casting is more difficult than spin-casting or bait-casting, basic fly casting is easy to learn. Anyone can become a decent caster. Fly casting does not require strength, but it does require proper timing and technique. Certainly, you can expect to feel awkward when you make those first casts, but that awkwardness will soon dissipate as you develop a feel for the rhythm of the cast and the loading of the rod.

Learning Sources

Anglers generally learn how to fly cast from any of four basic sources. The most convenient source is a fly-fishing friend or acquaintance willing to help you out. Professional instructors at local fly shops or fly-fishing clubs are another source for instruction. If your situation allows, fly-fishing classes and schools are excellent means of learning how to fly cast. Instructional videos,

Fishing Vocab

Loading is the process by which a rod flexes or bends from the weight of the fly line during the back cast. This flexing then powers the rod to propel the line, leader, tippet, and fly forward.

too, can get you started in the art of fly casting. Such videos are available at fly shops and are often included in fly-fishing kits. Videos are fine for do-it-yourselfers, but an actual teacher can readily identify and help correct errors, something that speeds up the learning process.

Bad Cast

When learning to fly cast, it's a good idea to wear protective eye gear just in case an errant maneuver causes the line or fly to approach your face.

Practicing

Regardless of your source for learning the basics of fly casting, practice is important for development of the skill. Initially, you will simply want to develop a feel for proper casting mechanics and timing. Once you start feeling comfortable with casting, you can work on accuracy. Don't expect to drop the fly on a dinner plate, but work at placing the fly between two objects. At this point in your development, avoid concentrating on distance. It's more critical to develop a sound technique than to work at making long casts. During your practice sessions, don't be too hard on yourself when things don't go perfectly. Instead, try to enjoy the fun of casting.

Before using a fly for practice, remove the hook point and barb by snipping the fly at the lower end of the shank. Also, avoid practicing on hard surfaces like pavement because such surfaces will damage fly lines and leaders.

The Overhead Cast

The overhead cast is the standard cast in fly-fishing, and the only cast you need to know to get started. This basic casting motion is often compared to the motion used in painting a ceiling or in hammering a nail for hanging a wall picture. The numerals on a clock dial are also used to set a framework for describing casting motions. To visualize this, picture twelve o'clock as being directly overhead and the rod as a hand on the clock. The rhythm of the cast occurs between eleven o'clock and one o'clock. Let's look at the overhead cast in five steps.

Step One: The Starting Position

Step one is the starting position. Begin by stripping 20 to 30 feet of line from the reel and laying the line out in front of you on the water or the lawn if you are practicing in the backyard.

Grip the rod handle as if you were shaking hands with it, making sure that the thumb is extended on top of the cork handle.

Using your off hand, grab the line below the first eye and pull your hand to the area of your belt buckle. An alternative line-holding method is to place the line under the index finger of your casting hand and then pinch the line against the bottom of the rod handle.

Place your off foot slightly out in front, and turn your body slightly in the direction of your casting hand.

Then position the rod at a 45-degree angle with the rod tip pointed at the line and in the direction of the target.

Step Two: The Back Cast

Step two is the back cast. Note that the rod is an extension of the forearm, and the elbow is the pivot point for forearm and its rod extension. Also, be certain not to bend the wrist; keep the wrist stiff.

Begin the back cast by smoothly lifting the line off the water or lawn. Again, the back cast motion occurs between eleven o'clock and one o'clock.

Once the rod reaches eleven o'clock, accelerate the rod to the one o'clock position and stop. The back cast is a crisp motion that involves a burst of rod speed.

Step Three: The Pause

Step three is the pause. When the rod reaches one o'clock with the abrupt stop at the end of the back cast, be sure to keep a stiff wrist. Also, keep the line high. You don't want to drop your arm or let the line fall below head level. As the line extends and straightens out behind you, the rod will flex or load from the weight of the line. Ideally, you want to feel the rod load, but when starting out, it's okay to turn your head and watch the line straighten.

Step Four: The Forward Cast

Step four is the forward cast or the power stroke. As soon as you feel the line pulling at the rod as it loads or as soon as you watch the line straighten behind you, begin the forward cast, which is actually a reversal of the back cast. Starting at the one o'clock position, push the rod in an accelerating motion to eleven o'clock and stop.

Step Five: The Presentation

Step five is the presentation. As the line straightens out in front of you, slowly lower the rod tip to a horizontal position. You are actually using the rod tip to follow the fly to the water or to the ground in the case of backyard practice. If done properly, the line, leader, and fly will straighten out and fall delicately to the water.

Real Fishing

While making long casts is fun, accuracy is more important than distance. In actual stream-fishing situations, most trout are caught within a 35-foot or so radius of the angler.

False Casting

False casting is a technique that doesn't allow the fly or the line to touch the water. Instead, the caster flicks the line backward and forward between the eleven and one o'clock positions. False casting serves a number of purposes such as increasing length of line, lining up the cast with the target, or drying a soaked dry fly. To increase the length of line and thus make longer casts, you simply feed more line through the guides with your off hand on each forward stroke. False casting is also great for practice and developing a feel for the rod loading. In essence, false casting is a repetition of the back cast and the forward cast motions.

Here are ten casting tips:

➤ Don't worry about distance; concentrate on 20 to 30 feet of line.

➤ Keep a rigid wrist; if a problem persists here, you can tape your wrist to the rod or stick the rod butt in your sleeve.

➤ Keep your forearm close to your body.

➤ Avoid dropping the forearm and elbow.

➤ Don't let the line fall below head level on the back cast.

➤ The casting rhythm is a pull and push motion between eleven and one o'clock.

➤ Accelerate the rod speed to an abrupt halt on back and forward casts.

➤ Avoid overpowering the cast.

➤ Let the rod do the work.

➤ Use a knowledgeable spotter; he or she can usually spot flaws more readily than the caster.

Casting Errors and Their Likely Causes

In general, people commit very similar casting errors when they first start the sport of fly-fishing. Here is a list of common casting errors and their probable causes to help you recognize and learn from your mistakes.

➤ If the line drops too low behind you on the back cast, you are likely bending your wrist or extending beyond the one o'clock guideline. Other causes may be a lack of power on the back cast or pausing too long on the back cast.

➤ If the line doesn't straighten on the back cast, you may be trying to use too much line.

➤ If the line doesn't lay out straight on the forward cast, you may not be putting enough power into your stroke.

➤ If the line makes a swooshing sound, you may be putting too much power into the stroke.

➤ If the line falls in a heap in front of you, you may be rushing the back cast and starting the forward cast prior to the line straightening out.

➤ If you are not getting desired distance, you may be rushing the back cast again.

➤ If the line snaps on the front cast, you may be pushing forward prior to the line straightening out on the back cast.

➤ If the line slaps the water, you may be dropping the rod past eleven o'clock on the forward cast.

Roll Cast

Even though the overhead cast is all you need to start fly-fishing, the roll cast is another cast you will want to use. Anglers use the roll cast in confined areas when obstructions behind them prevent the use of the overhead cast. The roll cast is so named because line rolls or makes a U-loop in the casting process. Easy to learn and execute, the roll cast is better practiced on water than dry land because the weight of water on the line and fly create resistance to load the fly rod.

Begin by laying 20 feet or so of fly line out in front of you on the water. Then grasp the line with your off hand and position that hand near the belt buckle area as you would with the overhead cast. Next, lift the rod to twelve o'clock and then ease it to one o'clock. At this point, your rod hand should be just behind your eye and slightly away from the body. Again, the rod will be angled over the shoulder at the one o'clock position. With the line hanging slightly behind you, pause and let the line on the water become still. Then make the forward cast, stopping the rod at nine o'clock or a 45-degree angle. The line and fly will go in the direction the rod tip is pointing. Be sure to maintain a stiff wrist and forearm. As you might guess, a longer rod makes for easier roll casting.

Five More Casts

Five additional casts you may want to add to your arsenal at some point are the backhand, the side cast, the double-haul, the S-cast, and the C-cast.

The backhand cast is actually the overhead cast. Instead of working the rod at the side of the body, though, an angler extends his casting arm across the chest and over the opposite shoulder prior to duplicating the motions of the standard cast.

The side cast can be made in a forehand or backhand style. Either way, the angler simulates the motions of the overhead cast but with the rod positioned horizontally to the water. In other words, the angler works the rod and line parallel to the water. This cast doesn't allow for the distance of the overhead cast, but the cast works well when obstacles prevent using the basic cast and when the angler wants to throw a fly under overhanging branches or under a dock.

The double-haul cast is a bit more complex, but it is used to add distance to the cast.

As the S-cast and C-cast names indicate, these casts lay down the line in S and C shapes to allow for a natural presentation of the fly.

Mending Line

The best fly presentations occur when the fly moves naturally in the current along with other drifting materials. A proper drift is often more important than a fly's size, color, and imitation quality. Because differences in current rate commonly exist between the rod tip and the fly, a fly may drift unnaturally fast or unnaturally slowly. Mending line is the technique of throwing line that is already in the water either upstream or downstream to allow a fly to drift drag free. If the line is moving faster downstream than the fly, the angler uses a short whipping motion of the rod to flip the line upstream. If the fly is moving faster downstream than the line, the angler uses a whipping motion of the rod to flip the line downstream.

Retrieving Line

Unlike spinning and bait-casting reels, where line is retrieved by using the reel handle, fly line is retrieved by hand. Once a cast is completed, the fly angler switches the line from his off hand to the rod hand where the line is tucked between a finger or fingers and the cork handle. Then the angler strips in line with his off hand. One foot increments are a common stripping length as the angler attempts to simulate a swimming creature, but anglers can strip in line at any speed and in any increments they so desire.

As line is stripped in, it is allowed to fall at the angler's feet. By stripping line with the off hand, the rod hand is in position to set the hook when a strike occurs. Once the hook is set, the angler initially fights the fish with his off hand as he works the line. For larger fish the angler should try to get the fish on the reel as soon as possible so the drag can do its work. For smaller fish, some anglers opt to fight the fish entirely by hand while others prefer to get the fish to the reel as they would a larger fish.

Bad Cast

Mishaps such as tangled leaders and flies catching in brush are routine occurrences for novice fly casters. Don't let such incidents frustrate you. Instead, correct the problem and take a few minutes to sit at water's edge and just enjoy your surroundings.

Reading the Water

Reading the water is a skill by which an angler looks at the water and identifies where the fish will most likely be. Obviously, experience plays a role in developing this skill.

In determining likely holding places for fish, an angler must consider a fish's three basic needs: comfort, safety, and food. For comfort, a fish needs oxygenated water within the fish's preferred temperature range. Regarding safety, a fish requires some type of protection from larger fish and other predators such as osprey. As far as food goes, a fish needs to be in an area where food is readily available.

Primer for Reading Water

If there were a primer for instructing anglers on how to read the water, it might contain four points. Number one is to look for visible cover such as shade. A second tip is to look for current obstructions such as boulders, points, and bridge abutments. Third, watch where leaves, foam, and other surface materials drift in the stream since trout foods will likely drift into those same locations. A fourth point calls for wearing a good set of polarized glasses. These glasses allow for a better view of underwater obstructions than do standard sunglasses. Polarized glasses also allow anglers to actually see fish in the water, and reading the water doesn't get any easier than that.

Reading Trout Streams

Here are fifteen signs to look for when reading the water of any trout stream:

➤ Undercut or eroded banks offer shade, shelter, deep water, and drifting food.

➤ Overhanging tree branches offer shade, falling insects, and protection from aerial predators.

➤ Downed trees offer shade and shelter; minnows hang here for the same reasons.

➤ Boulders offer protection from the current and drifting food passes on either side.

➤ Deep pools offer shade, safety, cool water, and baitfish. Fish the edges of the pool.

➤ Runs or smooth-water stretches offer feeding grounds. Again, fish the edges of the run.

➤ Tributary mouths offer incoming water, food, and meshing currents.

➤ Necked-down areas mean food is drifting by in a funnel-like fashion.

➤ Eddies offer a resting place from the current and drifting food.

➤ The base of rapids means oxygenated water and available food.

➤ The base of any waterfalls offers oxygenated water, available food, and a deep pool.

➤ The base of any dam, too, offers oxygenated water and available food.

➤ Structures of any kind offer current breaks, shade, shelter, and drifting food.

➤ Riffles and choppy waters offer a feeding area holding a bounty of insect life.

➤ Seams allow for resting in quieter water and darting into faster water to grab passing food.

Fishing Vocab

A **seam** is the edge between two contiguous currents that are moving at different speeds.

Fly-Fishing Accessories

When purchasing fly-fishing gear, or any angling gear for that matter, go for the best quality your budget can afford. The essential fly-fishing gear consists of rod, reel, line, leaders, and flies. Though not absolutely necessary for fly-fishing, but high on the list of should-have items, are the fly vest and footwear. A sleeveless fishing vest has plenty of pockets to hold all of your accessories. In addition, the vest has a large compartment in the back for holding large items such as rain suit, water bottle, or lunch. There is also a snap for attaching your net and keeping it out of the way. The two footwear choices are hip boots and chest waders. Hip boots are fine for knee-deep water; otherwise, you will want chest waders. Some models have attached boots while other models have a stocking foot that requires the separate purchase of boots. Most anglers prefer the stocking-foot style. When purchasing footwear, be sure to get something with nonslip bottoms such as cleats.

Bad Cast

Anglers can unintentionally transfer nonnative vegetation from one stream to another. To prevent such transfer, anglers should wash and dry their footwear when going from one stream to another. For some waters, certain types of footwear such as felt-bottom soles are prohibited because felt bottoms are more likely to carry unwanted species from water to water.

Among the fly-fishing accessories you will want to have are a fly box for storing flies, polarized glasses for reading the water, hat for sun protection, rain suit for those drizzly outings, clippers for line cutting, hemostats for removing hooks, small needle-nose if you want to flatten barbs, packages of extra leaders and tippets, floatant if using dry flies, split shot if fishing deeper water, and strike indicators for detecting bites. On the might-want list are wading staff, landing net, thermometer, tape measure, creel if keeping any fish, sunscreen, and insect repellent. Spray-on sunscreens and repellents are the way to go as they lessen the chances of contaminating the fly line, leader, and fly.

 # Ice Fishing

> ## In This Chapter
>
> ➤ What makes ice fishing attractive
>
> ➤ How to be safe and comfortable on the ice
>
> ➤ What gear ice anglers use
>
> ➤ What basic strategies ice anglers employ
>
> ➤ How to catch common ice fishing species

In this chapter, you'll learn about safe ice conditions and how to be safe and comfortable while on the ice. Also, you'll learn about the wide array of specialized gear used by ice fishermen. Then you'll learn the basic strategies ice anglers use as well as specific techniques for catching the most-pursued ice fishing species.

Attraction of Ice Fishing

People commonly complain about long winters, but that is not the case for ice anglers. From their perspective, winter, also known as the hard-water season, is too short. Ice fishing is something of an equalizer because an ice cover opens up a body of water and a winter landscape to all anglers.

While some anglers opt for solitude when ice fishing, the sport has much more of a social nature than other types of fishing. During the open-water season, shorelines, docks, streams, and boats might not allow for group fishing, but groups of family and friends are routine sights on the ice. In some cases, congregations of fishermen resemble a small village. Ice fishing derbies, too, play a role in the social aspect of the sport. Most derbies are annual affairs used as fundraisers by communities, civic groups, and sportsmen's clubs, and most derbies run for one day or one weekend, although some are part of week-long winter festivals, and others are season-long affairs.

Since good fishing spots and derbies do draw a large contingent of anglers to a relatively small area, the resource may be subject to overfishing. With this in mind, many derbies have conservation themes such as catch-and-release categories, minimum-length requirements exceeding state regulations, and random drawings for prizes.

Ice fishing is a great winter activity with plenty of benefits, two of which are fresh air and exercise. Spend a day on the ice performing routine ice fishing tasks such as walking to a fishing spot, carrying gear, auguring holes, setting rigs, tending rigs, running to flags, jigging from hole to hole, picking up the gear, and returning to the vehicle, and you'll be a tired individual. Ice fishing is a youth-friendly and pet-friendly activity, so take the kids and dog along. Another benefit is the possibility of a meal of fresh fish at the close of a winter day.

Bad Cast

Ice fishing regulations for many waters are different from regulations for those waters during the open-water season. For example, some waters may be closed to ice fishing while other waters may prohibit fishing for certain species such as brook trout. Also, regulations vary regarding the type and number of lines an angler may set. The point is you should always familiarize yourself with the ice-fishing regulations for any water prior to fishing there.

Safety on the Ice

Although perceived by some people as a somewhat risky activity, ice fishing is a very safe sport. The key is to venture forth only when ice conditions are favorable. General guidelines regarding ice safety are that ice 2 to 3 inches deep is safe for walking, ice 4 inches deep is safe for drilling holes and fishing, ice 5 inches deep is safe for snow machines and ATVs, ice 8 inches deep is safe for cars and light trucks, and ice 12 inches deep is safe for medium trucks and vans. When driving a vehicle on the ice, precautions call for going slowly, unfastening seatbelts, unlocking doors, and rolling down windows to facilitate escaping from the vehicle in the unlikelihood of going through the ice.

Ice Conditions

Ice conditions may or may not be consistent on a body of water. Two situations where ice could be thinner than the rest of the ice cover are underwater springs and current. Also, shallow areas and protected areas freeze first so they often have thicker ice than exposed areas that freeze later. First ice is good time to abide by the saying, "When in doubt, don't go out." Actually periods of deteriorating ice are usually more dangerous than periods when ice is forming. Last ice, rainy periods, thaws, consecutive days of unseasonably warm temperatures, and extended periods of sun can cause ice deterioration, and that deterioration occurs primarily around shorelines, islands, rocks, manmade structures, and shanties.

Checking on ice conditions is an important step in preparing for an outing. Local bait shops are excellent sources of such information because the shops are in daily contact with anglers. Some bait shops and fish and game departments regularly update their websites with current ice conditions. Also, consider doing some scouting by visiting potential fishing waters to check ice depth. If other anglers are there, politely ask them about ice depth and how the fishing is. Ice fishers are like other anglers in that they are usually willing to share information about their craft.

Safety Accessories

Among common ice fishing accessories for safety are cleats, picks, and ropes. Ice cleats strap over boots and provide insurance against slips and falls. Ice picks are handheld pieces of wood or plastic with a nail embedded in them, and they are used to pull an angler up on the ice in the rare case he or she ever falls through. A length of rope with an attached ring allows a person to aid an angler who has fallen through without having to approach the hole in the ice and risk breaking through, too.

Comfort on the Ice

If you are warm and dry, a day on the ice is an enjoyable experience. Such is not the case, though, if you are wet and cold. Comfort on the ice means dressing properly, and that means dressing in layers. Layering is important because you'll be spending time in the vehicle and auguring holes, actions that require less clothing than when you are sitting on a pail waiting for a tip-up flag to fly or gathering gear as the sun settles on the horizon. Layering begins with long underwear and ends with a wind-resistant outer layer. A hooded jacket or an underneath layer consisting of a hooded sweatshirt provides extra warmth when it's windy.

Critical to comfort as well as to protection from hypothermia and frostbite are protecting the extremities. Up to 40 percent of a person's body heat can be lost through the head, 20 percent through the hands, and 10 percent through the feet. Extremity comfort means wearing quality socks, foot wear, gloves, mittens, and hats, and it never hurts to have an extra pair of socks and gloves in the vehicle. My hat choice is a warm toque. To reduce foot sweating, which can lead to cold feet, it's best to put on your warm boots only after arriving at the fishing site.

Food and fluids also contribute to ice fishing comfort. Food helps the body produce heat, and fluids such as water and juices protect against dehydration, an overlooked ill of lengthy exposure to wind and cold temperatures.

A variety of ice fishing gear such as portable shelters and heaters allow for comfort, too, but commercially packaged hand warmers and foot warmers are hard to beat for cost, convenience, and effectiveness. Since people spend most of their winter hours indoors, a sunny day on the ice lends itself to sunburn, so applying sunscreen can provide protective comfort to facial skin.

Ice Fishing Gear

The gear used by ice anglers makes ice fishing unique, and there's a lot of ice fishing gear out there. An ice fisherman can easily spend thousands of dollars when purchasing gear, but you can get started for less than $100 and still catch plenty of fish. Most anglers begin with basic equipment and then add gear as they go from season to season. When starting out, it's worthwhile buying quality gear because as you get more into the sport, you're going to want that quality in your gear. Because of ice fishing's unique nature, I recommend hooking up with experienced anglers if you are new to the sport. In a single outing, they can teach you more about gear than you would learn in a full season on your own.

Gear Options Vary

In essence, people can make ice fishing as simple or as complicated as they want. Even though I have been hitting the hard water for five-plus decades, I opt to keep things pretty simple. I head to the water with a pack basket on my back, a 6-gallon bucket in one hand, and an auger on the other shoulder. The basket holds tip-ups, jig poles, ice scoop, terminal tackle, miscellaneous gear, and lunch. The bucket holds live bait, and a lid on the bucket allows the pail to also serve as a seat. The auger is gas powered.

I choose to travel light because I fish a lot of different waters, some of which require hiking through the woods, walking down a steep bank, or hiking to the far side of the lake. Also, if the fishing is slow in a selected spot, I'll pick up all my gear and relocate. Relative to most anglers on the ice, I'm typically at the low end of the gear scale.

I have an ice fishing friend, though, who is at the other end of the scale. Several years ago, he decided to sell his fishing boat and invest in ice fishing gear. He has an ATV to which is attached a portable shelter on a sled. Inside the shelter are sonar unit, GPS unit, cook stove, gas-powered auger, and the rest of his basic fishing gear. When he arrives at a fishing site, he drives the ATV and attached shelter off the trailer and heads across the lake to his fishing destination. At day's end, everything gets packed in the portable shelter, and he drives onto the trailer and then heads home. By the way, this friend missed having a boat after his first summer without one, so he now has a new boat to go along with his ice-fishing rig.

Making Holes

Ice fishing begins with making holes in the ice, and the three hole-making tools are the spud, manual auger, and gas-powered auger.

Spuds are simply large chisels, and because of the work involved in chopping through ice, especially when making a dozen or two holes, spuds work best on thinner ice. Although spuds are inexpensive, making holes with them is noisy and time consuming.

Hand augers are inexpensive and lightweight, and they make holes ranging from 4 to 8 inches in diameter. Making the larger holes requires some effort, but a sharp blade is critical to all cutting. Hand augers are particularly popular among panfish anglers who require small holes and who move from site to site in search of fish.

Gas-powered augers are the choice of most ice anglers. Despite being more costly and heavier than spuds and hand augers, gas-powered augers make for fast and easy hole cutting, important qualities since modern anglers are active ones who may drill several dozen holes on a given outing.

Fishing Vocab

An ice skimmer, sometimes called a scooper, is a large ladle-type device with holes in it. It is used to skim or scoop ice to clear out a hole. Anglers use skimmers to clear ice out of newly drilled holes and holes that freeze over during an outing. Metal skimmers significantly outperform plastic ones.

Jigging Rods and Tip-Ups

Ice anglers use two tools for catching fish: the jigging rod and the tip-up. Jigging rods are handheld while tip-ups are set on the ice.

Jigging rods typically measure 24 to 32 inches. The short length allows an angler to stand near the hole when making presentations, playing fish, and landing fish. Although jigging rods may be set in holders, a technique called dead-sticking, anglers usually hold the rod and jig their bait or lure, thus the name jigging rod.

Like other rods, ice fishing rods are available in various powers and actions. Lightweight rods are a good choice for smaller species such as bluegills, black crappies, and yellow perch, and medium-weight rods work well for trout and walleyes. Large species such as northern pike and lake trout call for a heavyweight rod. Fast action rods work well for ice fishing because they allow for detection of delicate bites and they have enough backbone for hook-setting. A spring bobber attached to the end of a rod is also effective for detecting light bites as well as for presenting tiny lures. Furthermore, rods with larger eyes don't ice up as easily as do rods with small eyes.

Fishing Vocab

A spring bobber is a strike indicator attached to the end of jigging rod. This light-wire device indicates the lightest of bites, so it is a sure way to put more panfish on the ice.

Tip-ups, sometimes called fish traps or setlines, have a frame made of wood or hard plastic, and the standard model sits across a hole with a spool submerged in the water. When a fish strikes and pulls out line, a trip mechanism causes a flag to spring up, and this flag is the angler's signal of a strike. When fishing in deep water or for species such as lake trout that make long runs, oversized spools are available. Also, flag extenders are available, and they allow for easier spotting when tip-ups are set at a distance or in deep snow. To aid strike detection in low-light or night conditions, sound and light indicators may be attached to the flag.

Ice Fishing Lines

A variety of ice fishing lines are available, the most common of which are monofilament, Dacron, and specialty lines. When spooling the reels on jigging rods, the key is to match line strength to the targeted species and line visibility to water conditions. Limp, low-stretch, sensitive lines work best for detecting bites.

When spooling tip-ups, I use Dacron line with a 6-foot, monofilament leader. Dacron line is easy to handle in freezing conditions, and by changing leaders I can use the same tip-ups for different species. For example, I can tie on 20-pound test leaders when fishing northern pike. If the next outing targets rainbow trout, I can tie on 8-pound test monofilament. More and more anglers are turning to fluorocarbon leaders when fishing in clear water conditions. Because lines commonly rub against the edges of the hole, anglers need to routinely check lines for wear.

Ice Fishing Lures

Ice anglers rely on three basic artificial lures: the jigging spoon, the jigging minnow, and the lead-head jig. The jigging spoon is a heavy spoon with a more slender design than the casting spoon. This spoon emits flash and injured-minnow action as it falls, glides, and darts toward bottom. Large jigging spoons are available for pike and lake trout, whereas the smallest sizes work for small-mouthed bluegills.

Jigging minnows, sometimes called swimming lures, have a horizontal rather than a vertical profile, and their gliding, swimming actions imitate an injured baitfish. Again, there are various sizes for various species.

The lead-head jig, too, comes in a variety of sizes, and jigs are commonly tipped with plastic baits such as grubs, tubes, and twister tails. The tiny ice jig is especially designed for panfish. Artificial ice fishing lures are routinely tipped with minnows, minnow pieces, and maggots.

Bad Cast

Minnows purchased at a bait store and then exposed to frigid air or water temperatures will weaken and die. To avoid losing your minnows, use a pail with an insulated insert, and when adding colder water to your bucket, do so in moderate doses so the bait has time to acclimate to the temperature change.

Sleds

Ice fishing sleds work great for hauling gear. These high-sided sleds are made of plastic, and they come in various sizes to hold auger, buckets, tip-ups, jig poles, cook stove, lunch, etc. Ice fishing sleds may be pulled by hand, snow machine, or ATV.

Shelters

An ice fishing shelter's most attractive feature is protection from the wind. Getting out of the wind provides comfort for anglers and allows for easy cooking with a gas or propane grill. For decades, all shelters were of the homemade variety.

Homemade shelters, commonly called permanent shacks, are commonly set up in a location at the beginning of the season, and then removed from that location at season's end. Because of the weight of homemade shacks, some type of motorized vehicle is necessary to haul them onto the ice. This means the shack cannot be set up until ice conditions are safe for vehicular access. Also, owners may have to remove the shelters prior to major thaws or prior to the end of the season. Another drawback of permanent shelters is the restriction to a certain area. On the other hand, most anglers set their shelters in a proven location such as a point, shoal edge, weed edge, drop-off, or soft-bottom flat. In a way, setting out a permanent shelter is almost like staking a claim to an area. Most shelters contain cooking, heating, sitting, and storage features.

Bad Cast

Ice shelters are not typically airtight, but anglers are cautioned about the possibility of carbon monoxide poisoning when propane stoves and heaters are being used. Always make sure a shelter has adequate ventilation.

In recent decades, portable shelters have grown in popularity among the ice fishing crowd. These shelters come in a variety of sizes and styles. Some shelters hold one angler while other shelters hold a small group of anglers. Portable shelters have a tentlike structure, and some have an ice-fishing sled for a base; others have hard-plastic flooring. Lighter shelters are easily pulled by hand, but the larger ones require an ATV or other vehicle for hauling. Portable shelters are designed for easy setup and easy breakdown, and in addition to providing protection from cold and wind, the shelters allow for angler mobility since an angler can fish different areas on a particular lake or even fish different bodies of water from outing to outing.

Electronics

Open-water anglers routinely move from spot to spot in search of fish, and more and more ice anglers are doing the same. Snow machines and portable shelters facilitate this active angling, but sonar units play a critical role, too. In searching for fish, a sonar unit allows for finding structure and structural edges. The units also identify where fish are holding in a water column, and anglers who know the workings of their units can interpret a fish's behavior to a particular presentation and then alter that presentation to entice a strike.

Sonar units for ice fishing come in compact cases. Flasher units are the most popular, but chart and LCD models are also available. When fishing shallower water, wide-angle cones are the way to go, and when fishing deep water, narrow-angle cones perform best. Ice fishing sonar units have revolutionized the sport, and any angler who uses such a unit should see his or her catches improve significantly.

In addition to sonar units, other electronic devices used by ice anglers include GPS units and underwater cameras. GPS units allow anglers to return to locations marked as waypoints on their units. For example, an angler can mark waypoints during the open-water season and then return to those spots for ice fishing. Also, some units come with preloaded information, and others have multimedia card slots for chips containing electronic charts of popular fishing waters. Underwater cameras are fun to use because an angler can see what is really there. Cameras, though, are somewhat harder to use than sonar units, and cameras present poor images in dark-water conditions.

Miscellaneous Gear

Miscellaneous items that find their way to the ice are line clippers, gaff, lantern for heat and light, knife, hand towel, fold-out chair, needle-nose pliers, mouth spreaders, measuring tape, and gear bag.

Fishing Strategies

The best ice fishing strategy is to set up where the fish are, and familiarity with a water body definitely increases the odds of setting up in a fish-holding location. For example, anglers who fish the same waters during the ice-covered months that they fish during the open-water months have a definite advantage in knowing where certain species of fish are likely to be.

Unfamiliar Waters

When fishing unfamiliar waters, lake maps make good guides because they indicate water depths and reveal likely holding places such as drop-offs, humps, and points. If maps are unavailable, you can start with visual clues. For example, bays and points are easily identified, and land features offer clues, too. If the shoreline is flat, the water near it is likely shallow. If the shoreline consists of a steep bank, there is likely deep water adjacent to shore. Also, shoreline makeup of gravel, boulders, sand, or swamp can indicate bottom makeup. Ultimately, verification of water depths and structures occurs by drilling holes and using a manual sounder or electronic depth finder.

Other anglers are also a visual clue to good fishing areas. When joining other anglers, be sure not to crowd them. Rather, set up on their fringes, and you'll likely be in a pretty good spot especially if the area is a bay or large flat.

Fish Needs

Fish needs in winter include cover, food, oxygen, and water temperature. Areas meeting those needs include weedy bays, submerged vegetation, points, medium and deep flats, shoreline and island drop-offs, mid-lake humps, quiet backwaters on rivers, and shoal edges. When setting up in these areas, be certain to set up with a purpose such as working a weed line, covering the various depths of a point, fishing along a drop-off as well in the adjacent deep water, or working the top and edges of a mid-lake hump.

On the Move

If you set up in an area and the fishing meets your expectations, then it makes sense to stay put. If the action is slow in an area, drill more holes and work those holes. If that effort proves unproductive, consider moving to another likely spot. In essence, the modern ice angler is a mobile one. Again, the key to productive mobility is to move and to do so with a purpose and a plan. An exception to the mobility guideline is when you are set up on a structure where a species such as walleye are known to move during a lowlight period such as dusk. Then it pays to fish in a waiting mode rather than a mobile mode.

Seasonal Adjustments

The hard-water season actually has three parts: early ice, mid-winter, and late ice. Early ice is a fairly short period when fish are found in the shallows, around shorelines, around weed beds, and near shallow and shoreline structures.

Mid-winter is the longest period of the ice fishing season and also the most challenging time to catch fish because they are more dispersed than during the early and later periods. With less light reaching them, shallow weeds die and no longer produce oxygen. As a result, fish abandon the shallows for deep water that is warmer and more stable. Mid-winter calls for fishing mid-lake humps, the mouths of bays, medium and deep flats, drop offs, deep-water points, and structural edges. Again, predator fish will move shallower in these areas to feed during lowlight periods of dawn and dusk.

Late ice offers the best fishing of the winter, but it is also the most dangerous time because ice conditions are deteriorating rather than strengthening. Late ice sees large concentrations of fish returning to the shallows, shorelines, and tributaries where the fish are drawn because of available forage, warming water temperatures, and prespawn positioning.

Using Tip-Ups and Jigging Poles

Where allowed, the combination approach of using both tip-ups and jigging poles works well. An angler can set the legal number of tip-ups and then move from hole to hole with a jigging rod. For example, five tip-ups and two hand lines are allowed on my home waters, so I usually set my tip-ups for northern pike, walleyes, or tiger muskellunge and then do some jigging for yellow perch, black crappies, or walleyes. Even though two hand lines are allowed, I find that a single one is all I need.

Setting Tip-Ups

Tip-ups allow for the presentation of live minnows at a desired depth. Where the use of multiple tip-ups is permitted, anglers can present their baits in various spots such as a weed edge, an opening in the weeds, above the weeds, and deep water adjacent to the weeds. If fishing is more productive in one spot, the other tip-ups can be adjusted accordingly.

The typical setup for presenting live bait consists of a hook at line's end and split shot placed a foot or so up the line to keep the minnow somewhat anchored. The angler attaches a clip-on sounder to the hook and lowers it to determine water depth. After determining the distance the bait should be from the bottom, the angler attaches a depth indicator such as a small bobber on the line where the line enters the tip-up spool. This way the angler does not have to sound for bottom depth every time he or she resets the tip-up. Minnows are generally hooked just below the dorsal fin.

Real Fishing

When using live minnows on tip-ups, the traditional hook-setting method calls for letting the fish make its initial run and setting the hook when the fish starts its second run. It is believed that species such as northern pike turn the bait and take it deeper into their mouths prior to the second run. I have good luck, however, using small treble hooks and setting the hook on the initial run. With this method, fish are usually hooked in the side of the mouth.

Jigging Presentations

When using jigging rods, the key is to have plenty of holes. The angler works one hole for a few minutes, and moves on to another hole if there is no action. The angler works all the holes and then starts the cycle again, making sure to focus on any holes that produced fish during previous tries. Throughout the day, an angler may want to drill additional holes if the current ones are not producing. Again, the new holes should be drilled with a purpose such as to move closer to the weed edge or to move to deeper water.

When jigging, anglers use a variety of motions to entice strikes, and this is where a sonar unit comes in handy because an angler can try different presentations and see how the fish react to each. Common presentations include lift and drop, hitting the bottom, sudden lift, long pause, twitching the rod tip, tapping the butt of the rod with a forefinger, leaving the lure motionless, etc.

Whether an angler is using tip-ups, jigging poles, or both, general guidelines call for pretrip preparation so the rigs are in working order, travelling light to allow for mobility, drilling plenty of holes to allow for covering a lot of water, and being quiet, especially when fishing on thin ice, bare ice, and in shallow water.

Common Ice Fishing Species

Ice anglers target a variety of cold-water, cool-water, and warm-water species during the hard-water season. Popular cold-water fish include lake trout, brown trout, rainbow trout, brook trout, and cutthroat trout. Popular cool-water fish include northern pike, walleyes, yellow perch, and black crappies. Bluegills and other sunfish are favorite warm-water targets. Because winter, especially early- and late-ice periods, often finds fish congregated in large numbers, fish may be subject to overharvesting, so anglers are encouraged to limit their catches.

Lake Trout

Lake trout are a prized quarry of ice fishermen. Whereas the open-water season typically finds lake trout holding tight to bottom in the deepest and coldest portions of a lake, the cold temperatures of winter create a comfort zone that encompasses the entire water body. Under the ice, lake trout are extremely active as they move throughout a lake in search of baitfish and small fish.

Even though lake trout are free to roam anywhere in the lake, prime fishing spots include points, rocky structures, and steep breaks at depths of 20 to 60 feet. Because lake trout are mobile, setting tip-ups baited with live minnows works well. For best results, set minnows around structures in the bottom half of the water column. Lake trout are great fighters capable of running all the line off a spool, so ice fishermen commonly use oversized spools with plenty of backing.

Even though lake trout are mobile, most anglers go in a search mode when pursuing this fish. Thus, jigging is the more popular technique because it allows for angler mobility and for working the entire water column. Common lures include jigging spoons, jigging minnows (airplane jigs), tube jigs, and bucktail jigs. Lake trout are attracted to the flash and injured-baitfish appearance of these lures, but tipping any lure with a minnow or minnow piece makes the offering even more appealing. The tipping also slows the fall of the lure, an action that appeals to lake trout.

Stream Trout

Brown trout, rainbow trout, brook trout, and cutthroat trout are sometimes called stream trout; however, ice fishing for these cold-water species occurs on ponds, lakes, and reservoirs. For the most part, these trout are stocked fish rather than native ones. Look for winter trout around shoreline flats, shoreline and island drop-offs, underwater springs, and points. During the late-ice period, also check out tributary areas.

Under the ice, trout are cruising fish that roam in search of aquatic insects, invertebrates, minnows, and small fish. The best fishing times are dawn, dusk, and during overcast conditions because trout are most active at those low-light times. Since trout are roamers, suspending 3-inch, live minnows below tip-ups works well. Tipping jigging spoons with a small minnow also entices trout hits as does the tipping of jigs with tube bodies or plastic grubs. Because trout feed on small prey, tiny ice jigs work well. Working the upper half of the water column should produce more trout than working the bottom half.

Northern Pike

Northern pike are a popular ice quarry because of their voracious appetite, large size, and fighting ability. You can expect a hooked pike to make any number of surging runs once it nears the hole, and landing a big pike through the ice is much more challenging than getting one into the boat. This cool-water species feeds actively all winter long. Favorite pike areas are large bays, shoreline and island drop-offs, points, and humps where the fish relate to edges. The very best areas have weed growth. In late winter, pike move to the shoreline shallows and near tributaries in anticipation of spawning after ice-out. Northern pike bite throughout the day, but early morning and late afternoon produce the biggest fish.

Jigging is not that popular among winter pike anglers. In fact, more pike are probably caught by anglers jigging for other species than are caught by those actually targeting northern pike. Still, jigging spoons and jigging minnows offer a flash and action that entice pike hits because of the injured-minnow look.

For the best results with tip-ups, set them on structural edges. Even though pike are not a schooling fish, packs of fish seem to hold in certain areas. Where multiple tip-ups are allowed, it's not uncommon to produce two or three pike from a single hole while the adjacent holes fail to yield even one fish. Live minnows in the 4- to 6-inch range are the most common pike bait, but fish will also hit dead minnows, particularly larger ones. Anglers looking for trophy pike often use 8- to 12-inch suckers on quick-strike rigs. Since a pike's eyes are set so the fish can see prey above them, pike rigs should be set several feet above bottom.

Real Fishing

I do a lot of ice fishing for northern pike in very clear waters so I use monofilament leaders rather than the more visible steel ones. Despite the pike's sharp teeth I rarely experience bite-offs. The monofilament leaders do become frayed, though, and I have to routinely replace them.

Walleyes

Because of their fine table fare, walleyes rank as the most popular game fish on many waters. A cool-water species, walleyes remain active throughout the winter, and they are quite mobile in their search for food. The most significant movement occurs at twilight when walleyes leave deeper water and move toward and onto adjacent structures. Prime walleye-holding areas include deep-water humps, weed edges, drop-offs, points, and other structures. Generally, the best fishing occurs in areas with the largest and most varied structure. Since walleyes feed heavily on yellow perch, look for walleyes wherever perch are found. In late winter, walleyes congregate near spawning tributaries, bays, and rocky areas, but regulations commonly prohibit fishing at that time in order to protect spawning fish.

Both jigging and tip-ups take winter walleyes, and jigging is the more popular technique. Jigging spoons, jigging minnows, and jigs work well especially when tipped with a minnow or minnow part. For the best results, use a slow presentation, and work the lure near bottom since walleyes generally hold within a few feet of bottom. Some walleye anglers like to use the dead-stick approach where they suspend a live minnow on a thin-wire hook and put the jigging rod in a holder. Tip-ups should be set near structural edges where the best action occurs at twilight when walleyes move in to feed. The favorite tip-up offering is 3- to 4-inch minnows hooked just below the dorsal fin on #6 or #8 trebles. Be sure to set the minnow within a few feet of bottom.

Yellow Perch

Ice anglers love this cool-water fish because of its abundant numbers and active feeding throughout the winter. Furthermore, they have a fairly aggressive nature that is likely due to competition with other fish in the school, and they feed throughout the day. Yellow perch also make excellent table fare.

Finding perch below the ice amounts to fishing around vegetated and soft-bottom areas because these spots hold the aquatic insects and small fish upon which perch feed. Prime winter locations where perch feed are weedy shorelines, weedy bays, flats with a sandy or soft bottom, tapering shorelines, flats with scattered or low-growing vegetation, mid-depth flats, and deep flats. Late spring offers the very best fishing of the winter because perch congregate on shallow, weedy flats and near tributaries.

Both jigging and setting tip-ups will take winter perch, though jigging is the more productive technique because it allows for easier mobility going from hole to hole. If a school of perch is located, jigging is the faster method of getting a bait or lure back to the fish. For the most part, yellow perch are not finicky eaters so jigging spoons, tipped jigs, and live minnows work well. Since perch commonly feed on small aquatic insects, smaller spoons and jigs tipped with maggots are very effective, too. Perch generally hold near bottom so baits and lures are best presented within a few feet of bottom. In mid-winter when perch move to deeper flats, working the bottom one-third of the water column is worthwhile. Tip-ups baited with live minnows work well for perch, particularly jumbo ones. The difficulty with tip-ups, though, is the action sometimes gets too fast for the time it takes to rebait and reset lines.

Black Crappies

Black crappies are another cool-water species that feeds throughout winter, and their tasty flesh makes them a popular quarry. Locating crappies presents a special challenge to ice anglers because the fish favor fairly deep water and they move around. Look for crappies near basins, deep holes, mouths of large bays, harbors, steep breaks, drop-offs, mid-depth flats, and deep flats. The best locations have structure associated with them. Catching crappies through the ice is a searching game, and once you locate a few, good numbers of crappies are usually in the area. Generally, early ice and late ice offer the best fishing.

Because of the searching nature of crappie fishing, jigging is a more effective technique than is setting live minnows below tip-ups. Still, tip-ups set along deep structural edges will take fish. Jigging, though, allows the mobility to move from hole to hole, and jigging makes it easier to work the water column for suspended crappies. Because crappies commonly suspend in deeper water, and they may be anywhere in the water column from the bottom to just under the ice; sonar units can significantly facilitate finding fish.

Slip bobbers, too, aid in presenting bait or lures in deeper water. The most popular presentation is a small minnow on a hook or jigging lure, although a maggot-tipped jigging lure frequently produces better results. Since crappies are soft biters that can inhale and quickly exhale a bait or lure, a sensitive setup such as a pencil bobber or spring bobber aids in detecting bites. Crappies commonly return to the same areas to feed, so once you find fish, those areas merit your attention on future outings. Because crappies are most active in the evening, at night, and in early morning, those are the times when you want to be on deep-water edges near points, weed beds, and other structures.

Bluegills

Even though bluegills and other sunfish such as the pumpkinseed are warm-water species, they remain fairly active throughout the winter, particularly during early- and late-ice periods. Bluegills like cover, their favorite of which is vegetation. In early and late season, look for bluegills around weedy bays, weedy shorelines, and weedy flats with 10 feet or less of water. During midwinter, look for bluegills in the same areas but at depths out to 20 feet or so. Prime midwinter locations include weed lines, flats with bottom weeds, and soft-bottom flats.

Bluegills are a schooling fish, so find one and the action is usually quite good. Since bluegills do not roam like yellow perch and black crappies, you can often continue to catch fish in a fairly small area. Bluegills are small-mouthed fish that tend to hold near bottom. Thus, tiny ice jigs tipped with insect larvae and presented near bottom is the go-to technique. Use subtle jigging actions such as quivering, twitching, and jiggling.

PART THREE

Most Common Freshwater Species

 # The Sunfish Family

In this chapter you'll learn about the members of the sunfish family whose technical name is *Centrarchidae*, translated to mean "nest builders." The sunfish are native only to North America. In addition to thirty native species, there are over twenty hybrids due to crossbreeding between species such as the pumpkinseed and blue gill or the black crappie and the white crappie.

Members of the sunfish family prefer warm-water habitat such as ponds, shallow lakes, and protected bays of deep lakes and large rivers. During spawning, the male builds a nest, protects the fertilized eggs, and guards the fry until they abandon the nest. The three major groupings in the sunfish family are the true sunfish, the crappies, and the black bass.

The True Sunfish

The most popular species in the true sunfish grouping include the bluegill, pumpkinseed, and redear sunfish, all of which have a brightly colored appearance that merits the fish being labeled as sunfish. The true sunfish are very popular among anglers because the fish are abundant, easy to catch, excellent table fare, and scrappy fighters. If there is a negative aspect to sunfish, it lies in their tendency to overpopulate and become stunted in waters where there is a lack of larger predators.

The true sunfish do well in a wide range of water temperatures and qualities. Their habitat preference is the quiet, warm, and weedy water of ponds, pits, lakes, reservoirs, and rivers. Like their largemouth bass cousin, sunfish prefer shallow-water habitat where favorite feeding times are morning and evening.

Bluegills

The bluegill, *Lepomis macrochirus*, is the most widespread of the true sunfish, and as a result, it is also the most popular among anglers. The bluegill once inhabited waters in the eastern half of the United States but can now be found in all states except Alaska. This sunfish earned its name from the light blue gill cover. Other identifying marks of the bluegill are the black ear flap as well as the black blotch on the lower rear of the dorsal fin. In the South, anglers commonly call the bluegill bream, which is pronounced brim.

Bluegills favor warm, quiet water with a fair amount of weed growth. They feed in water temperatures from 55°F to 85°F but feed most actively when temperatures range from 70°F to 80°F. Food choices include insects, crustaceans, small fish, aquatic vegetation, and plankton. Because bluegills are attracted to shoreline shallows and weed growth, the fish are accessible to a large number of anglers, whether it's a veteran angler looking for a tasty meal or a family looking to introduce youngsters to the fun of fishing. Despite their average size of only 7 to 8 inches, bluegills are scrappy fighters and fun to catch on light gear.

Real Fishing

True sunfish are the ideal species for introducing youths to the world of angling. Sunfish are willing biters, and they are readily accessible to shore anglers.

Pumpkinseeds

Pumpkinseeds, *Lepomis gibbosus*, are more colorful than other sunfish. The pumpkinseed's bright coloration consists of gold sides with green, orange, and red speckles, and a belly of reddish orange or bronze. Another identifying mark is the bright red tip of an otherwise dark ear flap. Once found in waters of the Midwest and eastern United States, the pumpkinseed has since been stocked in waters to the West Coast. The pumpkinseed is often called the common sunfish.

The pumpkinseed is smaller than the bluegill, and the pumpkinseed prefers slightly cooler water, too. A typical pumpkinseed measures in the 5- to 7-inch range. Like the bluegill, though, the pumpkinseed does well in shallow lakes and the protected bays of large waters where it feeds on insects, crustaceans, and small fish. Despite its small mouth, the pumpkinseed takes tiny baits aggressively. Because of its preference for near-shore habitat and its willingness to hit a grub or piece of worm, the pumpkinseed is a great starter fish for kids.

Redear Sunfish

The redear sunfish, *Lepomis microlophus*, is often called a shellcracker by southern anglers because of the fish's ability to grind up snails. Redear sunfish can be found in the south-central part of the United States and throughout most of the eastern half of the country except for the very northeastern portion. Stockings have taken place in some western states. Redears have a thicker body than other sunfish, and anglers identify them by the red or orange edge around the ear flap, a feature that earned this species its name.

Redear sunfish like clear water and weed growth, but the fish will hold around cover such as downed trees, logs, stumps, and standing timber. Also, they tend to hold in deeper water than bluegills and pumpkinseeds. Redears are bottom feeders that dine on snails, small fish, and insects. Various live baits work well for redears that average a slightly bigger size then their bluegill cousins. As is the case with other sunfish, the best shellcracker fishing occurs around spawning.

Locating Sunfish

Because of their preference for quiet, warm, weedy water, sunfish are fairly easy to locate. In addition to the cover provided by vegetation, the very best spots often offer additional cover in the form of downed trees, sunken logs, stump fields, and standing timber. Manmade structures such as docks and bridges are favored covers, too, and the best covers also have a depth change. Under bright conditions or during a cold front, sunfish hold a bit deeper and somewhat tighter to cover. When looking for schools of sunfish, move from cover to cover. If a fish is caught, work the area thoroughly, and when the action slows, move along to another spot. Once you have located a productive area, it will likely be a good fishing spot year after year.

Best Fishing Times

Sunfish are catchable year-round, but most anglers target sunfish in the spring because the fish are most concentrated at that time. As water temperatures warm, sunfish move into shallow, soft-bottom, vegetated areas where the fish feed actively.

Bad Cast

Avoid keeping small sunfish as they yield very little flesh when filleted. Such fish better serve the resource when they are released and allowed to grow to a larger size.

The best locations have direct exposure to the sun. These same areas serve as spawning grounds, so look for fish in those protected areas and shorelines that have sand or gravel bottom. After spawning, the smaller fish remain in the shallows, but larger sunfish move to deep weed edges, sloping breaks, and cover-providing structures. In early fall, sunfish move shallow again, and covers and edges near spawning areas are good bets. By late fall, sunfish have moved to deep water where they spend the winter.

Sunfish are catchable throughout the day and particularly so in the spring. Otherwise, the best fishing times are early and late in the day when sunfish leave cover and move shallow where they feed actively. At sunset, though, sunfish seek cover where they spend the night hiding from predators.

Fishing Strategies

Live bait ranks as the favorite offering for sunfish, and popular baits include worms, grubs, crickets, and grasshoppers. In addition to their visual appeal, these offerings appeal to the sunfish's good sense of smell. Generally, the bait is impaled on a small hook and suspended below a bobber, or the bait is fished a foot or so up the line with a sinker at line's end. Where legal, anglers often use multiple baited hooks. Always hook the bait in a way so that it has a lively appearance. Second to live bait in popularity is the use of tiny jigs with hair, marabou, or plastic bodies or jigs tipped with plastic or live bait such as a grub. Jigs may be suspended below a bobber or fished freely.

Whether you are fishing with bait or jigs, cast the offering to a desired spot, and let it sit for a minute or two. If there is no bite, ease the line in a couple of feet and let the offering sit for another minute or two. Continue this process until it's time to make another cast. If you catch a fish, then cast again to that same area. If you don't get a bite, cast to a new area. Because of their preference for shallow water and their aggressive nature, sunfish are a favorite target of fly-fishers. When conditions are calm, small poppers and terrestrials work well. Otherwise, bright nymphs are the flies to use.

Here are some tips for catching bluegills, pumpkinseeds, and redear sunfish:

> ➤ Sunfish have small mouths, so use tiny baits and jigs.

> ➤ Use a fine-wire hook (#8 to #12) for best hook-sets.

> ➤ Use a long shank hook to make for easier hook removal.

> ➤ Carry a set of hemostats for removing hooks.

> ➤ Use light line for more bites, and use light tackle for scrappier fights.

> ➤ Use a quick hook-set to prevent fish from swallowing the hook.

> ➤ Make long casts to avoid alerting fish in shallow water.

➤ Use a quiet approach to avoid alerting fish.

➤ Anticipate light bites since sunfish inhale rather than strike their food.

➤ Use a slow presentation rather than a fast one.

Crappies

Like the true sunfish, crappies can be found in waters in just about everybody's backyard. In addition to widespread availability, the crappie's popularity stems from its sporting and eating qualities.

The crappie group consists of the black crappie and the white crappie. Though the two species have overlapping ranges, black crappies are more abundant in the northern portion of the United States while white crappies are more plentiful in the southern part of the country. Crappies, pronounced crop, have soft mouths, a characteristic that earned the fish the nickname of papermouth. Among the crappies other common names are calico bass and specks.

Crappies are similar to the true sunfish in the types of water the fish inhabit, in their spawning behaviors, and in their food preferences. Crappies differ from the true sunfish in that they spawn at slightly lower temperatures, they handle lower-oxygenated water better, they are roamers in their habitat, they suspend varying distances from bottom, and they have larger mouths so they have a stronger tendency to feed on small fish.

Black Crappie

The black crappie, *Pomoxis nigromaculatus*, can be found in waters in the eastern two-thirds of the United States, along the West Coast, and in southern Canada. More abundant in the North, this fish has a silver- to shiny-green body with erratic dark green or black blotches. The crappie's thin body gives the fish something of a pancake appearance. Black crappies favor the quiet, clear, cool water characteristic of many northern lakes where the fish hang out around vegetation and wood cover. Black crappies have a strong tendency to travel in schools.

Black Crappie.

On most waters, black crappie populations are extremely cyclical. In other words, some years the success of the spawn is phenomenal, and other years the spawn is very poor. Highly successful spawns result in a strong year-class of fish, and when those fish reach maturity, the crappie fishing remains good for several years. A poor year-class of crappies means below-average fishing until a strong year-class surfaces again. On many waters, black crappies and walleyes seem to have opposing cycles, and this makes sense as high numbers of crappies mean more predation on walleye fry, and high numbers of walleyes mean more predation on crappie fry and young.

White Crappies

White crappies, *Pomoxis annularis*, can be found in the eastern two-thirds of the United States, some western states, and southern Canada. More abundant in the South, the white crappie is lighter in coloration than the black crappie. The white crappie has silvery- to olive-colored sides and a darker dorsal area. Other features include the eight or so vertical bars along its length, and the bars are formed by dark-green markings. Also, the white crappie has six spines in the dorsal fin, whereas the black crappie has seven or eight spines.

White crappies favor warmer water and murkier water than black crappies, so the whites do well in silted rivers and lakes. White crappies thrive in southern reservoirs, especially in the newer, highly fertile impoundments. Like the black crappie, the white suspends above bottom near the cover afforded by brushy shorelines, downed trees, flooded timber, and mid-lake structures.

The success of white crappie spawning varies from year to year. When there is a good spawn and food is plentiful, a strong year-class of whites results in several years of excellent fishing. White crappies have a strong tendency to hang near cover, but the white crappie has less of a schooling tendency than the black crappie.

Locating Crappies

In the spring, look for crappies in bays, along shorelines, and in tributaries. The best spots have vegetation and woody cover, and firm bottoms of gravel or sand attract more fish than soft, muddy bottoms. In the summer, look for crappies in these same areas, but focus your efforts on deeper water in the 10- to 20-foot range. Favorite summer hangouts include weed lines, shoreline breaks, and submerged structures, particularly where there is a combination of weeds and rocks. Areas of flooded timber are also good bets because the standing trees allow crappies to find shade throughout the day.

In early fall, crappies move to shallow vegetation where they feed aggressively. Good spots during fall include weed lines, submerged vegetation, rock piles, mid-lake humps, and tributaries. By late fall, crappies move to deeper water adjacent to their favorite structures where they spend the winter months.

Crappies, by nature, are a roaming and sometimes suspending species, but they don't roam aimlessly. Instead, crappies move from cover to cover and structure to structure, where they seek both food and safety.

Best Fishing Times

Crappies are catchable year-round, but spring offers the best fishing of the year. Action begins when water temperatures approach 50°F, and crappies move shallow to feed. Spring means good concentrations of crappies in tributaries and near-shore areas where the crappies remain through the spawn, which typically occurs in the range of 62°F to 65°F. For best results, anglers focus on brushy shorelines, manmade brush piles, fallen trees, docks, and other woody cover. Crappie fishing remains good after the spawn when fish move to weed lines and other structural edges adjacent to spawning sites. Night fishing for crappies can be productive during the summer months when anglers focus on lighted areas such as marinas and bridges.

Crappies are less active during the day than their true sunfish cousins because crappies are low-light feeders. The best fishing hours of the day occur in the early morning and again in the evening when crappies move en masse to feed in the shallows. As you would expect, overcast days offer better fishing than do sunny days. When fishing during bright conditions, look for crappies in shaded areas, in deeper water, and tighter to cover. Check out those same areas during cold-front conditions.

Fishing Techniques

Catching crappies is relatively easy. The angler's challenge lies in locating fish. Good areas are generally well known as the same spots produce quality fishing year after year, and such spots are easily identified by the concentration of boats or shore anglers. Still, veteran crappie anglers know the importance of staying on the move. Once a fish is caught, though, it's time to settle in and work the area since crappies are a schooling species. If the action slows, continue to move until you find another productive spot. It's always worth returning and refishing a spot that produced fish earlier in the day. Some anglers, where legal, use a multiple-rod trolling system to locate crappies. This method can be especially effective when the fish are suspended adjacent to structure.

Suspending a 2-inch minnow below a bobber is the time-honored technique for catching crappies. An equally effective technique is suspending a small hair, marabou, or plastic jig below a bobber. Tipping the jig with a live grub usually translates to higher catch rates. Whether using a minnow or jig, work the offering with a retrieve of short twitches. When fishing deeper water, use a slip bobber or use no float at all to get the minnow or jig to the desired depth. Because crappies have a large mouth and feed on minnows, small spinner-type lures work well, too.

Here are some tips for catching crappies:

➤ Crappies have a delicate mouth so set the hook and play the fish gently.

➤ Use light line and tackle for a scrappier fight.

➤ Use a slow presentation in spring when water temperatures are cold.

➤ Use a quiet approach so as not to alert the fish of your presence.

➤ Where legal, consider placing some crappie-attracting, manmade brush piles.

➤ Use specially designed extra-long poles for placing bait or jig in a precise spot.

➤ Fish the north side of a lake in early spring because waters there warm first.

➤ Work your bait or jig deeper and closer to cover during bright conditions and cold fronts.

➤ Work your offering at various depths to 20 feet or so to find suspended fish in the summer.

➤ Look for crappies in areas of sparser vegetation than you would look for the true sunfish.

Black Bass

Most people don't think of bass as sunfish, but black bass are members of the sunfish family. The three most popular bass are the largemouth bass, smallmouth bass, and spotted bass, and they are likely called black bass because of their dark appearance as fry and their dark upper half as adults.

The black bass rank as North America's favorite game fish for various reasons. First of all, bass thrive in waters from coast to coast. In addition to their native waters in the eastern two-thirds of the United States, southern Canada, and northern Mexico, bass have been stocked in waters throughout the United States and southern Canada. Also, bass inhabit a wide range of waters from small ponds to massive reservoirs. Other factors contributing to the bass's popularity are its aggressive feeding nature, susceptibility to a variety of presentations, and great fighting ability.

Fishing Vocab

B.A.S.S. stands for the Bass Anglers Sportsmen Society. This organization has served as the authority on bass fishing for more than forty years. The organization advances the sport through advocacy, outreach, and an expansive tournament structure, and connects directly with the passionate community of bass anglers through its Bassmaster media vehicles.

More so than other sunfish, bass are pursued for sport rather than for food. Much of the sport fishing interest in bass likely stems from Ray Scott's founding of the B.A.S.S. in 1968. B.A.S.S. has also played a key role in the popularity of catch-and-release fishing among the bass-angling fraternity.

Largemouth Bass

The largemouth bass, *Micropterus salmoides*, is so named because the fish has a large mouth with the upper jaw extending beyond the eye. Popular nicknames include bigmouth and bucket-mouth. Largemouth bass have a brownish to greenish body with a dark horizontal band extending along their length from head to tail. This species can be found in nearly every state and in a variety of waters from farm ponds to large water systems. Largemouth bass favor quiet, weedy areas where the fish inhabit water depths from a few feet to 20 feet, and these fish do especially well in fertile waters. Though largemouth bass can tolerate water temperatures in the 80s, they are more active in 65°F to 75°F water.

Fishing Vocab

Crayfish, sometimes called crawdads or crawfish, are a freshwater cousin and smaller version of the lobster, and crayfish are a common prey of many game fish, particularly members of the black bass family.

Common prey includes crayfish, minnows, and small fish, especially juvenile sunfish. In clear water, largemouth bass feed by sight, but when waters are murky, the fish rely on their lateral line to detect prey. More so than other sunfish species, largemouth bass are loners rather than schooling fish. Still, a number of largemouth bass may appear in the same area if that area offers both food and cover.

Locating Largemouth Bass

Largemouth bass are a shallow-water fish, inhabiting depths from only a few feet out to 20 feet or so. These fish are drawn to cover and objects in quiet water particularly where aquatic vegetation abounds. Favorite holding areas include weed beds, weed lines, weedy shoals, lily pads, islands, points, drop-offs, brush, downed trees, logs, stumps, standing timber, creek beds, boulders, docks, bridge pilings, and various manmade structures in impoundments.

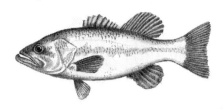

In the spring, look for largemouth bass in the shallows along mainland and island shorelines where the fish feed and spawn. During the summer, some bass will remain near shoreline cover, but others will move to deeper structures such as weed lines and weedy shoals. In early fall, largemouth bass again move to the shallows where the fish feed heavily.

During late fall and through the winter, largemouth bass move to deeper structures, breaks, and weed lines where feeding tapers off. Cold-front conditions cause bass to move deeper and hold tighter to cover. Strong, gusting winds also drive the fish deeper.

Best Fishing Times

Like other members of the sunfish family, largemouth bass move to warming shallow areas in the spring in search of prey and in preparation for the spawn. Because bass are vulnerable to angling pressure at this time of the year, some waters have closed seasons while other waters have catch-and-release-only regulations. On waters with open seasons, anglers can expect first-rate fishing, and sight fishing for spawning bass is particularly popular.

In the summertime, food is abundant so feeding windows are often brief. Still, the best fishing times are early in the morning and again in the evening when largemouth bass take advantage of low-light conditions to move shallow to feed. Night fishing can also be productive in the summer. For best results, try using a surface lure with a steady retrieve. With the lower angle of the sun in early fall, largemouth bass frequent the shallows (10 feet and less) to feed, so autumn promises good action.

From spring through fall, stable weather patterns find largemouth bass in predictable feeding patterns. In clear waters, expect bass to feed primarily in the morning and evening. In turbid waters, bass often bite throughout the day. Also, moderate winds tend to create lower-light conditions and to stir up organisms and algae. This makes baitfish and small fish active, which, in turn, brings the largemouth bass into the shallows to feed. Anglers can expect good fishing prior to a cold front, but once the front arrives, the action slows noticeably for a few days.

Fishing Techniques

Casting lures is the primary technique used by anglers pursuing largemouth bass. Part of the appeal of fishing for largemouth bass stems from the fish's willingness to hit a variety of lures fished anywhere in the water column from the surface to the bottom. Surface lures may be the most exciting ones to use because the angler sees the strikes as a bass explodes through the water's surface when the fish attacks the lure. Popular surface lures include chuggers, crawlers, poppers, and buzz baits, and they are most effective when fished under calm conditions in the morning, in the evening, and on overcast days. Plastic frogs and mice worked across the tops of weed beds are standard largemouth bass catchers, too. Bass bugs fished on the surface are the favorite lure for fly-fishermen seeking largemouth bass.

Spinner baits are also a go-to lure throughout the season. The lure can be retrieved near the surface or allowed to sink to a desired depth prior to beginning the retrieve. Cold water and turbid water call for a slow retrieve; warm water and clear water call for a faster retrieve. Plugs, too, work throughout the season. Select a small-lipped minnow plug for fishing over submerged vegetation or in shallow water, and select a large-lipped crankbait for fishing deeper water and structures. Vibrating crankbaits, also called lipless crankbaits or rattle baits, work well at a variety of depths because the lure can be retrieved just below the surface or allowed to sink to bottom prior to retrieving. Vibrating crankbaits work well over submerged weeds and in murky water where fish hone in on the vibrations emitted by the lure's action.

Bad Cast

Lipping (grabbing a fish by its jaw) is the standard method for landing largemouth bass. This technique works great when using single-hook lures. When using lures with multiple sets of treble hooks, though, an angler should consider using other and safer techniques for landing their catch.

Soft plastics come in an amazing array of sizes, colors, and shapes with the most popular styles for largemouth bass being worms, crayfish, and lizards. The final word regarding lures, though, emphatically ranks the plastic worm as the number-one choice among largemouth bass anglers. This versatile lure can be fished on a Carolina rig for deep water and in current; it can be fished in the weedless, Texas style for working in vegetation; and it can be fished wacky style around shallow cover. For best results when using plastic worms, work them along or near the bottom. Also, don't expect to feel a solid strike as largemouth bass tend to inhale worms. To detect a bite, you have to develop a good feel so that you sense the "tick" indicating the worm has been inhaled. Other means of detecting bites are to feel the resistance of the fish when you begin to move the worm and to watch for the line to stop moving or for the line to begin moving off to the side.

Jigs, too, are popular lures that can be fished at a variety of depths and speeds with various angler-imparted actions. Standard bass jigs have a lead head and a rubber skirt for the body. These and plain jigs can be tipped with pork trailers, plastic grubs, and plastic crayfish. Some jigs have weed guards to allow for fishing the lures in and around vegetation. Tube jigs are also productive bass offerings.

Live baits such as minnows and crayfish work well for largemouth bass. In the South, suspending oversize shiners below a bobber or balloon is a favorite technique when looking for big bass. Because bass are prone to swallowing live baits, anglers are encouraged to use a quick hook-set when they plan on releasing their catch.

Smallmouth Bass

Smallmouth bass, *Micropterus dolomieu*, have brownish or bronze sides with a series of dark vertical bars, a coloration that has earned this fish the nickname of bronzeback. Smallmouth bass are easily distinguished from their largemouth cousin because the upper jaw extends to the middle of the eye rather than beyond the eye. As you would expect, the smallmouth bass has a smaller mouth, too.

Found in much of the eastern half of the United States and into Canada as well as in some states in the western half of the country, smallmouth bass inhabit streams, rivers, lakes, and reservoirs. This bass likes clear, cool, moving water with hard bottoms of gravel or rock, so streams and rivers with summer temperatures in the 55°F to 75°F range offer the most ideal habitat. Smallmouth bass favor deeper structures than do largemouth bass.

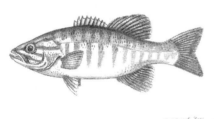

Smallmouth bass don't grow as big as largemouth bass. Whereas 10 pounds is considered a big largemouth bass, a 5-pound smallmouth bass is a big one. Still, smallmouths are often more prized because of the fish's fighting and leaping ability. Many anglers claim that pound for pound the smallmouth bass is the best-fighting game fish of all. Another attractive feature of the smallmouth is its schooling tendency. If you can catch one fish, the odds are that more fish are in the same area. A cool-water species, the smallmouth bass preys on crayfish, minnows, and small fish such as yellow perch and sunfish. Like the largemouth, smallmouths rely on sight for feeding in clear waters and lateral line for feeding in turbid water.

Locating Smallmouth Bass

Smallmouth bass are a structure-oriented fish, so look for them in the 5- 25-foot depths near rocky points, rocky shorelines, rip-rap, break walls, island and mainland drop-offs, shoals, and hard-bottom flats. In rivers and streams, smallmouths seek out current breaks caused by rocks and boulders. Seams and eddies are prime holding areas, too.

In early spring, smallmouths congregate in quiet water near spawning sites. Look for breaklines and out-of-the-current places. As temperatures approach the low 60s, smallmouths can be found in shallow, hard-bottom, gravelly locations where they spawn. Throughout the summer and into early fall, look for bass on structural edges and in current breaks out to depths of 20 feet or so. By late fall as water temperatures approach the 50°F mark, smallmouths migrate to deep, quiet water where they spend the winter in a relatively inactive state.

Best Fishing Times

Spring offers first-rate smallmouth action because the fish congregate in near-shore areas where they feed and spawn. Since males stay on the nest to protect eggs and fry from predators, males are especially easy to catch. Some waters have closed seasons or catch-and-release-only seasons during the spring to protect spawning fish. During the summer, the best fishing times are morning, evening, and overcast days, times when smallmouths move to shallow waters and onto structures to feed. The evening hours can be especially good for catching smallmouths.

Even though smallmouth can be caught throughout the summer, the fish seem to have longer feeding windows in the early season as the water warms from the 60s into the low 70s and again in early fall as temperatures cool from the 70s to the low 60s.

Fishing Techniques for Smallmouth Bass

Live bait ranks as the top fishing technique among smallmouth bass anglers. Minnows work well throughout the season while crayfish and worms produce best during the summer months. Bait is generally fished on a #2 or #4 hook at line's end with split shot placed a foot or so above or on rigs with a weight on the bottom and the bait a foot or two above the weight. Baits can be still-fished, cast out and worked slowly back, or drifted through an area. If you plan on releasing your catch, use a quick hook-set to prevent bass from swallowing the bait and hook.

Casting lures is another popular and effective technique for catching smallmouth bass. When targeting smallmouth instead of largemouth bass, anglers tend to use smaller lures. Popular lures include in-line spinners, diving plugs, and jigs. In-line spinners work well in shallow water where the flash and vibration simulate a fleeing baitfish. Diving plugs work well along structural edges and over deep shoals. Working the plug so that it emits an injured-minnow appearance produces the best results. Crayfish-imitating plugs fished along rocky-bottom areas are a favorite summer lure. The jig ranks as the most effective artificial lure for catching smallmouths. Bass jigs, tube jigs, and plastic-tipped lead-head jigs have the versatility to be fished at different speeds, in varying water depths, in a wide range of current flows, and with different actions.

Real Fishing

Taking a float trip down a small river is an excellent way to catch smallmouth bass. My fishing partner Bob Flavin and I often made such trips in a 14-foot canoe. Ironically, we spent more time out of the canoe because we would wade in the shallow, rocky, moving-water sections where we cast spinners. These areas produced the majority of our catches, so don't be afraid to get out and do some wading on your next float trip.

Surface lures and plastic worms are less popular among smallmouth anglers than largemouth bass anglers. Still, both lures will take smallmouth. Use surface lures in the spring and early fall and on summer evenings, times when smallmouth bass inhabit shallow water. When fishing plastic worms, use small ones for the best results. Since smallmouth bass inhabit shallow streams, the fish are a favorite of fly-fishers who cast bass bugs, streamers, and wet flies.

Spotted Bass

Spotted bass, *Micropterus punctulatus*, are primarily found in waters from Ohio down to the states along the Gulf Coast from Texas to western Florida, but the species has been stocked in other states. More of a regional bass than the smallmouth and largemouth, the spotted bass is also called the Kentucky bass or the Kentucky spotted bass. The spotted bass has light green to brownish sides with a lateral band comprised of dark blotches. The fish's lower half has horizontal rows of small, dark spots, which earned the bass its name. Though the spotted bass looks like its largemouth cousin, the lower jaw of the spotted bass does not extend beyond the eye. The spotted bass differs in appearance from the smallmouth because the spotted lacks vertical bars. Smaller than both smallmouth and largemouth, spotted bass average less than 1 pound in their northern range and maybe 1.5 pounds in the southern range.

Spotted bass inhabit the pools and runs of clear streams and small rivers with sluggish flows. The fish also thrive in reservoir systems where they hold near deeper structure than their smallmouth and largemouth cousins. Look for spotted bass in rocky areas where the fish feed on crayfish, minnows, small fish, and other prey. To aid in the eating of crayfish and other crustaceans, the spotted bass has a teeth-like patch on its tongue.

In the spring, spotted bass migrate upstream to spawn in shallow water with a gravel bottom. During the summer, these fish relate to areas of mild current in streams and rivers and to structures in reservoirs. To catch spotted bass, use smallmouth techniques. Whereas you might work the 10- to 20-foot depths for impoundment smallmouths, try the 20- to 30-foot depths for spotted bass.

CHAPTER 19

The Catfish Family

In this chapter you'll learn about the members of the catfish family, the largest family of freshwater fish. From an angling perspective, the most popular species in the family are the black, brown, and yellow bullheads, and the channel, flathead, white, and blue catfish. Despite their somewhat ugly appearance, these species rank behind only bass and panfish on the list of most popular species for U.S. anglers. The easiest way to distinguish a bullhead from a catfish is by the tail. Bullheads have square or rounded tails; catfish, other than the flathead, have a forked tail.

Catfish have very poor eyesight, but they have four pairs of barbels, or whiskers, that allow the fish to find

Bad Cast

The sharp spines on the fins of a catfish contain toxin, and an angler handling enough catfish will get stung. Now the catfish doesn't really sting a person, but in the handling process, anglers bring the sting upon themselves. Generally, the stung area will turn red and be sore for a few days. Treatment of the sting calls for the application of a disinfectant and then monitoring the area for infection.

food through the senses of touch and taste. Furthermore, the sense of smell and the lateral line help catfish find food in low-light and turbid-water conditions. Once these fish capture prey, the sandpaper-like teeth that angle inward prevent that prey from escaping. Other characteristics of the catfish family include a smooth skin with no scales and sharp spines on the dorsal and pectoral fins.

Members of the catfish family once had a range east of the Rockies from southern Canada into Mexico, but stocking has introduced the species into the western states. Wherever catfish are found, they have a seasonal popularity, but these fish are most popular among anglers in the South and Midwest. People love catfish because they are omnivores that readily bite on a variety of offerings. Also, catfish have an excellent sporting quality in that they rank among the biggest freshwater game fish in North America. In addition to their fighting ability, catfish are even more prized for their eating value.

In late spring and early summer, members of the catfish family build nests where eggs are laid and fertilized during the spawn. For all species, the male remains to guard the eggs and fry from predators, but in some cases the female, too, provides protection.

Bullheads

The most popular bullheads are the black, brown, and yellow, and their square or rounded tails help anglers distinguish these fish from their catfish cousins that have forked tails. Bullheads need very little oxygen, so they survive in poorer water conditions than other freshwater fish. In waters lacking large predators, bullheads often overpopulate and become stunted.

Real Fishing

On those spring evenings when the bullheads are biting, I'll usually limit my catch to two dozen or so fish. Because I am a morning person, I don't like to clean fish upon returning home in late evening. Fortunately, bullheads are a hardy fish and, unlike most fish species, will survive until the next day. To ensure their liveliness, I split the catch into several buckets, fill the buckets with water, and put them in a dark corner of the garage.

Because bullheads are easy to catch, they make a great fish for kids. Other positive aspects of bullheads are their abundance, near-shore presence, scrappiness, and eating quality. Fishing for bullheads requires only basic gear and simple techniques. All you need is your fishing rod, a container of worms, hooks, and sinkers.

From a habitat perspective, bullheads do well in ponds, small lakes, and slow-moving streams and rivers. These fish favor shallow, quiet, murky areas with soft, weedy bottoms. While some anglers bait their hooks with items such as stink baits, liver, chicken innards, and cheese, worms are really the best bait. The key is to present the bait on or near bottom where bullheads forage for food. Where legal, anglers use multiple rods and multiple-baited hooks. Although bullheads will hit live minnows and slow-moving lures, these are not standard offerings.

Bullheads will bite throughout the day, especially in murky waters, but the best action usually occurs in the evening because bullheads are nocturnal feeders. Under low-light conditions, bullheads cruise the shallows looking for worms, eggs, insect larvae, small fish, plant material, etc. Bullheads will also bite throughout spring, summer, and fall, but the fastest fishing of the year takes place in late spring as water temperatures gradually increase through the upper 50s and into the 60s. Spring-caught fish are the most prized for eating because of the firm flesh. Once waters warm, bullhead flesh may become mushy and lose its textural appeal.

Real Fishing

Preparing bullheads for the table amounts to skinning the fish and removing the fins and intestines. For bullheads weighing over a pound, though, I prefer filleting. Because of the bullhead's thick rib cage, I don't use the standard technique of cutting through the rib cage as you would with panfish. Instead, I remove the skin, and then work the knife around rather than through the rib cage. The fillets seem to cook up better than thick-bodied whole fish.

Black Bullheads

Black bullheads, *Ictalurus melas*, have a dark back, green to gold sides, dark barbels, a rounded anal fin, and a rounded tail with a small notch. These bullheads are found in most states, southern Canada, and northern Mexico, but they lack a significant presence in the coastal states. Nicknamed the horned pout in some areas, black bullheads are most active when water temperatures range from 75°F to 85°F, and the species has a high tolerance for waters of

Black Bullhead

poor quality. After the spawn, both males and females guard the nest and fry. Most black bullheads weigh less than 1 pound, but 2-pound fish are a possibility.

Brown Bullheads

Brown bullheads, *Ictalurus nebulosus*, have a brownish back, blotchy sides of yellow to brown, a square tail, dark barbels, and a rounded anal fin. Sometimes called horned pout, the brown bullhead has a range covering most of the eastern half of the United States and most states along the West Coast. Much of the brown's range overlaps with the black bullhead so hybridization does occur. Brown bullheads thrive in traditional bullhead waters as well as in larger lakes and streams where weeds are present. The species prefers slightly cooler water temperatures than the black bullhead, but brown bullheads can survive in waters over 90°F. One or both parents may protect the eggs and fry. Smaller than the black bullhead, the average brown bullhead weighs ½-pound or so.

Yellow Bullhead

Yellow bullheads, *Ictalurus natalis*, have yellow to yellowish-brown sides and thus the name yellow bullhead. Other features include a rounded tail, straight edge on the anal fin, and pale-colored barbels. These light-colored barbels along with the fish's yellowish sides make for easy identification. Sometimes called the yellow cat, the yellow bullhead is found in most of the eastern half of the United States and in the Southwest. These bullheads prefer clearer water and slightly cooler temperatures than other bullheads, but the yellow bullheads may be even more tolerant of pollution and poor oxygen levels than their cousins. For the most part, just the male protects eggs and fry after the spawn. Like the brown bullhead, the yellow bullhead averages ½ pound or so.

Fishing Vocab

As the name suggests, a fish farm is a place that produces fish, and catfish are the most commonly raised species. The majority of farm-raised catfish find their way to supermarkets, restaurants, and pay-to-fish places.

Catfish

The most popular catfish are the channel, flathead, white, and blue, and these species are most easily distinguished from their bullhead cousins because of the catfish's forked tail and generally larger size. Catfish populations like waters with slow-moving current, so these fish do well in larger rivers, lakes with large tributaries, and impoundments. Quite mobile in their search for food and comfortable water temperatures, catfish tend to settle in woody cover such as logs and fallen trees. Favorite hangouts, the best of which offer woody debris, include drop-offs, deep river bends, deep holes, tributary mouths, and the slack-water areas in tail waters below dams. When water levels recede, look for catfish in deep holes, and when water levels rise, check out backwaters and tributaries.

Catfish have a varied diet that consists of insect larvae, crustaceans, minnows, small fish, plant life, eggs, and more. Because of their varied diet, catfish bite on a wide variety of natural, homemade, and commercial baits. Scent is a key attractant in any catfish bait, and catfish anglers practice patience as they allow the scent of their baits to disperse. Of course, if action doesn't occur within a reasonable period, it's time to move to another catfish hole. Whether an angler uses a slip sinker or a bobber, it's important to get the bait to bottom. Also, be sure to rebait your hook regularly.

If water temperatures are favorable, catfish are catchable year round. The best action occurs during the late spring and summer months and when water temperatures reach 60°F and beyond. The slowest fishing occurs in winter and when water temperatures drop into the 50s and lower. Catfish feed during low-light periods so evenings, overcast days, windy days, shaded areas, and turbid water conditions make for good fishing.

Because catfish love woody cover, anglers use fairly heavy gear to help pull hooked fish away from obstructions. Another reason for using stout gear is the chance of hooking a big catfish, and catfish do get big. In fact, what catfish lack in regard to beauty of appearance, they make up for in the beauty of their size. On a final note, if you are after bigger catfish, use natural baits rather than prepared ones.

Channel Catfish

The channel catfish, *Ictalurus punctatus*, ranks among the best-eating freshwater fish, so it is the catfish of choice for many anglers as well as for many involved in fish farming. This species has sides that vary in color from blue gray or green gray to silver, and the channel catfish is most readily identified because its forked tail has dark spots. In fact, the fish is often called a spotted cat. The channel catfish has a range covering most of the United States into southern Canada, but the species lacks a significant presence in some costal states.

Although channel catfish are found in lakes, the species favors large rivers that have clean, firm bottoms of sand, gravel, and rock. Favorite hangouts include areas below dams and locations out of heavy current flow. Channel catfish are very much a schooling fish. They spawn in small

channel catfish

streams and tributaries once water temperatures reach the mid-70s, and the male protects the nest and fry.

Willing biters, channel catfish will hit just about any offering, including minnows and even lures. Still, the standard catfish offerings of dead baits and prepared baits produce the most consistent results. Spring is the best season of the year for channel catfish, and evening is the best period of the day as catfish move shallow to feed as the sun sets. Medium-action bait-casting rigs are standard fare. Even though channel cats average just a few pounds, double-digit weights of 10 to 12 pounds are quite common.

Flathead Catfish

The flathead catfish, *Pylodictis olivaris*, ranks second behind the channel cat on the list of favorite catfish. Sometimes called the mud cat, these fish have brownish or yellowish sides with dark mottles. The two most distinguishing features of the flathead catfish are its square tail and its distinct flathead. This flat head earned the fish its name and gives the fish an even uglier appearance than its cousins. Flathead catfish have a range covering the central United States and extending into Mexico.

This species does live in reservoirs and lakes, but large rivers with hard bottoms and submerged wood offer the best habitat. Along such rivers, the favorite hangouts are deep pools, sluggish runs, and areas below wing dams, power dams, and other manmade structures. Flathead catfish are less prone than their cousins to eat homemade or commercial baits, so serious anglers use live bait such as suckers and panfish (if legal), although flatheads will bite on fish pieces and crawlers.

Flathead catfish have a reputation of being night biters and great fighters. Much of the fighting reputation stems from the fish's large size. Although flatheads average less than 5 pounds, fish can reach weights of 100 pounds.

Real Fishing

The International Game Fish Association was formed in 1939 for the purpose of maintaining records on various game fish. The organization currently recognizes the following world records for catfish: channel catfish (58 pounds from Santee-Cooper Reservoir in South Carolina), flathead catfish (123 pounds from Elk City Reservoir in Kansas), white catfish (19 pounds, 5 ounces from Oakdale, California), and blue catfish (124 pounds from Mississippi River in Illinois).

White Catfish

The white catfish, *Ictalurus catus*, has blue-gray to blue-black sides, a forked tail, and white barbels, the fish's most distinguishing feature. Whites have a natural range of the Chesapeake Bay region and states along the East Coast, but fish have been introduced elsewhere. Whites can survive in very sluggish flows, backwaters, reservoirs, and ponds. The white catfish's limited range likely accounts for its lack of widespread popularity because the species does offer quality fishing opportunities, not so much for size of fish but for the ease of catching.

The white catfish makes an excellent catfish for kids because it readily hits a variety of baits and bites during the day. Since whites also make excellent table fare, they are a common stocking in pay-to-fish places. Compared to their catfish cousins, the whites are small with the average catch being less than 1 pound, and 3 pounds is a big white.

Blue Catfish

The blue catfish, *Ictalurus furcatus*, is the largest in the catfish family, a characteristic that along with the fish's fighting ability makes it a more prized game fish than other catfish. Gray-blue to silvery-blue sides earned this catfish its name, and a deeply forked tail earned the fish its nickname of forktail cat. Unlike the channel cat, the blue catfish has unspotted sides. The fastest growing of all catfish, blues have a range pretty much limited to the southeastern United States where the fish prefer clear, swift streams with a bottom of sand, gravel, boulders, and bedrock. Favorite hangouts include deep holes, rip rap shorelines, and the waters around wing dams, dams, and shoals.

Blue catfish form schools, and they may do some feeding during the day, but most feeding gets underway at dusk and continues into the night. Cut fish, live fish, and crawlers are good baits, but blues do not hesitate to take stink baits, too. The average catch of a blue catfish weighs several pounds, but fish in the teens are very common, and fish between 20 and 100 pounds are a possibility.

The Perch Family

In this chapter, you'll learn about the three most important members of the perch family. You'll learn the seasonal patterns of these fish, the best times to fish for them, and the most common techniques anglers use when fishing for each species

The perch family is a large one, second only to the catfish family in numbers of member species. Most members of the perch family, though, are darters and measure only a couple of inches. As far as freshwater anglers are concerned, the three important game fish belonging to the perch family are the yellow perch, walleye, and sauger. These three species are cool-water fish with longer bodies than species in the sunfish family, and they are schooling fish that do not protect eggs and fry after the spawn.

Yellow perch are the most widely distributed of the three species and walleyes are the biggest. The sauger is the walleye's little cousin, and all three game fish are highly valued for their eating quality.

Yellow Perch

Yellow perch, *Perca flavescens*, rank high on the freshwater angler's list because of the fish's abundance, wide distribution, ease of catching, year-round availability, and fine table fare.

Yellow perch are colorful fish sporting dark green tops, orange-colored pectoral fins, and yellow or gold sides with a series of green vertical bars. Perch do not have the sharp teeth characteristic of walleyes and sauger.

For the most part, yellow perch can be found across the northern half of the United States and southern Canada, although stockings have introduced perch elsewhere. A cool-water species, perch like clear rivers, lakes, and reservoirs with some vegetation and a firm bottom of sand, gravel, and rock. Still, perch do well in weedy, soft-bottom waters, too. The species spawns in tributaries and shallows when water temperatures creep into the 40s. Ideal spawning sites include scattered weeds and brush over a firm bottom. Gelatinous strings of eggs are deposited on the weeds and brush, but adults do not protect the eggs or fry.

Yellow perch travel in schools of generally the same size fish, and the schools roam in search of food such as fish eggs, insects, minnows, snails, crayfish, and small fish. Sport-caught perch average 7 to 8 inches and ½ pound, although some waters have stunted populations. Perch measuring 12 inches or more, sometimes called jack perch or jumbos, are especially prized by anglers.

Daily and Seasonal Habits

In the morning, yellow perch gather in schools for feeding purposes. In addition to morning feeding, perch also feed throughout the day and into evening. Unlike crappies, perch don't see well in low-light conditions, so the fish scatter to cover with the approach of sunset where they remain until the sun rises. When feeding or seeking cover, yellow perch tend to move shallower to weed lines, weed openings, moderately vegetated flats, and vegetated shoals.

Prior to spring spawning, yellow perch congregate in bays and at tributary mouths near spawning grounds. During the spawn, the fish move into the shallows at night and retreat to deeper water in the morning. Once spawning is completed, perch remain in the general area where their favorite hangouts include weed edges, drop-offs, and shoals in large bays as well as areas of quiet water in tributaries and at tributary mouths. Throughout spring, yellow perch feed actively.

Yellow Perch

Yellow perch remain in their spring locations into early summer when warm water temperatures drive this cool-water species to deeper water. Although some fish hold deeper, most perch occupy depths of 15 to 30 feet during the summer months. Favorite locations include mainland points, island points, shoals, deep-water flats, and drop-offs, all of which must have vegetation to attract perch. Other prime summer haunts include weed lines and openings in weed beds.

As water temperatures begin to cool in early fall, perch move to shoreline structures such as drop-offs and weed lines, to large bays with breaklines, mid-depth flats, and holes, and to tributary mouths with quiet water areas. Perch roam these locations in search of baitfish and small fish that abandon the shallows as water temperatures drop and vegetation begins to die off. Perch remain in these areas into late fall and through winter, although midwinter sees large perch move to adjacent deep water prior to their return to spawning locations.

Fishing Techniques and Best Fishing Times

Yellow perch are easy to catch because they are not finicky eaters and their roaming and schooling tendencies force them to compete for food. Once you locate a school of perch, you can expect good action until the school moves off. To locate yellow perch, shore anglers must move from spot to spot, and boat anglers have the luxury of drifting through an area until fish are found.

Anglers pretty much use two basic techniques when targeting yellow perch. Number one is the use of live baits such as small minnows and crawler pieces. Whether the bait is suspended below a bobber or bottom-fished with a weight, the key is to get the offering a foot or two above bottom since yellow perch are a near-bottom-dwelling species. Also, be sure to use small hooks (#8 or #6) and baits because perch have fairly small mouths.

The second technique is casting small jigs tipped with tiny minnows, crawler pieces, grubs, or plastics. For shallow-water fishing, the jig may be suspended below a bobber. Again, be sure to get the jig within a foot or two of bottom.

You can catch perch year-round, but spring offers the best fishing because yellow perch congregate in large numbers in near-shore areas where the fish feed aggressively for a three-month period. Spring is the time when perch are most available to shore and dock anglers. While summer-caught perch tend to run on the small side, spring and fall are the best times for jumbos. Because yellow perch don't see well in low light, they prefer to feed during bright conditions. This means perch may feed throughout the day, although the best fishing often occurs in mid-morning and early evening. (See discussion of ice fishing yellow perch in chapter 17.)

Walleyes

Walleyes, *Stizostedion vitreum*, are the largest member of the perch family, and the fish earned its name because of its large, glassy eyes. Other walleye features include light green sides with gold specks, a light-colored belly, forked tail, spiny dorsal fin, white tip on lower tail, and sharp teeth. Walleyes were originally found in the northern states and Canada, but stocking has resulted in the fish's presence throughout much of the United States and

Canada. The walleye is an especially popular game fish in southern Canada, the Great Lakes region, and the Midwest.

Sometimes called marble eyes, walleyes do well in large lakes with some turbidity, in rivers with a moderate current, and in reservoirs with a number of tributaries. The fish spawn in shallow water over gravel and rocks in tributaries, along shorelines, and on shoals. Spawning takes place where current or wave action facilitates egg development. Water conditions at the time of the spawn dictate the success of the spawn and the number of walleyes in a particular year-class. A highly successful spawn can result in several years of excellent fishing once those fish reach legal size.

Bad Cast

Walleyes are called walleyed pike in some areas and pickerel in other areas. These names are misnomers, though, as walleyes are members of the perch family and not the pike family.

Walleyes are more adaptable in their choice of prey than are most other species, and walleyes have a roaming nature that allows them to find various prey. Baitfish and small fish, especially yellow perch, are the species' primary food, though walleyes also feed on leeches, crayfish, snails, and aquatic insects. The average walleye weighs a couple of pounds; a 7-pounder is a really

nice fish, and one over 10 pounds approaches trophy status. The walleye is something of an event species since opening-day derbies, community festivals, professional derbies, amateur derbies, ice fishing derbies, and fish dinners center on this fish. (See discussion of ice fishing walleyes in chapter 15.)

Best Fishing Times

Because of the nature of the walleye's eyes, the fish sees well in changing-light and low-light conditions, times when their favorite prey, the yellow perch, does not see well. Throughout the year, walleye fishing is best in the low-light periods of early morning, evening, darkness, windy days, and days with cloud cover and in the changing light periods of sunrise and sunset. In clear water and when conditions are calm and bright, walleyes stop feeding earlier in the morning and begin feeding later in the evening. In low-clarity water, walleyes have longer feeding windows. When weather conditions are stable, feeding patterns remain the same from day to day. During cold fronts and strong thunderstorms, the fishing drops off as walleyes move deeper and may not feed for several days.

Spring is by far the best season for walleye action because large numbers of fish congregate near spawning sites, many of which are near shore and accessible to shore anglers. Good fishing spots include tributaries, gravelly shorelines, shoreline points, drop-offs, and flats. In rivers, look for walleyes to hold in slack water areas near spawning sites. Young males remain near spawning areas longer than mature fish.

Walleyes can be caught throughout the summer, but the schools of spring will have dispersed throughout a water system. Instead of finding schools of fish, anglers are more likely to encounter small groups of walleyes. When looking for summer walleyes, focus on two things: structure and food. Walleyes hold in deep water near rocky points, rocky shorelines, rocky bottoms, holes, tributary mouths, shoals, and current breaks. During low-light periods, walleyes move shallow to the adjacent structure to feed. If there is adequate prey in the area, walleyes remain in the vicinity. Otherwise, the fish roam to better feeding grounds.

Real Fishing

My home fishing water has a three-fish daily limit for walleyes, and the minimum length is 18 inches. In the fall, I like to take some walleyes and freeze them for eating during the winter months. When doing so, I self-impose a maximum limit of 24 inches because smaller fish are better eating, and I like to release larger fish so they have the opportunity to spawn in the spring.

As the water cools and the angle of the sun lowers in fall, walleyes again move shallow. The fish also congregate in schools so anglers who locate fish can have some of the best fishing of the year, especially for larger fish. Prime locations include drop-offs, weed lines, holes, slack water areas, and tributary mouths, where baitfish and small fish move as water temperatures cool. Good fishing typically holds up until water temperatures drop through the 40s, at which time the fish move to deep water. Even though their metabolism slows, walleyes feed throughout the winter on structural edges near deep water and in areas with concentrations of yellow perch.

Fishing Techniques

Popular walleye offerings include live bait, jigs, plugs, crawler harnesses, and blade baits; live bait ranks as the overall favorite. Effective live baits include crawlers, minnows, and leeches. Jigs are the top-producing artificial lure and the most versatile. Plugs work well because they imitate small fish, a primary prey of walleyes. Crawler harnesses offer a combination of flash and bait, and blade baits present both flash and vibration.

Live bait may be still fished in a location or drifted through an area. Some anglers use a weight on the bottom and a baited hook above; others use a baited hook at line's end with split shot above. Using slip sinkers is another option as is suspending the bait below a float. No matter what system you use, be sure to get the bait near bottom.

Anglers usually cast and retrieve jigs, but jigs can also be fished vertically when employing a controlled drift through an area. When drifters encounter a group of walleyes, it's time to set up near the fish and do some casting. The jig's versatility stems from its various styles, weights, colors, tipping options, and angler-imparted actions. Jigs with bucktail or plastic bodies take plenty of walleyes, but for the best results, try enhancing the jig with a crawler piece, small minnow, or leech.

Bad Cast

Because walleyes often hang around rocky structure, it's common to get bottom rigs, jigs, and crawler harnesses snagged. Instead of getting frustrated with such hang-ups, just accept them as part of fishing for walleyes. As your fishing skills improve, you will develop a better feel for what's happening at line's end, and you will encounter fewer snags.

Plugs may be cast or trolled. Casting is popular in spring and fall, and at night when walleyes patrol the shallows. Otherwise, anglers troll plugs. When trolling, the key is to get the plug near bottom, something that can be easily accomplished by the use of big-lipped crankbaits, in-line weights, downriggers, or diving planers.

Crawler harnesses may be trolled in the same fashion that plugs are. The rigs may also be drifted through an area when wind and current conditions are favorable. When presenting crawler harnesses, the keys include maintaining a proper speed for the blade(s) to turn, getting the rig near bottom, and hooking the crawler so it is fully extended.

Anglers fish blade baits similarly to jigs, except blade baits are used more often for vertical presentations rather than cast-and-retrieve ones. Also, anglers don't ordinarily tip blade baits with bait. Blade baits are most often used when fishing for deep-water walleyes.

Here are some walleye tips:

➤ A slow presentation seems to work better than a fast one.

➤ Using a stinger hook on jigs will likely double your catch.

➤ Use your electronics to locate fish; then set up in that area.

➤ Walleyes are light biters, so set the hook when you feel anything different at line's end.

➤ Light lines and fast-action rods are best for detecting bites.

➤ Most of the time, walleyes hit a jig as it falls rather than when it rises.

➤ For best results, troll into the wind or current rather than with it.

➤ Use natural colors in clear water, brighter colors in stained water, and dark colors at night.

➤ Use a quiet approach because too much boat activity can shut down a school of fish.

Saugers

Sauger, *Stizostedion canadense*, look very similar to walleye, but a sauger can be identified by the black spots on its dorsal fin and the lack of a white spot on the base of the tail and the anal fin. In some areas, the sauger is referred to as a sand pike, but the sauger is a member of the perch family, not the pike family. The sauger's range extends from southern Canada through the Great Lakes and the Mississippi, Missouri, Ohio, and Tennessee rivers.

Saugers do best in large rivers and lakes that have cool-water temperatures and firm bottoms of gravel and rock. Saugers and walleyes are similar also in that they live in the same waters and habitats. Still, the walleye is the more popular fish because of its size as an average-size walleye is bigger than a large sauger.

Saugers are pretty much identical to walleyes in seasonal behaviors, so the

Fishing Vocab

A saugeye is a hybrid created by the breeding between a sauger and a walleye.

strategies for locating and catching walleyes also work for taking saugers. Generally, though, saugers hold in a bit deeper water because their eyes are more sensitive to light. Also, on some waters saugers migrate in large numbers in late fall and early winter to the waters below large dams. In such cases, the sauger fishing is at its best of the year.

CHAPTER 21

# The Pike Family

> ## In This Chapter
>
> ➤ What species belong to the pike family
>
> ➤ What characteristics and behaviors pike display
>
> ➤ How to catch pike, muskellunge, and pickerel

In this chapter you'll learn about species in the pike family, including northern pike, muskellunge, chain pickerel, and redfin pickerel. Members of the pike family are usually the largest predators in their waters. Although pike meat has a good flavor, these fish are more prized for their sporting value because of their size, aggressive nature, and fighting ability. Pike are carnivores with needle-sharp teeth, large mouths, and long, slender bodies designed for attacking prey. Members of the pike family do not build nests, and the fish do not protect eggs and fry as do members of the sunfish and catfish families. Instead, pike scatter their eggs randomly and then abandon them.

Northern Pike

The northern pike, *Esox lucius*, is sometimes called the great northern pike, water-wolf, freshwater barracuda, snake, and hammer handle. The wolf and barracuda nicknames give testimony to the northern pike's ferocious nature, and the snake and hammer handle refers to the long, slender profiles of young pike.

Northern pike have dark-green to light-green sides with rows of light roundish spots. Pike are often described as having light markings on a dark background, which contrasts with muskellunge that have dark markings on a light background. Other distinguishing pike features include the five or fewer pores on the underside of the lower jaw and the scaling on the entire cheek and on the top half of the gill cover. The primary northern pike range extends across the northern half of the United States from the East Coast to Montana and throughout Canada and Alaska, but pike have been introduced into waters in the South and West.

Northern pike rank as the most popular member of the pike family. Extremely aggressive in nature, pike hit a variety of baits and lures, put up an impressive fight often consisting of leaps, thrashing, and long runs, and have a tasty flavor. Because pike have Y-bones that require a special filleting technique and because the fish grow to a large size, many anglers view the pike as a sport fish and practice catch-and-release rather than keep the fish for the table.

Bad Cast

Because northern pike and other members of the pike family have mouths full of ultrasharp teeth, anglers are advised to use caution when handling these fish, particularly when removing hooks. To keep fingers away from the sharp teeth, always use needle-nose pliers for hook removal, and if the bait or lure is inside the mouth, use mouth spreaders to facilitate unhooking..

A cool-water fish, the northern pike does well in a variety of habitats in streams, rivers, lakes, and reservoirs. The fish's favorite areas, though, are shallow, weedy bays that hold abundant prey and provide cover for pike that like to lash out at unsuspecting prey. Other ambush spots favored by northern pike are shoreline drop-offs, weed lines, shoal edges, tributary mouths, breaklines, and slack-water areas. Northern pike prefer water temperatures in the 60s so large pike often move to deep water in the summer even though smaller pike may remain in warm, weedy bays.

Northern Pike

Territorial in nature, northern pike are sight feeders that prey primarily on baitfish and other fish but have been known to eat frogs, mice, ducklings, and more. These fish average 3 to 4 pounds on most waters, but 10- to 20-pound pike are always a possibility.

Seasonal Patterns

Spawning takes place in early spring just after ice-out as water temperatures ease into the low 40s. Preferred spawning sites include tributaries, marshes, vegetated shorelines, and weedy bays, where pike scatter and fertilize eggs on thick vegetation. The eggs and fry are subject to predation because the parents provide no protection. Late spring offers some of the best fishing of the year because numbers of pike linger near spawning sites where the fish feed actively until water temperatures begin rising through the 60s.

Summer finds northern pike scattering throughout a water system where the fish become loners. While midsummer fishing is usually the slowest of the year, early summer and late summer action is pretty good on most waters. Good spots for summer pike are weed lines, weedy shoals, points, deep holes with mild current, necked-down areas, and any area where yellow perch or walleyes are present.

Bad Cast

Some anglers falsely believe that northern pike fishing is slow during the summer because the fish lose their teeth and have sensitive mouths. In reality, though, pike do not lose their teeth all at once, although some teeth may be lost and regenerated during a fish's lifetime. A more logical explanation for slow fishing in the summer is the fact that pike inhabit deep, cool waters then, which makes them harder to locate.

As water temperatures cool in the fall, northern pike move to shallower water in search of prey. Good fishing usually holds up until late fall when fish retreat to deep water and the action slows. Prime fishing spots include weed lines, areas of scattered weeds, points, tributary mouths, and wind-blown shorelines with drop-offs.

Unlike many species, northern pike feed actively throughout the winter. This means ice anglers can have good fishing for a period of four months or more. The keys to locating winter pike are the same as they are for other times of the year. Look for weed lines, areas of scattered weeds, structural edges in quiet water, and areas holding yellow perch or walleyes. As a general rule, winter pike will be shallow in early and late winter, and they will go deeper in midwinter.

Fishing for Northern Pike

Northern pike are daylight feeders, and the fish tend to be most active in the early morning, in the evening, and on overcast days. Early afternoon usually means slow fishing, and night fishing is even less productive. Fishing also slows once water temperatures reach the upper 60s, but pike often go on feeding sprees before the arrival of severe thunderstorms or cold fronts.

Because of their predatory nature, northern pike readily strike a variety of baits and lures. Live minnows, though, are the favorite offering of spring anglers who suspend the minnow below a float in shallow water and a favorite offering of ice anglers who suspend the minnow below a tip-up. Casting artificial lures is also popular in the spring as it is during summer and fall. Spoons, in-line spinners, spinner baits, jigs, surface lures, minnow plugs, crankbaits, and swim baits are effective lures for taking pike, and the key is to select a lure to match the fishing conditions. For example, a surface lure works well over weeds, and a jig works well for deep water. Lures such as spinners and spoons can be fished at various depths by allowing the offering to sink to a desired depth prior to beginning the retrieve.

Real Fishing

When handling northern pike, the standard practice is to grip the fish firmly in the area just behind the gills. The grip involves placing your palm on the fish's back with your thumb on one side and fingers on the other. Some anglers perform this grip on the gill plate, but excessive pressure may damage the gills. Instead of using the standard grip, I have good luck landing and handling pike by inserting my fingers under the gill plate and getting a firm grip on the gill plate to hoist the fish. When using this grip, be sure to keep your fingers out of the gills to avoid damaging them as well as your fingers, which can easily be cut by the gill rakers.

Trolling artificial lures, like casting them, is an effective pike technique throughout the open-water season. Spoons and crankbaits rank as the top two trolling lures. Either one will catch fish, but I prefer the plug because of its more natural appearance. Trolling keys amount to getting the lure to the desired depth and presenting it along a weed line or structural edge where pike lie in wait for passing prey.

Because of the northern pike's accessibility in shallow, weedy areas, this freshwater fish is a favorite of fly fisherman.

Here are some northern pike fishing tips:

➤ Use a slow presentation in cold water and a fast presentation during the summer.

➤ Pause your retrieve periodically because pike readily attack a stationary lure.

➤ Pike often hang in loose packs, so work the area whenever a fish is caught.

➤ A pike's eyes are designed for seeing prey overhead so keep your offering several feet off bottom.

➤ Use a leader to prevent bite offs.

➤ Monofilament leaders induce more strikes than steel leaders in clear water.

➤ Studies indicate most pike are caught in less than 16 feet of water.

➤ Fast-action rods work best for good hook-sets in the pike's toothy and strong mouth.

➤ Expect the pike to make a surge once it nears the boat.

Muskellunge

The muskellunge, *Esox masquinongy*, is considered by many to be the king of all freshwater fish, and catching a muskellunge is no everyday thing. In fact, the muskellunge has been called the fish of 10,000 casts and the fish of 100 hours, and pursuing this fish has been compared to big game hunting. Some people say the odds of catching a muskellunge are comparable to the odds of winning the lottery. While these descriptions are something of an exaggeration, they do make the point that catching a muskellunge is a challenge.

Real Fishing

I took my brother-in-law, Cody Richardson, to a river in Ontario, Canada, for his first-ever trip for muskellunge. I explained how to operate the reel and how much lead core line to let out to get the lure down 15 feet because we were trolling a weed line in 18 feet of water. Cody got his rig set, and I turned my attention to setting my rod when Cody said, "Mike, I got one." Believing he had caught the edge of the weed bed we were trolling, I said, "No you don't. It's just weeds." Cody responded, "No, I've got a fish." Indeed, he literally caught his first muskellunge, a 16-pound fish, within his first two minutes of fishing. He should have bought a lottery ticket that day.

Despite the poor odds of catching a muskellunge, the number of anglers pursuing this species continues to grow across North America. A certain mystique surrounds the muskellunge, and anglers who pursue this fish rank among the most dedicated and passionate of all anglers. At one time, muskellunge were subject to overharvesting, but modern fishers subscribe to a catch-and-release philosophy.

Fishing Vocab

Muskie Fever is not an affliction. Rather, it is an overpowering desire to pursue muskellunge. Some cases of muskie fever even last a lifetime, and if you develop muskie fever, you will know it because the muskellunge will excite you just as the approaching summer vacation excites students during the final days of the school year.

Also called muskie, lunge, and maskinonge, the muskellunge shares a strong resemblance to the northern pike. Identifying features of the muskellunge, though, are the six or more pores on the lower side of each jaw, the cheek and gill covers that have scales on the upper half only, and the sides with dark marks (spots or bars) on a light background.

Their primary range extends across southern Quebec and Ontario and across the northern United States from Vermont to the Midwestern states. Because of the fish's popularity, though, its range continues to grow with stockings elsewhere. Still, the muskellunge has a significantly smaller range than its northern pike cousin.

Muskellunge and northern pike like the same habitat, but when both species appear in the same water, one species does better than the other. If any water has a thriving muskellunge population, those fish will keep the pike numbers down. If any water has high pike numbers, muskellunge numbers will be low because pike spawn earlier than muskellunge, and pike fingerlings prey on muskellunge fry

Fishing Vocab

The tiger muskellunge is a sterile hybrid cross between a northern pike and muskellunge. Sometimes called norlunge, tiger muskellunge are often raised in hatcheries and introduced into waters that contain stunted populations of panfish due to a lack of large predators.

Muskellunge spawn in mid- to late spring when pairs of fish scatter and fertilize eggs on vegetation in shallow water. Because muskellunge are a top predator, nature does not allow for high numbers of fish. Thus, fertility rates are quite low, and the resulting fish density is quite low. Like northern pike, muskellunge are a cool-water species that does well in weedy lakes and slow-moving rivers with abundant vegetation. Also like their pike cousin, the muskellunge tends to hold around weed lines, submerged vegetation, weedy shoals, points, tributary mouths, necked-down areas, and current confluences.

Muskellunge have needle-sharp teeth and large mouths that facilitate their penchant for eating 8- to 18-inch fish such as suckers, yellow perch, bullheads, smallmouth bass, and walleyes. The largest member of the pike family, muskellunge average 10 to 20 pounds on most waters. Anglers consider a 40-inch fish a good one, a 50-inch fish a special accomplishment, and a 50-pound fish a real monster.

Real Fishing

Some muskellunge waters are essentially trophy waters that have minimum lengths of 50 inches or so. Ironically, when most anglers catch such a trophy, the fish is released and a photograph or replica mount serves as a memento of the catch. If your objective is to catch a monster muskellunge, your best bet is to fish one of these trophy waters. With a minimum length of 48 inches in some areas and 50 inches in others, my home water of the St. Lawrence River is trophy water for muskellunge.

Best Fishing Times

Fall is the favorite season of the year for muskellunge anglers because the fish do their heaviest feeding then. As water temperatures drop out of the 70s and through the 60s and then the 50s, muskies go on the prowl. Feeding windows are longer in the fall, and fish that held in deep water during the heat of summer move to shallower structural edges. On many waters, late fall sees the action slow in numbers of fish, but late fall often produces the largest muskellunge of the year.

Some waters have a closed muskellunge season in the spring to allow for spawning. On waters where the season is open, muskellunge roam the shallows and are catchable. Fishing remains decent through late spring and early summer until water temperatures warm and the muskellunge move to deeper water and feed less actively. Though not considered a prime fishing time, midsummer does yield its share of muskellunge because summer is a time when high numbers of anglers take to the water.

Anglers can increase their odds of catching a muskellunge by fishing in the early morning and in the evening. On clear waters, night fishing is a good bet, whereas low-clarity waters offer better action during daylight. Overcast, drizzly days with a light to moderate wind usually mean good fishing. On windy days, action is better in wind-blown areas than in wind-protected areas. Muskellunge fishing is also good in the period prior to significant weather changes such as thunderstorms and strong cold fronts. More so than other anglers, muskellunge fishermen pay attention to the feeding times predicted by tables based on the positions of the sun and moon.

Fishing Strategies

Casting, trolling, and drifting are the three techniques used for presenting baits and lures to muskellunge, and casting far surpasses the other two in popularity. Muskellunge anglers have a wide array of casting lures at their disposal, and those lures include bucktails, spinner baits, soft baits, jerkbaits, jigs, crankbaits, surface baits, and more. Which lure a person uses is a matter of personal preference since all types will catch fish. For the most part, casting is restricted to water depths in the 5- to 18-foot range, although jigs and swim baits work fine for deeper water. At the end of each cast, some anglers perform a figure eight with their lure; other anglers perform the maneuver only when they see a fish following the lure.

Trolling is not legal on all muskellunge waters, but where the technique is allowed some anglers opt to troll because it offers the advantages of covering a lot of water and of having the lure constantly in the water. Diving plugs are the favorite trolling lures. Some anglers speed troll in shallow water with short lines only 20 to 30 feet behind the boat, whereas anglers in large, open waters may use downriggers to present their lures. Flatlining a diving plug 100 or more feet behind the boat is the most common trolling method. Successful trolling involves getting the lure to a desired depth and presenting that lure as close to structural edges as possible.

Drifting through an area while presenting a live sucker or working oversize plastic baits such as tubes is gaining in popularity as a technique because the method catches fish. This method seems most effective in late fall when muskellunge move to deep water and a slow presentation entices strikes. Drifting works best on rivers where a mild current moves the sucker or tube along naturally. Drifting on lakes requires the right wind or some method of boat control such as paddles, oars, or electric motor.

Here are some muskellunge fishing tips:

> ➤ Put in your time on a good water, and you will catch fish.

> ➤ Look for large muskellunge to hold on deep structures.

> ➤ Speeding up a retrieve entices more strikes than slowing down the retrieve.

➤ Use an erratic retrieve to give a lure the appearance of an injured fish.

➤ Use a long rod for easier casting of large, heavy lures.

➤ Select lure colors that match natural forage.

➤ If a follow occurs, return to that location at a later time.

➤ When night fishing, use larger lures.

➤ When trolling, use different arm motions to give lures an erratic action.

➤ Keep hook points needle-sharp to ensure good hook-sets.

Chain Pickerel

The chain pickerel, *Esox niger*, has dark, chainlike, vermiculate markings on its sides, markings that earned the fish its name as well as the nickname of chainsides. Another feature that distinguishes the pickerel from its cousins is the complete scaling on the cheek and gill cover. The chain pickerel's range includes the states along the East Coast and along the Gulf Coast to east Texas, but populations are most abundant in the waters of Maine, Rhode Island, Massachusetts, Connecticut, New York, and New Jersey.

Chain pickerel are smaller than northern pike and muskellunge with the average size running just a couple of pounds. Still, this species is an aggressive feeder that strikes hard and puts up a good fight. The combination of small size, Y-bones in the flesh, and feisty nature make the chain pickerel more of a sport fish than an eating fish. For fishing fun, it's hard to beat catching pickerel on light tackle.

Chain Pickerel

Like pike and muskellunge, pickerel spawn in shallow bays and marshy areas where eggs are scattered and fertilized on vegetation. This species likes the clear, quiet water of ponds, bays, and other backwaters, where the fish seek cover and prey in and around vegetation. Weeds are critical for good pickerel habitat, although the fish hold around features such as stumps, fallen trees, and docks, where the pickerel lie in wait to ambush their prey. Chain pickerel feed primarily on minnows and small fish,. Frogs, crayfish, etc. are secondary foods.

Fishing for Pickerel

An easy-to-catch fish, chain pickerel offer year-round action because the fish feed actively as water temperatures rise through the 50s, 60s, and 70s, and then again as water temperatures drop through the 70s, 60s, and 50s. During the winter, chain pickerel are a popular quarry for ice anglers. Live minnows are the favorite offering during the winter, and minnows work well year-round if they can be kept from burying themselves in the weeds.

Casting lures is the primary technique for catching pickerel during the open-water season because these fish readily hit spoons, spinners, plastic worms, surface lures, minnow plugs, and vibrating crankbaits. Because pickerel favor the same habitat as largemouth bass, pickerel are a common incidental catch of bass anglers. Use any largemouth bass technique, and you are likely to have success catching chain pickerel, although pickerel anglers generally employ a faster retrieve than do largemouth bass anglers. For best results, work your lure along the weed line, in openings in the weeds, around woody cover, and over the top of vegetation.

The chain pickerel is truly a fun fish. To make the fishing even more fun, use light tackle, fish with a surface lure, or fly cast a streamer.

Redfin Pickerel

The redfin pickerel, *Esox americanus*, has light-colored sides of brown to green with dark, wavy vertical bars that distinguish the fish from its cousin with chainlike markings. Like the chain pickerel, though, the redfin has completely scaled cheeks and gill covers. Reddish-brown to reddish-orange lower fins account for the fish's name. Redfin pickerel are found in states along the East Coast and in many states in the eastern third of the United States, where the fish favor weedy ponds, weedy backwaters of lakes, and slow-moving, weedy streams.

The smallest member of the pike family, redfin pickerel seldom weigh more than a pound or exceed 10 inches in length. And even though their white flesh has a sweet flavor, the fish's small size and Y-bones prevent it from being common table fare. Still, the redfin pickerel's aggressive feeding nature and scrappiness once hooked make the species a fun fish for anglers casting tiny spinners, spoons, or plugs on ultralight tackle or for anglers casting flies on a fly rod.

CHAPTER 22

The Trout Family

In This Chapter

➤ What species belong to the trout family

➤ What characteristics the various species display

➤ How to catch trout, char, Pacific salmon, whitefish, and grayling

In this chapter, you'll learn about the members of the trout family. These fish are known as salmonids so some sources label the fish as members of the salmon family. Either way, salmonids are divided into three subfamilies, and the three subfamilies are generally further divided into five groups: trout, char, Pacific salmon, white fish, and American grayling. All salmonids have an adipose fin.

Trout

Names can get a little confusing when it comes to the trout grouping. For instance, the Atlantic salmon is really a trout, and some fish such as brook trout and lake trout are actually char. Anyway, here's a look at the seven most popular species in the Salmoninae subfamily of the Salmonidae trout family: the brown trout, rainbow trout, steelhead, cutthroat trout, golden trout, Atlantic salmon, and landlocked salmon.

Fishing Vocab

An adipose fin is a fatty-tissue fin located between the dorsal fin and the tail of some species.

Brown Trout

The brown trout, *Salmo trutta*, is so named because of its golden-brown coloring. Other identifying features include large black spots, a scattering of reddish spots, and a square tail. Introduced to North America from Germany, this fish is often called the German brown, and the species now exists throughout the western one-third and northern one-third of the United States as well as in East Coast states to the Carolinas. Anadromous brown trout live in the Atlantic Ocean and Great Lakes.

Fishing Vocab

A redd is a spawning bed made by trout and salmon.

Fishing Vocab

A tiger trout is a hybrid resulting from the breeding between brown trout and brook trout.

Real Fishing

Despite the challenges of wading, line tangles, and retying in the dark, night fishing on streams is a good way to catch wary brown trout, particularly large ones. Among the top-producing offerings is a surface fly that imitates a mouse.

Brown trout prefer slower-moving and warmer streams than do rainbow and brook trout. Even though these fish can tolerate water temperatures into the low 70s, browns prefer temperatures from 55°F to 65°F. Spawning occurs in the fall when water temperatures drop into the 40s, and females make several redds in the gravel bottoms of tributaries and mainstream riffles.

Brown trout are commonly recognized as the hardiest, wariest, smartest, and hardest to catch of all trout. This species is a somewhat finicky feeder that focuses on specific hatches and often feeds nocturnally. Favorite foods include aquatic insects, minnows, and terrestrials.

Trolling is the technique of choice for pursuing brown trout on the Great Lakes and other lakes, particularly in the spring when fish move to the warming shallows to feed. Favorite offerings include plugs and spoons that imitate natural forage. Spin-casting and fly-fishing are popular on streams. Spin fishers use live minnows, worms, insects, spoons, or spinners, and fly-fishers cast the traditional dries, nymphs, or streamers. The best stream fishing occurs during the fall when brown trout spawn, especially in those tributaries that see runs of anadromous fish. Prime fishing periods during the summer include dawn, dusk, and after dark.

Rainbow Trout

The rainbow trout, *Salmo gairdneri*, is known for its beautiful coloration consisting of silver sides, pink bands along its length, and black dots on its sides and tail. Rainbows are easy to raise in hatcheries so the species has a widespread presence, including inhabiting nearly every state, the western provinces of Canada into Alaska, and parts of Mexico. Because of its preference for clean, cool, oxygenated water, the rainbow trout thrives better in western waters than in eastern ones.

Rainbow trout like swifter water than do their brown trout and brook trout cousins. Preferring water temperatures around 60°F, this species does well in temperatures from 50°F to 70°F. Rainbow trout ascend tributaries for spawning in the late winter and spring, and females create redds in areas with a clean, gravel bottom. Spawning occurs around the 55°F mark.

Rainbow trout are easier to catch than browns, and once hooked, rainbows love to jump in an attempt to shake free, a behavior that endears them to anglers. This species feeds primarily on aquatic insects; other foods include small fish, salmon eggs, and crustaceans.

Bad Cast

Like other stream trout, rainbow trout are wary of predators such as people, other mammals, birds, and larger fish. To avoid putting fish in a negative mood, you should utilize quiet, stealth, and camouflage when stream fishing.

Stream rainbows provide real sport for anglers using light spinning tackle or lightweight fly rods. Spin fishers use baits such as small minnows, worms, eggs, or even small marshmallows; and lures such as flashy spoons and spinners. Because rainbow trout feed heavily on insects including those on the surface, both wet and dry flies are effective. Trolling is the standard technique when targeting rainbows in lakes, and the most popular lures are wobbling plugs and spoons. For the most part, lake rainbows are larger than stream rainbows, and the fish hold in the top 20 feet of the water column.

Steelhead

The steelhead, *Salmo gairdneri*, is a migratory rainbow trout. Some steelhead are anadromous and migrate into Pacific coastal streams; other steelhead are the Great Lakes type that migrate into lake tributaries. The Great Lakes steelhead was first introduced from the Pacific Coast in the late 1800s. Because steelhead commonly reach double-digit weights, the species is highly prized by anglers. Other praiseworthy traits include the fish's power, speed, and leaping ability.

Steelhead are chrome colored, and fish develop the stripe of a rainbow during the spawn. Spawning runs vary seasonally in different areas, and fish may enter a tributary several months prior to spawning and remain in the tributary for several months after spawning. It is generally believed that spawn-run steelhead strike more out of instinct or reflex than due to a feeding behavior. Unlike Pacific salmon, steelhead may live to spawn several times.

Slip trolling in a drift boat is perhaps the most effective way to catch steelhead. Slip trolling involves the use of oars to approach a promising pool stern first. The rower maneuvers the boat so that wobbling plugs are eased into the hole and allowed to work the area. The rower is essentially holding the boat in place and sliding the boat sideways and backwards while the plug does its work. Once a hole has been adequately worked, anglers move to the next hole and repeat the process.

Shore anglers and waders work pools, too. Spin fishers cast spoons and spinners or drift eggs and spawn imitations, and fly-fishers present egg and flesh patterns. No matter what offering an angler uses, it's critical to get the bait or lure near bottom. Obviously, the first anglers to reach a hole have the best odds of catching fish. Otherwise, early morning offers the best fishing opportunities. Even though steelhead are good eating, many anglers treat them as a sport fish and practice catch and release.

Cutthroat Trout

The cutthroat trout, *Salmo clarki*, has a patch of red or orange on its throat that earned the fish its name. Other identifying features include reddish orange on the gill cover, black spots on the sides and tail, and a patch of teeth at the base of the tongue. Sometimes called the native trout or cut, the cutthroat trout has a range covering the western one-third of the United States and the coastal provinces of Canada into Alaska. Cutthroats live in rivers and lakes, and there is an anadromous strain along the Pacific Coast.

Like brook trout, cutthroat trout are wilderness fish found in the cleanest, coolest headwaters and tributaries. Ideal temperatures range from the mid-50s to 60°F. Spawning gets underway when temperatures reach the upper 40s, and coastal cutthroats spawn from late winter into summer, and river and lake fish spawn in the spring. Females make redds in gravel, and the eggs and fry are left unprotected. Some cutthroat trout spawn only once, but others spawn several times.

Cutthroat trout are opportunistic feeders so they may be found anywhere in the water column. Popular prey includes freshwater shrimp, aquatic insects, terrestrials, minnows, crayfish, fish eggs, frogs, salamanders, and more. Cutthroat trout lack the wariness of other trout, so the fish are easily caught on baits, spinners, spoons, and flies. In most waters cutthroat trout weigh up to only a few pounds, but the fish are strong fighters and make for great sport on light tackle.

Fishing Vocab

A cutbow is a hybrid resulting from breeding between a cutthroat trout and a rainbow trout.

Golden Trout

The golden trout, *Salmo aguabonita*, has gold sides, a crimson band along its length, a spotted tail, and white tips on its dorsal, pelvic, and anal fins. Considered by some anglers to be the most beautiful of all trout, the golden trout is primarily found in mountainous lakes and streams of the West. Reaching such waters often requires hiking. Golden trout spawn in early summer to midsummer when water temperatures hit 50°F. Lake fish spawn in inlets and outlets, and stream fish spawn in tributaries or gravel areas of the main stream. Females dig several redds, and after spawning the fish return to the lake or to their home pools.

The slow-growing golden trout averages only ¼- to ½ pound, and the fish prefer water temperatures around 60°F. Primary feed consists of small crustaceans and aquatic insects such as caddis flies and midges. At times, the golden trout can be choosy about what it eats, so matching the hatch produces the best results. Generally, though, the fish will hit small spoons and spinners, baits such as worms, eggs, and insects, and flies, especially those that match native insect life.

Atlantic Salmon

The Atlantic salmon, *Salmo salar*, is really a trout even though it is called a salmon. This fish is a highly prized game fish, and many anglers consider it the premier species of all trout and salmon. Even though the flesh is fine eating, the Atlantic salmon is valued more as a sport fish, and most anglers pursue them with a fly rod and practice total catch and release. The Atlantic salmon is a challenging fish to get on line's end, but once there the fish displays outstanding fighting ability with its long runs and impressive leaps.

Atlantic salmon have silver to yellowish-brown sides with dark spots and a slightly forked tail. Their range extends along the Atlantic coast of Canada down to Cape Cod. These fish are anadromous and migrate to their natal tributaries in summer and early fall. Spawning occurs in the upper stretches of streams when water temperatures drop into the 40s. Like other trout, the Atlantic salmon digs redds in gravel areas and covers the eggs. Unlike their Pacific salmon cousins, Atlantics live to spawn more than once. The young generally spend two years in the stream before venturing to sea, and male Atlantics often winter in the stream after spawning.

Atlantic salmon prefer water temperatures in the upper 50s, and primary foods include crustaceans, insects, and small fish. Still, this species doesn't feed when it enters spawning tributaries, but fish do strike out of instinct or as a reflex action. This nonfeeding behavior makes catching Atlantic salmon very challenging, and this challenge is part of the allure of pursuing Atlantics.

Stream fishing for Atlantic salmon is pretty much a fly-fishing venture, sometimes as an angler choice and other times as required by regulations. Prime holding spots include slick-water runs as well as the heads and tails of pools. Anglers familiar with a specific tributary know that the flow has favorite lies that seem to hold fish year after year. Fishing for Atlantics is quite often a sight-fishing affair that is very much a game of skillful casting and patience. An angler selects a pool or lie and casts repeatedly in hopes of enticing a strike. If there is no activity, the options are to move to another spot or to let the lie rest for fifteen minutes or so before renewing casting and mending efforts, usually with a different fly at line's end.

Like fishing for many species, the best fishing times are early morning and in the evening. Because Atlantic salmon are powerful fish that typically weigh in the 5- to 15-pound range, 7- to 9-weight rods are the norm. Because these fish make long runs, reels should have plenty of backing. Atlantic salmon tend to take a wet fly on the swing, and Atlantic salmon anglers know that a strike may occur on the first cast or the twenty-first cast.

Landlocked Salmon

The landlocked salmon, *Salmo salar,* is actually the Atlantic salmon in landlocked form. Native to Maine and stocked in several other states, this fish lives in natural lakes and impoundments that have large tributaries for spawning. Most waters with landlocked salmon rely on stocking efforts to maintain populations. Smaller than Atlantic salmon, landlocked salmon may average just a couple of pounds.

Landlocked salmon feed year-round, but the best fishing occurs in spring and fall when water temperatures range from 45°F to 60°F. At these times, the fish gather in shallow water and near the surface to feed, and their favorite feeding areas are tributary mouths and outlets where smelt and alewives are present. Early morning promises the best fishing, but the evening hours can also be productive. Casting will take fish, but anglers generally troll streamers, plugs, or spoons that imitate smelt or alewives in size and color. Once surface temperatures rise into the 60s in late spring, landlocked salmon seek the thermocline in the 52°F to 58°F range until waters cool again in autumn. Summer fish can be hard to locate, and anglers rely on lead core line, downriggers, or diving planers to get their offerings to the desired depths.

Char

Like the trout group, the char group is a Salmoninae subfamily of the Salmonidae trout family. Also, like the trout group, names can be misleading because the Arctic char is the only member of the char group that has char in its name. Other members of the char subfamily are the brook trout, lake trout, Dolly Varden, and bull trout. While the true trout have dark spots on a light background, the char are distinguished by red or pale spots on a dark background. Char have only a few teeth at the front of the bone in the center of the mouth, whereas trout have teeth along the length of that bone.

Brook Trout

The brook trout, *Salvelinus fontinalis*, is a beautiful fish with light spots, blue spots, and red dots on dark sides. Other features include white-edged lower fins, a nearly square tail, and dark vermiculations (wavy, wormlike marks) on the fish's upper body. Breeding males are particularly colorful. The brook trout's range includes the eastern Canadian provinces, the western one-third of the United States, the Great Lakes region, and the northeast states extending down to Tennessee. Some anadromous brook trout exist on the Atlantic Coast and in Lake Superior.

Also called brookies and speckled trout, this species is a wilderness fish found in mountain streams, ponds, and lakes. Brook trout prefer water temperatures in the mid-50s, and their favorite holding places include the uppermost reaches of streams and the cold-water springs in lakes and ponds. Whenever brook trout thrive in waters, it is a sure sign of a healthy environment. Unfortunately, human development and pollution have eliminated brook trout from many of their native waters.

Brook trout spawn in the fall when water temperatures are in the 40s, and females make redds in gravelly, riffled sections of streams. This species can also spawn in shallow, gravelly areas of lakes where moving water aerates fertilized eggs. Primary prey includes aquatic insects, terrestrials, crustaceans, and baitfish.

Brook trout are a favorite of anglers because the fish are easy to catch, feisty fighters, and first-rate eating. Also, this species bites throughout the day, although late afternoon and early evening provide better action. Stream brook trout run smaller in size than their lake counterparts. By anyone's standards, though, a 12-inch fish is a nice one, a 2-pound fish is a great catch, and anything over 4 pounds is of trophy quality.

Brook trout readily strike a variety of offerings, and spin fishermen on both streams and

Lake Trout

lakes have good luck with worms, minnows, leeches, spinners, spoons, and jigs. Since these fish are primarily subsurface feeders, fly-fishermen rely on wet rather than dry flies. Trolling a spinner and worm combination is a traditional technique on lakes where favorite hangouts include inlets, outlets, cold-water springs, and woody cover.

Lake Trout

The lake trout, *Salvelinus namaycush*, is the most popular char. It has white spots on a dark-green to black body, white-edged lower fins, and a forked tail. The lake trout has a range extending from Alaska across Canada to the New England states, the Great Lakes, and the Finger Lakes in New York. Populations also exist in cold-water western lakes. Also called laker, togue, mackinaw, and gray trout, lake trout favor colder and deeper water than other game fish. This species prefers temperatures around 50°F and comfortably handles depths of more than 100 feet.

Like the brook trout, this char spawns in the fall, but instead of spawning in tributaries, the lake trout spawns in gravely rocky areas of the main lake. Spawning typically occurs in depths of 10 to 20 feet where the fish have cleared an area, and the female ejects her eggs. Males reach sexual maturity around age five, whereas females reach maturity several years later.

Fishing Vocab

A splake is a hybrid resulting from breeding between the male brook trout and female lake trout.

After ice-out, lake trout move shallower for warmer water and food. During the summer, the fish relate to deep-water structures before returning to the shallow structures for spawning in the fall. Comfortable water temperatures of winter allow lake trout to patrol the shallows and upper reaches of the water column in pursuit of baitfish. No matter what the time of year, lake trout like structures such as points, humps, rocky shoals, and drop-offs.

Lake trout rely primarily on their strong vision for finding prey, but the fish also use their lateral line and sense of smell. Favorite baitfish species include ciscoes, smelt, alewives, and sculpin. Lake trout are hunters, and although not a schooling fish, groups are often found in the same area because of structures, comfortable water temperatures, and available baitfish. A slow-growing fish, lake trout of 10 to 20 pounds are common in prime waters.

Trolling ranks as the most popular technique for catching lake trout, and productive lures include diving plugs, flashy spoons, and wobbling lures or cut bait behind attractors such as cowbells. To reach desired depths, anglers use in-line weights, wire line on a roller-tipped rod, or downriggers. Jigging with heavy spoons is another effective technique for taking lake trout. Whether trolling or jigging, keys to success include getting the lure near bottom, using a slow presentation, and working areas with structures.

The best fishing times for lake trout are spring and fall when the fish migrate to structures around the 20-foot depths. At these times, lake trout are available to shore anglers, especially where deep water is adjacent to the shoreline structure. Bottom fishing with dead or cut bait is popular in the spring and fall, but casting jigs or spoons and trolling spoons or plugs are also effective techniques.

Arctic Char

The arctic char, *Salvelinus alpinus*, has light spots (red, pink, or cream) on a dark background that lightens in color from the back to the belly. Like other members of the char family, this species has a forked tail and white-edged fins. The arctic char has slightly larger spots than the Dolly Varden, but the fish look so similar that in some locations the two species are simply called char and are not distinguished.

With a northerly distribution, the arctic char is found in Alaska and across northern Canada. This anadromous species uses rivers that empty into the Bering Sea, the Arctic Ocean, and inland lakes in the Arctic, but there are landlocked populations in southwest Alaska, northern New England, and southern Quebec. Landlocked arctic char prefer habitats similar to lake trout, and landlocked fish are smaller than sea-run fish, with the former weighing a pound or so and sea-run fish commonly reaching weights of several pounds.

Arctic char spawn in the fall in water temperatures around 40°F. Spawning occurs over rocky areas, and fish remain in pools or lakes through the winter. Preferring water temperatures in the 45°F to 50°F range, arctic char are not fussy eaters, feeding on plankton, eels, crustaceans, insects, and small fish. The arctic char is considered an easy-to-catch species that offers good fighting and good eating. Effective lures include colorful streamers and flashy spoons.

Dolly Varden

The Dolly Varden, *Salvelinus malma*, has silvery to greenish sides with pink-colored spots, and the fish looks very similar to the brook trout, arctic char, and bull trout. According to legend, this fish earned its nickname from a Charles Dickens' character, Miss Dolly Varden, who wore a green dress with pink spots. The Dolly Varden is primarily anadromous, and the fish's range extends along the Pacific Coast from Washington to Alaska. Also, the more colorful landlocked Dolly Varden inhabits some cold-water streams and lakes in a number of western states.

This species spawns in the fall when water temperatures drop into the mid- to upper 40s, and spawning generally occurs in home streams. Like other char, the female digs redds in gravel areas. Females live to spawn several times, but males commonly die after spawning due to the stress caused by competing with other males. Dolly Varden in lakes spawn in tributaries or in shallow, gravelly areas of the lake.

Preferring water temperatures in the 50 to 55°F range, Dolly Varden are sometimes looked down upon because of their preference for eating salmon eggs and fry. Overall though, anglers consider the Dolly to be a good-eating, easy-to-catch fish that hits a variety of offerings such as eggs, spinners, spoons, and streamers. The key is to get the offering near bottom.

Bull Trout

The bull trout, *Salvelinus confluentus*, is a lesser-known char with a range limited to some northwestern states and western provinces, although some anadromous bull trout live in Alaska. Often confused with the Dolly Varden, the bull trout has greenish sides with pink or orange spots, white-edged lower fins, and a forked tail. A distinguishing feature, though, is the bull trout's somewhat wider and flatter head.

Protected by regulations in some waters, the bull trout is a wilderness fish that does best in deep, cold, infertile lakes and in the deep pools of large undeveloped flows. Bull trout begin migrating to spawning tributaries in late spring or early summer even though spawning does not occur until fall when water temperatures drop into the upper 40s.

Some anglers look down upon the bull trout because of its preference for eating eggs and fry, but the species also preys upon aquatic insects, crayfish, clams, and snails. Because of the bull trout's preference for deep water, the fish is not popular among fly-fishermen. The most productive angling methods include trolling spoons or plugs and jigging, and the average weight of a caught fish runs a couple of pounds.

Pacific Salmon

Like the trout and char, Pacific salmon belong to the Salmoninae subfamily of the Salmonidae trout family. Pacific salmon are highly valued for both food and recreation. These species have a range extending along the Pacific Coast from Alaska to California, and the fish have also been introduced into the Great Lakes. Pacific salmon populations can be harmed by such stresses as commercial overfishing, industrial pollution, and manmade developments, most notably dams that block the fish's migratory runs.

Pacific salmon are anadromous, returning to their native streams to spawn and subsequently die. Prior to entering spawning tributaries, salmon stage in large numbers near tributary mouths. Fish sport a silver color when leaving the sea or lake, but they turn black during their migratory run. Upon their deaths, Pacific salmon become the primary source of food and nutrients in their spawning tributaries.

chinook salmon

Off-shore trolling is the primary technique for salmon in the open waters of the sea or the Great Lakes, and trolling, casting, and drifting are effective techniques once salmon enter spawning tributaries. North America's five members of the Pacific salmon grouping are the chinook salmon, coho salmon, sockeye salmon, pink salmon, and chum salmon.

Chinook Salmon

The chinook salmon, *Oncorhynchus tshawytscha*, is the largest and fastest-growing of the Pacific salmon. The chinook, sometimes called the king salmon, ranks as the most popular salmon among sport fish anglers. The runs of this powerful and hard-fighting fish can be measured in football field lengths, and battles commonly last twenty to thirty minutes or even longer. An average fish weighs 18 pounds or so, and fish in the 30- to 40-pound range are an everyday occurrence where salmon are congregated.

Chinook salmon have silvery sides, small dark spots on the back and tail, and black gums that earned the fish the nickname of black-mouth salmon. This species has a range extending along the Pacific Coast from California to Alaska and in the Great Lakes. The fish treat the Great Lakes as though it were the ocean and make spawning runs into a lake's tributaries. Chinooks feed primarily on small fish, but they also eat shrimp and crustaceans.

Depending on their location, chinook salmon spawn between June and November, and fish are referred to as spring, summer, or fall chinooks. Most chinooks have a four-year life span, but some may live up to eight years before spawning. Fish locate their native streams by scent, and spawning takes place over large gravel areas where the female digs her redds. The female guards her nest for a short period prior to her expiration. Spawning in the Great Lakes is usually not too fruitful, so populations are commonly maintained by hatchery operations.

Fishing Vocab

Parr are young salmon or trout that have dark vertical bars on their sides called parr marks. *Parr* is generally used to identify salmon up to the age of two years prior to the fish moving to sea.

It is estimated that nearly 90 percent of chinook salmon are caught by trolling herring, plugs, spoons, or flies. Since an erratic action produces the best results, anglers commonly use dodgers in conjunction with their lure or bait. Trolling works for open-water and tributary-run salmon, whereas drifting spinner and salmon-egg combinations and casting spoons, spinners, eggs, or flies work for stream-run fish. Chinook salmon don't feed upon entering their spawning tributaries, but the fish readily strike offerings, especially herring, wobbling plugs, and salmon eggs.

Coho Salmon

The coho salmon, *Oncorhynchus kisutch*, ranks as the second most popular of the Pacific salmon. Commonly called the silver salmon, the reddish flesh of this fish offers fine eating, and its fighting and leaping abilities provide plenty of sport. The coho has silvery sides, blue-green back, dark spots on its sides, back, and upper portion of the tail, and grayish gums. Like the chinook, the coho has a range along the Pacific Coast of the United States and Canada and in the Great Lakes, where hatchery operations sustain fish populations.

Coho salmon begin entering rivers in the summer, but the species spawns in fall and early winter, a bit later than the other Pacific salmon. Once water temperatures reach the upper 40s to low 50s, females dig redds in shallow gravel areas with moving water. Females guard the nests for a brief period before they die, and parr remain in the stream for a year or two. With a typical life span of three years, coho salmon average 6 or so pounds in weight.

Fishing Vocab

A smolt is a young salmon at that stage of life (usually one or two years) when the fish leaves fresh water and heads to the ocean.

Schools of coho salmon seek out water with temperatures around 55°F and abundant baitfish such as herring, smelt, or alewives, so that is where open-water anglers concentrate their trolling efforts. Considered an upper–water column fish, the coho favors the top 30 feet where anglers utilize the same trolling techniques employed when pursuing chinook salmon, although trolling speed is increased for coho salmon. Tributary-run coho salmon do not actively feed, but they do strike baits and lures. Common offerings include herring, salmon eggs, colorful streamers, wobbling plugs, spoons, and spinners.

Sockeye Salmon

The sockeye salmon, *Oncorhynchus nerka*, is best known for its food value especially among commercial anglers because the fish's red flesh offers fine eating. The sockeye has silvery sides and a bluish-green back, but the fish lacks the small black spots of the chinook and coho salmon. The species' range extends along the Pacific Coast from California to Alaska; however, no Great Lakes population exists.

Sockeye salmon spawn in rivers in late summer and early fall when water temperatures drop to 50°F or so. Females dig redds, and both sexes protect the nest prior to dying. During the spawn, the sockeye's head turns green, and the sides turn red. Noteworthy of sockeye spawning is the large number of fish that congregate in a small area. Sockeye have a four-year life span, but some fish may live up to eight years.

Fishing Vocab

The **kokanee salmon** is a small landlocked version of the sockeye salmon. Although stocked in some eastern states, the kokanee is really a fish of deep, cold western lakes. Trolling streamers is the standard technique for pursuing this nonmigratory salmon.

Sockeye salmon primarily feed on plankton, but they also eat small crustaceans. This species does not readily hit bait and lures, so they are harder to catch than chinook and coho salmon. Despite the challenge, sockeyes can be taken on small spinners and spoons, flies, and small hooks with eggs or colored yarn. Sockeye salmon average 5 pounds or so, and once hooked, the fish put up a strong fight and display their leaping ability.

Pink Salmon

The pink salmon, *Oncorhynchus gorbuscha*, is the smallest of the Pacific salmon, averaging around 4 pounds, and the species has more value for commercial fishermen than it does for recreational anglers. The pink salmon has silver sides and black spots on its back, upper sides, and tail. This species earned its name from its pink flesh, which offers good eating but is less preferred than the flesh of chinook, coho, and sockeye salmon. Like the other salmon, pinks have a range extending along the Pacific Coast from California to Alaska and have been introduced into Lake Superior.

With a life span of two years, pink salmon appear in heavier runs during alternate years in many waters. Spawning takes place in early to late fall when water temperatures reach the mid-40s. During the spawning run, males develop a large hump just ahead of the dorsal fin, and that feature has earned the fish its nickname of humpback salmon or humpy. Females dig redds in gravelly riffles, and males compete to fertilize the eggs.

Because pink salmon do not feed during spawning runs and because the species feeds on small foods such as plankton and crustaceans, pinks can be hard to catch. Still, the fish can be taken on yarn flies, small spinners, and small wobbling spoons.

Chum Salmon

The chum salmon, *Oncorhynchus keta*, has more of a commercial value than a recreational value. Even though this species is good eating and hard fighting, sport fishermen rank it behind the chinook, coho, and sockeye salmon. Since natives sometimes fed this salmon to their dogs, the fish is often called the dog salmon. For the most part, chum salmon occur as incidental catches by anglers pursuing other species of Pacific salmon. With a four-year life span, chum salmon average 8 to 10 pounds.

Real Fishing

Despite the nickname of dog salmon, the chum salmon is a good eating fish. When trolling wobbling plugs for chinook salmon on Alaska's Nushagak River, we would occasionally hook into a chum salmon, and those fish found their way back to camp to be smoked, grilled, or made into salmon spread for sandwiches.

Fishing Vocab

A **kype** is an obvious upward projection on the lower jaw of male salmon or male trout that develops during the spawning run.

Chum salmon have silvery sides, but the fish are easily identified by the series of vertical bands along its length. In addition to the standard range of Pacific salmon, chum salmon are found in the Yukon and Northwest Territories. Chum salmon spawn in the fall when water temperatures range from 45°F to 55°F, although some rivers see a run of summer-spawning fish. Like the other Pacific salmon, the female chum digs redds in gravelly riffles. After guarding the nest for a few days, the female dies. During the spawning run, males develop a hooked upper jaw and a kype.

Whitefish

Whitefish belong to the Coregoninae subfamily of the Salmonidae trout family. Members of this grouping include whitefish, ciscoes, and inconnus, and the two family members most pursued by anglers are the lake whitefish and the mountain whitefish.

Lake Whitefish

The lake whitefish, *Coregonus clupeaformis*, is often called the common whitefish. This species has silver-colored sides, large scales, a small head, and an underslung mouth, and its range includes the Great Lakes region, all of Canada, and Alaska. As the name suggests, lake whitefish live in lakes, and the fish spawn on shoals when water temperatures are in the low 40s. Unlike their trout, char, and salmon cousins, lake whitefish do not make nests or redds for spawning. Lake whitefish have both commercial and sport fishing value. Anglers cast jigs or bottom fish with bait during the open-water season, and the same presentations are used for ice fishing. Chumming with canned corn, cooked rice, or chopped minnows effectively lures whitefish into an area. Since lake whitefish rise to the surface to feed on insect hatches, fly-fishing will take fish, too. The average size for angler-caught lake whitefish is 1 to 2 pounds.

Mountain Whitefish

The mountain whitefish, *Prosopium williamsoni*, has a significantly smaller range than the lake whitefish. That range primarily includes the northwestern states and British Columbia. Sometimes called the Rocky Mountain whitefish, this species favors streams along the western slopes of the Rocky Mountains, although these fish also live in lakes. Similar in appearance to the lake whitefish, the mountain whitefish has silvery sides, large scales, a small head, and an underslung mouth.

Mountain whitefish spawn in streams from late fall to early winter when water temperatures are in the low 40s. Like lake whitefish, mountain whitefish do not build redds nor do they protect their young. Because mountain whitefish compete with trout, some anglers look down upon the species even though it puts up a feisty fight. Favorite hangouts include pools and slow-water stretches, where anglers present flies or small baits to fish that average ½ pound or so. Unlike many of their trout, char, and salmon cousins, mountain whitefish offer winter fishing opportunities.

Grayling

Grayling belong to the Thymallinae subfamily of the Salmonidae trout family, and the single North American species belonging to this group

Artic Grayling

is the American grayling. The most distinguishing feature of the grayling is its large sail-like dorsal fin.

American Grayling

The American grayling, *Thymallus arcticus*, has a bluish-gray and silver body with small black spots in the front portion, a small sucker-like mouth, and the unique sail-like dorsal fin. Referred to as the Arctic grayling in some sources, the American grayling has a range extending across Alaska, Yukon, Northwest Territories, and the northern portion of the western provinces. This grayling is also present in some western states.

The American grayling inhabits the cold, clear water of both lakes and rivers, and the fish spawns in tributaries and rivers after ice-out when water temperatures reach the mid- to upper 40s. Like the whitefish, grayling do not make nests or redds. Instead, the eggs are released and fertilized over gravel bottoms.

The American grayling makes for great sport fishing because these fish congregate in schools and they are not fussy eaters. Since their diet is comprised of insect larvae, aquatic and terrestrial insects, and fish eggs, grayling are a perfect quarry of fly-fishers because these fish readily hit a variety of dry and wet flies as well as egg patterns. The grayling has a small mouth so spin fishermen have their best luck with tiny spinners or baits placed on small hooks.

Grayling size varies in different waters. In the western states, grayling may weigh less than ½ pound, whereas prime waters of the north may see fish averaging 2 or more pounds. Without a doubt, the best American grayling fishing exists in Alaska.

CHAPTER 23

The Temperate Bass, Herring, Minnow, and Sturgeon Families

In This Chapter

➤ How striped, white, and yellow bass and white perch behave

➤ The characteristics of American and hickory shad

➤ The characteristics of carp

➤ The characteristics of sturgeon

In this chapter, you'll learn about the temperate bass family, which includes the striped bass, white bass, yellow bass, and white perch. You will also be introduced to the American shad and the hickory shad, the two most popular members of the herring family. Then you'll get details on the common carp, a member of the minnow family whose status as a game fish is growing. Finally, you'll learn about North America's largest game fish, the members of the sturgeon family.

Temperate Bass Family

The members of the temperate bass family are true bass that received their name because of their preference for moderate water temperatures. The four temperate bass include the striped bass, white bass, yellow bass, and white perch. Striped bass are both anadromous and landlocked; white bass and yellow bass are both freshwater species; white perch live mainly in freshwater, but some are anadromous.

Unlike other bass that are members of the sunfish family and build and protect nests, the temperate bass scatter their eggs randomly and then abandon them. Temperate bass are a schooling species, and once anglers locate a school of feeding fish, the action can be some of the most exciting of all freshwater fishing.

Striped Bass

The striped bass, *Morone saxatilis*, is the most popular temperate bass because of the fish's size, aggressive feeding nature, fighting ability, and table fare. Sometimes called striper or rockfish, this first-rate game fish has silvery sides with seven or so dark stripes running along its length, and these horizontal stripes give the fish its name. The striped bass has two spines on the back of its gill cover and two patches of teeth on its tongue.

Anadromous striped bass have a range along the east, west, and gulf coasts, whereas landlocked fish have been widely stocked in large southern reservoirs. Anadromous stripers gather at the mouths of large rivers until water temperature and water flows induce the upstream run to natural and manmade barriers. Landlocked fish make a similar run up tributaries or into the shallows where spawning occurs when water temperatures reach the upper 50s. Striped bass commonly travel the channel when migrating to and from spawning grounds.

Spring offers the best fishing of the year for anadromous and landlocked stripers because of fish concentrations, and prime spots include waters below dams, areas of slack water, eddies, tributaries, and channels. After the spawn, striper fishing is very much an open-water affair, although the edges of sandy flats and large points commonly hold fish. In the cooler water of spring and fall, stripers roam the upper 30 feet of the water column, but look for fish in the 40- to 60-foot range during the summer. Winter fishing is usually slow in the northern part of the range, but the southern range offers good fishing, particularly in deep basins above dams and near warm-water discharges.

Striped bass are famous for their aggressive attacks on schools of baitfish such as threadfin shad and gizzard shad, but stripers also prey on crustaceans and insects. The fish sometimes feed during the day, particularly on overcast days, but early morning and evening mark the most active times as fish move shallow or to the surface in low-light conditions.

Since striped bass have a roaming tendency, the key to successful angling is to locate a school of fish. Once fish are found, the action can be some of the best freshwater fishing has to offer. Many anglers locate stripers by witnessing the surface activity of fleeing baitfish or diving birds. Otherwise, anglers rely on fishing structural edges or using electronics to locate fish. The angling techniques of trolling and drifting also facilitate locating fish.

Fishing Vocab

Jump Fishing is a technique that involves locating a school of surface-feeding stripers and then moving in to fish for them. Schools are commonly located by the activity of gulls that join stripers in the feeding frenzy. When you are jump fishing, stop and cast to the fish from a distance so you do not alert the school.

Trolling with plugs or jigs works well for striped bass, particularly in the summer when fish may be more scattered and holding in deeper water. Planer boards allow for covering a wide area, and downriggers allow for getting lures to desired depths. Drift fishing with live minnows, cut bait, or jigs works well year-round, and the use of worms or eels works during the anadromous runs.

Casting ranks as the most thrilling way to catch striped bass, especially when the fish are chasing baitfish to the surface in late summer and fall. Casting is also popular in the spring and during low-light periods when stripers are more likely to inhabit shallow depths. Effective lures include jigs, shallow-running plugs, and surface lures. Success often requires that the lures match the color and size of the baitfish that the stripers are chasing. Generally, the most reliable colors are black and silver or white.

White Bass

The white bass, *Morone chrysops*, is essentially a smaller version of the striped bass. Averaging less than one pound, white bass are free-roaming, schooling, aggressive-feeding, and good-tasting fish. Sometimes called the silver bass, the white bass has silvery sides with dark stripes along its length, and the stripes above the lateral line are more distinct than those below. Unlike the striped bass, the white bass has only one patch of teeth on its tongue and only a single spine on the back of its gill cover. White bass are found throughout the eastern half of the United States and in a limited number of waters in the southwest.

This freshwater species likes the cool, deep water of clear rivers, lakes, and reservoirs. White bass spawn in tributaries, and strong year-classes of fish seem to appear every three years or so. Like the striped bass, the white bass

Fishing Vocab

A wiper, also called a whiterock, is a hybrid resulting from breeding between the white bass and the striped bass. Hatchery-raised wipers have been introduced in many southern reservoirs.

feeds most actively in the morning and evening with evening being the more productive time. Overcast days are better than sunny ones, and surface feeding occurs most heavily in summer and early fall. Fishing at night is popular during the summer on some waters.

Jump fishing is a favorite technique of white bass anglers. Once a feeding school is located, the fun kicks into high gear for anglers using light tackle. Popular offerings include marabou jigs, small crankbaits, and live minnows. Again, the key is to match the size and color of the natural prey. Once alerted, white bass shut down quickly, so anglers are reminded to use a quiet approach in their fishing areas.

Yellow Bass

The yellow bass, *Morone mississippiensis*, has a grayish-green back, yellow to gold sides, and dark stripes along its length. The yellowish sides are the distinguishing feature between white and yellow bass, and these sides give the yellow bass its name. The yellow bass has a fairly limited range, and the fish's scientific name gives indication that this range is in the central portion of the United States.

Sometimes called the streaker, the yellow bass is similar to the white bass in its schooling, roaming, feeding, and fighting qualities. But yellow bass hold more often in deep water and do less surface feeding. Yellow bass are also somewhat smaller in size and considered better table fare. Fishing strategy involves locating a school of fish and then casting small jigs, spinners, spoons, or plugs, or tossing out live worms or minnows.

White Perch

The white perch, *Morone americana*, has a dark back, silvery-green sides, and a white belly. Sometimes called a silver perch, the white perch lacks the stripes of its cousins and is the smallest member of the temperate bass family, averaging only a ½ pound or so. The fish's native range included the Atlantic Coast from Quebec to the Carolinas as well as the Great Lakes, but the white bass has been stocked in other waters.

Fishing Vocab

Brackish water refers to water having a lower salinity than seawater. Brackish water is commonly found where a freshwater stream or river empties into an ocean.

Able to survive in saltwater, brackish water, and fresh water, white perch prey on whatever is seasonally available. Favorite foods include insects, crustaceans, eggs, and baitfish. While white perch pursue baitfish on the surface less frequently than the other temperate bass, whites routinely surface feed on insects in the evening and after dark.

White perch are willing biters, and catching fish amounts to locating a school. Effective angling techniques include casting small jigs, spoons, and spinners, fishing with live bait such as worms or minnows, and fly-fishing with dry flies or wet flies. White perch are fairly inactive in the winter, but fishing can be good the rest of the year. A quiet approach is necessary for catching white perch just as it is for the other members of the temperate bass family.

Bad Cast

In some waters, anglers look down upon white perch because the species feeds on the eggs of walleyes, sauger, and white bass.

Herring Family

For many freshwater anglers, members of the herring family such as gizzard shad, threadfin shad, and alewives are important for their baitfish value, but two members of the family, the American shad and the hickory shad, are highly prized for their sporting and eating value. Known for their fighting and leaping abilities, these shad are often called the poor man's salmon. Shad are a good eating fish; their roe is used for caviar and their flesh is commonly pickled or smoked.

Primarily plankton eaters, shad don't feed once they enter a coastal river, but the fish do strike lures. These silver-colored, slender-bodied fish enter spawning flows in large numbers, which in turn attracts throngs of anglers and is cause for celebration in many communities. Males are called buck shad while females are called roe shad.

American Shad

The American shad, *Alosa spapidissima*, has a green to blue top with silvery sides, large scales, rows of dark spots behind the gill cover, and a forked tail. Sometimes called the white shad, this fish is the largest and most widespread shad. The American shad's native range extends along the entire East Coast from Canada to Florida, but the fish has been stocked along the West Coast from Alaska to California.

American shad spawn when water temperatures reach the mid-60s. Fish in the northern part of the range return to sea post-spawn, and those in the southern portion of the range commonly die after the spawn. Like other members of the herring family, the American shad eats primarily plankton, but the fish will also eat eggs, crustaceans, and small fish. American shad do grow to 7 or 8 pounds, but the average catch weighs a couple of pounds.

Hickory Shad

The hickory shad, *Alosa mediocris,* has a green to gray top, silver sides, large scales, black spots behind the gill cover, and a forked tail. Very similar in appearance to the American shad, the hickory can be distinguished by the extension of its lower jaw beyond the upper jaw. Found from Canada to Florida, the hickory shad is really more of a southern fish.

Capable of reaching weights of 2 or 3 pounds, hickory shad generally average 1 pound. What hickory shad may lack in size, though, they make up for in their leaping, acrobatic fight. These fish spawn when water temperatures are in the low 60s. Some fish return to sea during summer; others die. In addition to plankton, hickory shad prey on eggs, small fish, crustaceans, and insects.

Fishing for American and Hickory Shad

Despite not actively eating once they enter spawning tributaries, shad instinctively strike at lures. Generally, the fish move at night and settle in pools where they rest during the day. The heads and tails of pools hold the highest concentrations of fish, so these are the best fishing spots. When migrating up and down tributaries, American and hickory shad tend to follow channels.

Fishing Vocab

A shad dart is a small, flat-headed, lead-headed jig with a bucktail body.

Shad do feed after spawning and prior to their return to sea, so coastal tributaries and backwaters offer angling opportunities into early summer. Early morning generally is the best time for shad fishing, followed by evenings and overcast days. Favorite lures include shad darts, small spoons, and flies, and bright colors, especially silver and gold, produce better catches than natural, dull colors. Tiny silver spoons and ⅛-ounce shad darts rank as the top two offerings.

Whether an angler trolls or casts, two keys are to get the lure to bottom and to impart erratic lure action. Once a fish is hooked, play the fish easily as shad have a soft mouth. The fact that shad are accessible to shore anglers and waders gives additional meaning to the nickname poor man's salmon.

Minnow Family

Some two hundred members of the minnow family can be found in North America. Minnows are small fish used as bait by freshwater anglers, and the most common minnows include chubs, shiners, and dace. The one member of the minnow family that grows to large sizes is the carp.

Common Carp

The common carp, *Cyprinus carpio*, was introduced into the United States in the late 1800s. The fish has very large scales, sides that vary in color from brown to gold to yellow, and a pair of barbels on each side of the jaw. Carp are found throughout the United States and southern Canada, but the fish is most prevalent in the eastern states. The carp's widespread presence can be attributed to the fish's tolerance for a wide range of water conditions and its prolific breeding.

Carp are bottom feeders with a sucker-like mouth. The species has a strong sense of taste in its barbels and mouth, and carp detect food by their sense of smell. Common foods include vegetation, algae, aquatic insects, and crustaceans, which the carp ingest by grubbing on the bottom. In the process of scouring the bottom for food, carp often destroy native plants and the habitat of native fish. As a result, carp are considered second-class citizens by anglers in many waters.

Despite their disfavor with some anglers, carp are fast growing in popularity as a game fish, not so much for their food value but for their sporting value. After all, carp numbers are thriving, the fish grow to a large size, and they are great fighters. Carp offer anglers the easiest way to routinely catch freshwater fish that weigh between 10 and 40 pounds. Worldwide interest in the species has grown, and the United States and Canada have become popular destinations for carp anglers from around the globe.

Common baits for carp include corn, worms, dough balls, processed baits, and homemade baits. Since carp feed on the bottom, the baits must be presented there with either a weight or a properly set float. Most fishing is done from shore, so anglers use ultra-long rods for casting and heavy rods for handling these big fish. Where legal, anglers chum the waters with corn, commercial products, or homemade recipes to lure fish into the area.

Fishing Vocab

Legering is a technique that allows bait to be cast a long distance and presented on bottom to entice carp to bite. The best legering setups use the least amount of weight possible to cast the bait out and to prevent carp from feeling resistance when they pick up the bait. Legered rods are usually set in rod holders and have some type of strike indicator.

Since carb grub for their food instead of chase it, carp fishing is a sit-and-wait style of fishing that requires patience. Carp offer year-round fishing opportunities, but the very best action typically occurs in late spring and early summer when water temperatures are in the mid-60s and the fish move shallow to feed and spawn. Carp fishing is likely to continue to grow in popularity as more North American anglers adapt to the sophisticated equipment and systems utilized by the European carp anglers who revere the common carp and practice total catch-and-release of their quarry.

Sturgeon Family

The sturgeon is the oldest and largest game fish in North America. The fish's long physique, scaleless body, rows of scutes on back and sides, mouth that's located on its underside, sharklike tail, and barbels give it a prehistoric look. Sturgeon are slow-growing fish that may live as long as humans. Over the years, though, commercial fishing, pollution, and manmade developments have seriously affected habitat and caused a decline in sturgeon numbers. Fortunately, today's management plans, stocking efforts, closed seasons, and catch-and-release fishing have combined to make a brighter future for sturgeon populations. The most popular sturgeon are the lake sturgeon, the Atlantic sturgeon, the white sturgeon, and the shovelnose sturgeon.

Fishing Vocab

Scutes are bony plates characteristic of the sturgeon, armadillo, and turtle.

Sturgeon are bottom feeders that rely on their barbels to feel and taste for food. Common sturgeon foods include worms, insects, small fish, crayfish, clams, snails, fish eggs, leeches, and aquatic vegetation. Favorite holding places and good fishing spots are the deeper water below dams and falls as well as the deeper water of channels, outside river bends, and the waters downstream of natural and manmade structures. Popular sturgeon baits include night crawlers, dead minnows, and cut bait. Because sturgeon feed on the bottom and because the fish inhabit deep water with current, anglers must use enough weight to get their bait to bottom for best results. Evenings and after dark are prime feeding times. Obviously, heavy tackle is required to handle these monstrous fish.

Lake Sturgeon

The lake sturgeon, *Acipenser fulvescens*, is the most common sturgeon. In addition to the standard sturgeon features, the lake sturgeon has brownish to dark-gray sides and a long, somewhat cone-shaped snout. The lake sturgeon can be found across much of Canada, the Great Lakes region, and the Mississippi River drainage. Even though the fish is most commonly found in lakes, as the name suggests, lake sturgeon are also found in rivers. This species prefers clear, cool, deep water with bottoms of sand, gravel, and rock.

Lake sturgeon enter tributaries to spawn from April through June when water temperatures range from the upper 50s into the low 60s. Spawning takes place in moving water in relatively shallow areas of rock and gravel where the fertilized eggs stick to rocks, vegetation, or wood.

Lake Sturgeon

Females may take over twenty years to reach sexual maturity, and the fish may spawn every five years or so. Males may not reach sexual maturity until their late teens.

Lake sturgeon are powerful fighters and great leapers. Fish average 10 to 50 pounds, and weights well over 200 pounds have been recorded. All signs indicate that modern management efforts for the lake sturgeon are enhancing fish habitat and fish numbers.

Atlantic Sturgeon

The Atlantic sturgeon, *Acipenser oxyrhynchus*, ranks as the second-largest sturgeon; it grows to lengths of 12 feet and reaches weights of 800 pounds. Greenish gray or brown in color, this sturgeon has a range extending from Canada to the Gulf of Mexico. The anadromous Atlantic sturgeon migrates to rivers in the spring to spawn, with the Hudson River possibly seeing the strongest run of fish. Females may not reach sexual maturity until nearly twenty years old, and males mature at around twelve years of age. After spawning, females return to the ocean, but males may remain in the river until fall. Young sturgeon remain in the river for a period of three to seven years.

More so than other sturgeon species, the Atlantic sturgeon is protected by various regulations, so fishing opportunities are limited.

White Sturgeon

The white sturgeon, *Acipenser transmontanus*, is the largest of all freshwater fish. Gray in color with a short snout, this sturgeon carries the name white because the lower half of its body is white in color. White sturgeon, also called Pacific sturgeon, have a range extending from Alaska to California with the Pacific Northwest having the highest populations. Most white sturgeon are anadromous, but some have become landlocked and spend their entire lives in rivers such as the Columbia.

These sturgeon spawn in late spring as water temperatures rise through the 50s. Ideal spawning sites include the waters below dams, waterfalls, and rapids where there is a rocky bottom and current. Females reach sexual maturity at ages varying from thirteen to twenty-five, and they may go eleven years between spawns. Males mature at ten or so years, and their spawning cycle runs every five years or so. White sturgeon can reach weights of 1,400 pounds.

Shovelnose Sturgeon

The shovelnose sturgeon, *Scaphirhynchus platorynchus*, is a small sturgeon averaging only 2 pounds or so in weight. With a brown body and white belly, the shovelnose sturgeon is easily identified by its flattened, shovel-shaped head. This species has a range limited to the Mississippi Valley region where it prefers the fast-moving flows of larger rivers. In late spring, shovelnose sturgeon migrate upstream or into tributaries where the fish, like their white sturgeon cousins, spawn in swift water below dams, falls, and rapids. Females reach sexual maturity around seven years of age, and males reach maturity at about five years of age.

Shovelnose sturgeon prefer sand or gravel bottoms that contain their favorite foods, snails and clams. Despite their diminutive size compared to other sturgeon, shovelnose sturgeon are great fighters and leapers, and the fish provide excellent sport on light tackle.

AFTERWORD
Final Cast

Fishing has made my life richer than it might otherwise have been, and I was blessed to have parents who introduced me to the sport. My mother bought me my first reel with Green Stamps earned from her grocery shopping. She also arranged outings with her father, Clarence Seguin, and those outings rank among the most memorable of my life. Providing for a family of nine children, my father often worked two jobs. Even though free time was a luxury, he made sure I went fishing. Fortunately, we had the opportunity to fish together after his retirement from school administration, and many of the spots we discovered together are places where I take my clients to this day.

Like my parents, I introduced my two sons to the world of fishing. Matthew lives in Baltimore, Maryland, and he is an avid fly-fisherman. Luke lives in Canton, New York, and he has a case of muskie fever.

Fishing is more than a hobby for me. It is my way of life. I live in the northern reaches of New York State where nearby fishing opportunities include the St. Lawrence River and its tributaries, Lake Ontario, the trout waters of the Adirondack Mountains, and the wilderness waters of the provinces of Ontario and Quebec. For me, socializing means a fishing trip with family and friends, and work means joining fellow outdoor writers to do some fishing research or guiding clients for a day on the water.

Fishing has been a blessing in my life, and my hope is that fishing will be a blessing in your life, too.

BIBLIOGRAPHY

Allard, Tim. *Ice Fishing, The Ultimate Guide.* Beachburg, Ontario: The Heliconia Press, Inc., 2010.

Creative Publishing Editors. *The Complete Guide to Freshwater Fishing.* Minneapolis, MN: Creative Publishing International, 2002.

Lindner, Al. *The Secret Teachings of In-Fisherman.* Brainerd, MN: In-Fisherman Inc., 1987.

McClane, A. J., Editor. *McClane's New Standard Fishing Encyclopedia.* New York, NY: Random House Value Publishing, Inc., 1998.

McNally, Tom. *The Complete Book of Fly Fishing.* Camden, Maine: Ragged Mountain Press, 1997.

Meade, Tim. *Essential Fly Fishing.* Guilford, CT: The Lyons Press, 2008.

Perich, Shawn. *Catching Panfish.* Chanhassen, MN: Creative Publishing International, 2006.

Schultz, Ken. *North American Fishing.* Blue Ridge Summit, PA: Carlton Books Limited, 2001.

Sorenson, Eric. *The Angler's Guide to Freshwater Fish of North America.* Stillwater, MN: Voyageur Press, Inc., 2000.

Steinberg, Dick. *Freshwater Gamefish of North America.* Minnetonka, MN: Cy DeCosse, Inc., 1987.

Steinberg, Dick and Ignizio, Bill. *Panfish.* Minnetonka, MN: Cy DeCosse, Inc., 1987.

Vick, Noel. *Fishing on Ice.* Champaign, IL: Human Kinetics, 2000.

INDEX

The Smart Guide Series

Making Smart People Smarter

THE SMART GUIDE TO

GREEN LIVING

The most complete guide to green living ever published

How green living benefits your health as well as the Earth's

How green living can save you lots of money

Why the green economy and job market is an attractive, new, lucrative frontier

Julie Kerr **Gines**

Available Titles

Smart Guide To Astronomy
Smart Guide To Bachelorette Parties
Smart Guide To Back and Nerve Pain
Smart Guide To Biology
Smart Guide To Bridge
Smart Guide To Chemistry
Smart Guide To Deciphering A Wine Label
Smart Guide To eBay
Smart Guide To Fighting Infections
Smart Guide To Forensic Careers
Smart Guide To Forensic Science
Smart Guide To Freshwater Fishing
Smart Guide To Golf
Smart Guide To Green Living
Smart Guide To Healthy Grilling
Smart Guide To High School Math
Smart Guide To Hiking and Backpacking
Smart Guide To Horses and Riding
Smart Guide To Life After Divorce
Smart Guide To Making A Fortune With Infomercials
Smart Guide To Managing Stress
Smart Guide To Medical Imaging Tests
Smart Guide To Nutrition
Smart Guide To Patents
Smart Guide To Photography Essesntials
Smart Guide To Practical Math
Smart Guide To Single Malt Scotch
Smart Guide To Starting Your Own Business
Smart Guide To The Perfect Job Interview
Smart Guide To The Solar System
Smart Guide To Understanding Your Cat
Smart Guide To US Visas
Smart Guide To Wedding Photography
Smart Guide To Wedding Weekend Events
Smart Guide To Wine

THE SMART GUIDE TO

BACHELORETTE PARTIES

Planning your dream
bachelorette party

Planning non-racy bashes,
spa parties, dinners and
Girls' Getaways

How to hire a hot male
dancer

The most complete guide
to bachelorette parties
ever published

Sharon **Naylor**

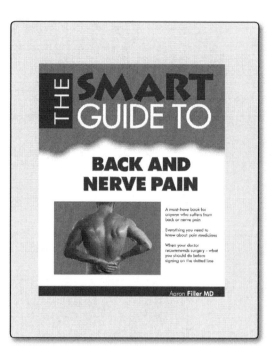

THE SMART GUIDE TO

BACK AND NERVE PAIN

A must-have book for
anyone who suffers from
back or nerve pain

Everything you need to
know about pain medicines

When your doctor
recommends surgery – what
you should do before
signing on the dotted line

Aaron **Filler MD**

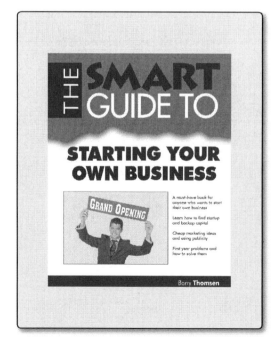

THE SMART GUIDE TO

STARTING YOUR OWN BUSINESS

A must-have book for
anyone who wants to start
their own business

Learn how to find startup
and backup capital

Cheap marketing ideas
and using publicity

First year problems and
how to solve them

Barry **Thomsen**

THE SMART GUIDE TO

FRESHWATER FISHING

A complete guide to
everything you need to
know to catch freshwater
fish

Practical advice for the
novice and seasoned
angler alike

Detailed information on
more than 50 popular
freshwater species

Mike **Seymour**

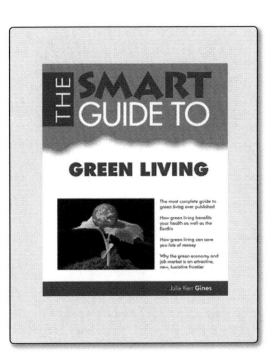

THE SMART GUIDE TO

GREEN LIVING

The most complete guide to green living ever published

How green living benefits your health as well as the Earth's

How green living can save you lots of money

Why the green economy and job market is an attractive, new, lucrative frontier

Julie Kerr **Gines**

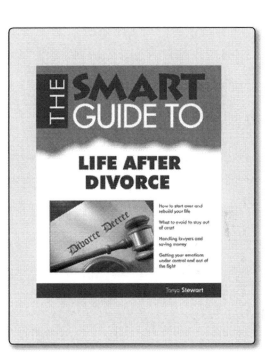

THE SMART GUIDE TO

LIFE AFTER DIVORCE

How to start over and rebuild your life

What to avoid to stay out of court

Handling lawyers and saving money

Getting your emotions under control and out of the fight

Tanya **Stewart**

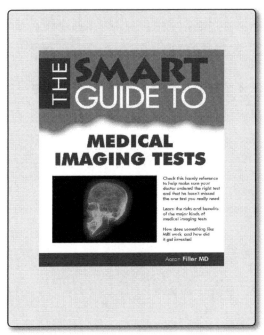

THE SMART GUIDE TO

MEDICAL IMAGING TESTS

Check this handy reference to help make sure your doctor ordered the right test and that he hasn't missed the one test you really need

Learn the risks and benefits of the major kinds of medical imaging tests

How does something like MRI work, and how did it get invented

Aaron **Filler MD**

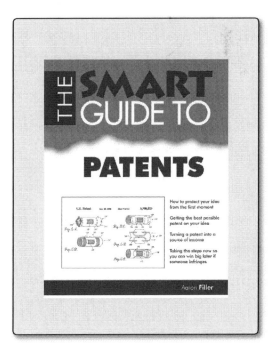

THE SMART GUIDE TO

PATENTS

How to protect your idea from the first moment

Getting the best possible patent on your idea

Turning a patent into a source of income

Taking the steps now so you can win big later if someone infringes

Aaron **Filler**

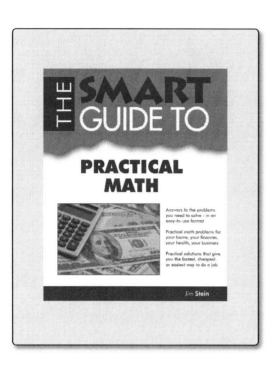

THE SMART GUIDE TO

PRACTICAL MATH

Answers to the problems
you need to solve - in an
easy-to-use format

Practical math problems for
your home, your finances,
your health, your business

Practical solutions that give
you the fastest, cheapest,
or easiest way to do a job

Jim **Stein**

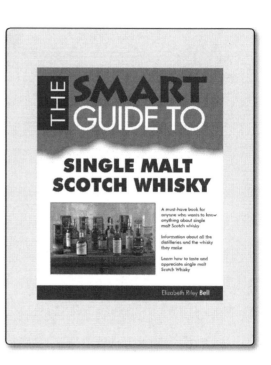

THE SMART GUIDE TO

SINGLE MALT SCOTCH WHISKY

A must-have book for
anyone who wants to know
anything about single
malt Scotch whisky

Information about all the
distilleries and the whisky
they make

Learn how to taste and
appreciate single malt
Scotch Whisky

Elizabeth Riley **Bell**

THE SMART GUIDE TO

THE PERFECT JOB INTERVIEW

Get the job you want by
crafting and directing the
perfect interview

Learn novel ways to stand
out from the competition.

The absolutely best guide
to creating the magic factor
in an interview

Practice tips from a
seasoned hiring manager

David **Holmes**

THE SMART GUIDE TO

UNDERSTANDING YOUR CAT

If only cats could talk,
they'd tell us almost
everything in this book.

How to connect with
your cat

Everything you need to
know to make your cat feel
at home in your home.

Take a closer look at your
loveable feline friend.

Carolyn **Janik**

The Smart Guide Series

Making Smart People Smarter

Smart Guides are available at your local bookseller

or from the following Internet retailers

www.SmartGuidePublications.com

www.Amazon.com

www.BarnesandNoble.com

Smart Guides are popularly priced at $18.95

Smart Guides are also available in Kindle and Nook editions

ABOUT THE AUTHOR

Mike Seymour is a New York State and U.S. Coast Guard licensed guide. For the past 25 years, he has operated Captain Mike's Fishing Charter's on the St. Lawrence River where he guides for bass, walleyes, northern pike, muskellunge, and yellow perch. He spent five summers in Alaska where he guided for salmon on the Nushagak River. In addition to guiding others, Mike is an avid angler himself, and he might be found on any body of water from a mountain trout stream to one of the Great Lakes.

Mike is also an outdoor writer who holds memberships in the Outdoor Writers Association of America, Association of Great Lakes Outdoor Writers, and New York State Outdoor Writers Association, an organization for which he is a Past President. He has written thousands of articles that have appeared in numerous publications including New York Sportsman, New York Game and Fish, New York Outdoor Times, Lake Ontario Outdoors, New York Outdoor News, Central New York Outdoor Journal, Outdoors Magazine, Northern Tier Magazine, New York Outdoors, Musky Hunter, The Conservationist, Advance News, and The Plaindealer. Mike's weekly column has appeared in the Advance News every Sunday for the past 22 years. He has also written angling guides for St. Lawrence County and for the Adirondack Tourism Council.

He received a Bachelor of Arts Degree in English at Siena College in Loudonville, NY; a Master of Science Degree in Education at St. Lawrence University in Canton, NY; and a Master of English Education Degree from the State University of New York in Potsdam, NY. Mike taught high school English for 33 years, 30 of those at Canton High School in Canton, NY.

Mike resides in Canton, NY on the banks of the Grasse River with his wife, Mary Sue, and his golden retriever, Pike. He has two adult sons. Matthew lives in Baltimore, MD, and he is an avid fly fisherman. Luke lives in Canton, NY, and he has a case of "muskie fever." Mike currently serves on the St. Lawrence County Fisheries Advisory Board, on the Board of Directors for FISHCAP, on the Pro Staff of Suick Lures, and as the President of the Federated Sportsmen's Clubs of St. Lawrence County. Mike can be reached at fishmike@twcny.rr.com.

WITHDRAWN

31901051496299

Made in the USA
Charleston, SC
26 April 2012